WHY READ *A LIVING CANVAS*

How do we allow God to remake us in His own image? *A Living Canvas* sets out to answer this question. God created each of us uniquely to fulfill His plans and purposes for our lives.

A Living Canvas is a guide to restoration, a guide to setting the Church on fire with revival through true God-worship. We are God's living canvas. Each time we enter into true God-worship, we allow Him to transform us, to take us from glory to glory, until we enter into eternity. Until then, we are His unfinished masterpiece.

When our heart is right and when we seek His face, when we submit to Him, when we enter into the throne room of God face-to-face, we enter into a divine relationship with our Father and Creator. It is through this relationship we are remade in His image and we walk the path we were predestined to walk.

Jesus changed my heart. He taught me to draw close to Him in **prayer**, in **worship** and through the **Word of God**. All three are essential to an intimate and loving relationship with Him, but as a creative worshiper the focus of this book is worship, a worship unlike any you have ever experienced.

Throughout these pages, I share my testimony, my heart and the work God has been doing in me as a creative worshiper. Through my experience, inspired by the Holy Spirit and rooted in the Word of God, I offer instruction to believers at every level, including pastors and worship leaders who want to see God take them and their churches to a new level of power, anointing and His glory.

God is calling His people to worship, to prophesy over the "valley of dry bones." God wants to restore His great army. God wants revival, in your heart and throughout His Church! He wants intimacy, a close and loving relationship with every one of us.

I am a living canvas upon which God continues to work. His work is still unfinished, but what He has already done serves as my testimony, one that God has called me to share with you.

I share my adventures, from Haiti to the Philippines to India, through which God has revealed my identity in Christ and the plans and purposes He has for me.

You too can access the throne room of God through true God-worship. This book is dedicated to helping you get there.

It is there, face-to-face, God will show you who He created you to be. Jesus will reveal to you the plans and purposes He has for your life. But more important than any of this, Jesus will show His love for you, a love and devotion unlike anything else you will ever know.

Finally, for those who love to dance, love the arts or consider themselves creative types, I will teach you how to use these passions, gifts and talents to give glory to God through your creative worship.

A LIVING CANVAS

God's Unfinished Masterpiece

ILSE R. SPEARS

A Living Canvas
By Ilse R. Spears

Copyright © 2017 Ilse R. Spears

Cover Art & Design by M.L. Spears

Edited by M.L. Spears

Photography by Carlie Faulk

www.ilsespears.com

ISBN: 978-0-9996880-0-7

SCRIPTURE ATTRIBUTION & COPYRIGHTS

"As a pastor I have come to realize that true worship is what sets the stage for the Word of God to come forth. This is not just a series of good songs. This is when individuals and the congregation enter into a place of true worship. I have seen people getting empowered and set free during worship. This prepares the atmosphere for the logos Word to become rhema in the hearts of the listeners.

In her book, *A Living Canvas*, Ilse motivates and instructs the Body of Christ how to properly engage in worship. All this is from a very sound scriptural foundation. Great care is taken to direct worshippers to be and stay under authority. Worship is not something that is done just to fill a space. It is a vital ingredient in the conduct of services."

Pastor David Remedios, Trinity Christian Center

"Through *A Living Canvas*, you will be inspired to enter a greater dimension in your relationship with God. Few understand spiritual warfare also happens through creative worship. We are eyewitnesses as Ilse Spears effectively uses her tools of dance and worship to break through the strongholds of the devil and see people set free!"

Terry and Cary Nelson, Missionaries to Haiti

TABLE OF CONTENTS

ACKNOWLEDGEMENTS

I will be the first person to tell you that I am human with many faults. I do not profess to be an expert on worship and the arts, or a scholar of the Bible, but I do have a lot of life's experiences and insights to share that God has shown me over the course of my life.

My hope is that when you read this book God will reveal to you the heartbeat of true worship, deepen your desire to know Him more and give you the keys and tools that you can use to benefit you as you freely and extravagantly worship God with creative expression.

Growing up in Rhema South Africa Church, as a young girl I saw Pastor Lyndie McCauley as a powerhouse woman of God. I would sit in services and was inspired to "be like" Pastor Lyndie when I grow up - a woman passionate about God, His Word and life itself, walking in excellence in everything she does. I am honored and blessed to have had such an amazing role model, mentor and friend in my life. My girls just love her to bits too. Love you Pastor Lyndie!

Immigrating to the USA in my young adult years was difficult, but an amazing couple poured into my life in more ways than one. Pastors David and Yvonne Remedios have always supported me and my family spiritually and continue to encourage me to go deeper, to desire humility above all else and to never doubt God's plan for my life.

Through this powerful man and woman of God I was introduced to a very talented young man, Phil King. He has become a dear friend of my husband Mike, our girls, London and Dakota, and myself and has been an inspiration to our little family. In fact, his book, *Defending the Purity of Worship* is what inspired me to write this book. His passion for worship and holiness is contagious and causes you to want to live a life of purity.

Without the unwarranted devotion and friendship of an amazing woman of God, Joy Tate, I would probably have taken much longer to get this message out, a message that has burned in my heart for years. I am beyond grateful for her help, support and encouragement. Ms. Joy, you are truly a God-send to our family, and our girls love you very much.

If it weren't for both my parents, Anton & Renie Botha through their wisdom and consistency, and their dedication to serving God throughout my life, I would not be the person I am today. They have always been a constant in my life, supporting me, encouraging me, challenging me and loving me unconditionally. They are my biggest cheerleaders. I love you so much mommy and daddy!

God handpicked my husband, Mike Spears, just for me. He is a true gift. Not only is he handsome and talented, but also an amazing daddy. Our girls adore him and constantly shower him with love and affection as reciprocation of his tender love toward us.

He is the head of our home. He always makes us feel very important, loved and safe. His passion for God's Word, prayer and the presence of God in our lives is what inspires our little family to constantly dig deeper for more of God in our lives and to reflect a godly understanding and character. I love you my sweets!!

I also want to give credit where credit is due. I want to thank my husband Mike for his tireless editing work to help me get this book into print. Nearly two years in the making, the process was often grueling, frustrating and exhausting.

This book is a testimony to our unity as husband and wife, and our commitment to serving the Lord. (Joshua 24:15) Instead of breaking us, this book has strengthened us and prepared us for what God has next!

FOREWORD

By Ps Lyndie McCauley

It is my absolute joy to write this foreword for a most dynamic, beautiful and anointed woman of God and precious friend, my precious daughter in the Lord.

Ilse, I have watched you blossom over the many years into a true worshipper. Your love for God and very beautiful expression of love through dance and flagging is so moving and so powerful that every time I am blessed to be in a service you are ministering, I am drawn deeply into the flow of the Holy Ghost.

Your heart to express that love is written on the pages of this book and every page is filled with an adoration for Who God is, and for How He has loved you and reached out to you. Your heart is so pure and always crying out to God..."I worship you!"

Many have not understood the flow of your anointing, but I honestly believe that it is because they have never experienced the power that lies in your anointed expressive worship. I pray that they will have an opportunity to witness and receive for themselves from your gifting and from the powerful flow of the Holy Spirit.

Over the years I have seen many attempt to flow in this gift without any Presence at all, that is why I celebrate your gift and support you in the writing of this book. Well done beautiful woman of God! I love you dearly, and I am excited to see you continue to blossom in the years ahead to an even greater anointing. May thousands of lives be touched and changed as you draw them into His Presence.

I love you so very much,
Ps Lyndie McCauley

PREFACE

What is a living canvas? You and me, we are each a living and breathing canvas, prepared and ready for God, the Master Artist. He is working on us, even now, perfecting His work.

Everyone's walk with Jesus was predestined before we were born. He created us for an intimate and personal relationship with Him. As long as we are here on earth, we are separated from Jesus and the Father. It is through worship that we can enter the throne room of God, face-to-face, where God transforms us.

The Master Artist creates a masterpiece of your life as you surrender it to Him through your worship. We are God's living canvas. Each time we enter into true God-worship, we allow Him to transform us, to take us from glory to glory, until we enter into eternity. Until then, we remain His unfinished masterpiece.

Worship is something we must learn to incorporate into everything we do. *A Living Canvas* presents a worship that contrasts the worship we find in most of today's church services. Worship is so much more than a stirring 20 minutes of worship songs before the pastor's message.

True God-worship prepares the hearts of everyone in a service. It sanctifies hearts. It readies and opens them to receive the Word of God and the message delivered by the pastor. It creates an atmosphere through which God can reach and change His people.

Scripture reveals how worship is an essential part of a daily relationship with God. I hope to demonstrate how worship can be a transformative part of your daily life.

As you read, you'll hear two voices. At times you'll hear the passionate and heartfelt voice of a child of God. At other times you'll hear the teacher, sharing what I've learned through scripture, prayer and communion with the Holy Spirit.

My heart's voice is one filled with love and adoration for God. It's filled with passion and conviction as I share personal testimonies through my stories and experiences. Although these stories and experiences are profound, especially in how they directed the course of my life as a creative worshiper, I also wanted to share them in the context of God's Word. As I share these testimonies, I connect them to scripture and biblical principle, and this is where you will hear the voice of the teacher.

All that God has given me, I am eager to share. I believe we are about to experience an incredible move of God, and I believe God is using people with stories and experiences like these that I share in *A Living Canvas* to prepare us for what is coming.

INTRODUCTION

On the 9th of November 2003 God revealed a powerful message through His Word about the purpose He has for me. As I began to meditate day and night on the scripture below my spirit was ignited with a passion I had not experienced before. I surrendered my heart and mind to Him with the hope of fulfilling His purpose for my life on this earth, and devoted myself to share with others the message that He imprinted on my heart.

The scripture that sparked this pivotal moment in my life is:

> Going through the motions doesn't please you,
>   a flawless performance is nothing to you.
> I learned God-worship
>   when my pride was shattered.
> Heart-shattered lives ready for love
>   don't for a moment escape God's notice.
>
> Psalms 51:16-17 MSG

Throughout these pages I will expound on the voice and message of these two verses of scripture. As you read through these chapters I will take you on a journey where we'll explore the powerful revelation of God and discover how the power in our worship lies in our hearts and in the motive behind our worship.

Do you ever find it difficult to pray? Or, do you find it hard to enter into worship? Do you sense a lack of genuine fellowship with Jesus when you do? Worship changes everything. Worship will enrich your life in ways you never thought possible. Worship brings breakthrough.

For example:

- Worship establishes the motive of one's heart
- Worship provides a clear sense of purpose

- Worship develops a healthy attitude of gratitude
- Worship renews, refreshes and reconnects us with God

God gave each of us gifts and talents to serve and worship Him. He created us uniquely to achieve His plans and purposes for our lives.

Some of us are gifted and talented in the marketplace, serving as businessmen or entrepreneurs. Some are helpers, serving as nurses, doctors, policemen and firemen. Some of us are administrators, and we serve as accountants, office managers and secretaries. Others are gifted in the entertainment industry, serving as actors, musicians, painters, poets, artists and dancers.

Discovering our gifts and talents and how we are to use them for God's plans and purposes, and to advance His Kingdom on this earth is essential to unlocking the power of worship. When our gifts and talents are fully submitted to God and the leadership that God has placed over our lives, we begin to move closer to God, and our lives begin to align with the Kingdom of Heaven.

This book is directed toward those who are gifted and talented in the creative arts, but certainly not limited to those alone. Creative worship is for everyone!

Musicians and singers have found a place in the Church today, but many others with creative talents that want to worship in those gifts and talents, artists and dancers for example, have difficulty finding their place.

If you are a dancer, painter, actor, mime or poet, there may not be a place on the worship team or an opportunity to express your gifts and talents in a worship service at your church.

However, there is certainly a place in God's Kingdom for you, your gifts and talents. Just because you have not found your place yet, it doesn't mean you can't engage these gifts and talents as an expression of your worship to God. Helping you find and understand your place is one of the primary objectives of this book!

There is a burning desire in my heart to restore the arts back to God and in the Church where it belongs. The devil has had it for way too long. He has influenced the hearts and minds of many, causing their expression of worship to be twisted, sick, perverted and self-serving.

Just look around us. Look at the Hollywood culture and the kinds of movies coming out of it. So many are filled with murder, violence and evil, in which the central themes incorporate the spirit of the anti-Christ.

The music on secular radio glorifies sex, racism and hatred. Walk into secular art galleries and we need to cover our eyes because of the pornographic nature of the artwork, or they depict dark and evil creatures, portraying them as cute and adorable.

It is time for us, in true worship, to take a stand and present ourselves holy and acceptable to God and to offer our expression of worship to Him in the way in which it was intended and created; to worship Him in spirit and in truth.

The challenges of praise and worship are not relegated to ancient history. They are also an issue for us today as we struggle to understand true worship and its place in our lives and God's Kingdom. I will be tackling this issue head on, and I'll discuss what is true worship, the power of praise, how to worship, the benefits of worship, what it does in our churches, in our lives, in the world, in Heaven and in our relationship with God.

THE HEARTBEAT OF WORSHIP

For where your treasure is, there your heart will be also.

Matthew 6:21 NKJV

As a worshiper, I seek nothing more than to lay my head on the chest of Jesus, my Groom, and allow my heartbeat to come into sync with His. By moving to the rhythm of His heartbeat it will give me everything I will ever need. I can fix my eyes on His face as I seek to know Him more with each day. Ultimately, the world around me will pass away but my relationship with Jesus is eternal and everlasting. My worship is one of the ways I build that relationship.

When God created us, He didn't do so casually. We were not a mistake or just a passing thought. We were very carefully and purposely created.

> "Thou art worthy, O Lord, to receive glory and honour and power: for thou hast created all things, and for thy pleasure they are and were created."
>
> Revelations 4:11 NKJV

God created in man a need to worship. But God does not need our worship to be God. He accepts from man what He does not need; our heart of true worship.

The more we begin to understand God, the more we understand that He is leading man in an attitude of worship because in His presence is where we rightly belong, and worship leads us into His presence. Whether or not we realize it, we need to worship - and God wants our worship because He knows and wants what is best for us.

> All has been heard; the end of the matter is: Fear God [*revere and worship Him, knowing that He is*] and keep His commandments, for this is the whole of man [*the full, original purpose of his creation, the object of God's providence, the root of character, the foundation of all happiness, the adjustment to all inharmonious circumstances and conditions under the sun*] and the whole [*duty*] for every man.
>
> Ecclesiastes 12:13 AMPC

When we understand that we were created to worship and that our life on this earth is preparation for an eternity of worship, then reading this book will help you understand how to use your gifts and talents as an expression of worship. You will be challenged to look inward and determine what is in your heart, what's your motive, your focus, your passion that drives you, and what's your purpose as a creative worshiper.

IS JESUS RELIGIOUS?

Worship cannot be rationalized. Our mind is what holds us back. The mind tries to rationalize and figure out what worship is, but God challenges and instructs us to worship Him in spirit and in truth, leaving our mind out of it.

The mind is the battleground where religion is constantly attacking the freedom that Jesus brings. This statement may surprise you, but Jesus is not as religious as we think.

> "'These people honor me with their lips, but their hearts are far from me. They worship me in vain; their teachings are merely human rules.'"
>
> Matthew 15:8-9 NIV

Those who entertain a religious spirit will often portray the perfect outside image but in their heart, they contradict themselves. God makes it clear in this scripture that no matter what we do or say, if it does not match the intent of our heart, we are merely following human teachings, rules and ideas about worship.

Religion is a waste of time and effort because it is without the rewards of freedom and liberty. Only a true relationship with Jesus, a heart relationship with Him, can most certainly guarantee total freedom.

WHAT IS RELIGION?

In the book of Isaiah we read that we will never fully understand God with our mind because His ways and thoughts are higher than that of man.

"For as the heavens are higher than the earth, so are My ways higher than your ways, and My thoughts than your thoughts.

Isaiah 55:9 NKJV

We may not recognize it, but humankind desires boundaries, leadership and understanding. When there is a lack of understanding, when we don't follow the lead of God's Holy Spirit, man tends to institute rules and guidelines. This is where a fine line is crossed, where God's laws and principals are turned into man-made rules and guidelines, which in turn become religion.

God is not something we need to study. God is someone we need to know. Religion focuses on the *study* whereas relationship focuses on the *know*.

Here are some of the downfalls and affects religion has had on society and how the Church has lost its life-changing power.

- Religion tells us we must search for God. Yet, we have already found Him and can commune with Him through worship and prayer. Jesus came to abolish religion.

- Religion tells us we need big, beautiful churches in which to honor God. Jeff Bethke, a spoken word artist and author, puts it well in a poem when he wrote that religion builds huge churches with all the bells and whistles but has little to no impact on the lives of the poor by being the hands of Jesus feeding the poor and clothing the impoverished.

- Religion tells us there are certain dos and don'ts we must follow to be a Christian. Religion never addresses the core of a problem. It tells us how to modify our behavior to fit in the perceived mold of a Christian. We may look well dressed from the outside, but inside our world is falling apart.

- Religion tells us man and our churches hold the answers to our questions, the solutions to our problems. Religion keeps our focus on a horizontal plane looking to man for answers and not on a vertical plane that shifts our focus off man and onto God.

- Religion tells us if we act and look like a Christian we are a Christian. It's like saying that if we sit in a garage long enough we will turn into a car.

- Religion tells us the Holy Spirit is not necessary to have a relationship with Jesus. Religion has snuffed out the life force of God in our churches. It has driven the power out of our churches. It has evicted the Holy Spirit.

- Religion tells us if we cannot understand it, we cannot embrace it. Religion has said that if our mind cannot understand it then it is to be cast down, controlled or ignored.
- Religion tells us God and our relationship with Him requires an institution. Religion is the institutional aspects that surround a personal relationship with God.

God is not a human. He does not think like one or operate like one. (Isaiah 55:8-9) If we try to understand God and His ways without the Holy Spirit and without His teachings in the Word, then our minds and our worldly thinking will lead us into religion.

The Holy Spirit is our teacher, our revelator and our guide. Without the Holy Spirit in our life, home and church, we will never understand the ways of God.

God's Word instructs us to: 1) Worship Him in spirit (where our spirit connects with the Holy Spirit); 2) Worship Him in the truth of His Word (as who He created us to be).

> For God is Spirit, so those who worship him must worship in spirit and in truth."
>
> John 4:24 NLT

The Holy Spirit is the person of God who gives us freedom, and freedom from religion. To access this freedom, we must give the Holy Spirit access to us. One very powerful way to do this is through our worship. That is when we will see and experience how free, creative and radical God is in worship. True God-worship sets the worshiper free from their human limitations.

The bottom line is this: True God-worship cannot be realized without the Holy Spirit and the truth of God's Word.

BATTLE CRY
A Warrior Generation

God is raising up a warrior-generation, one by one, to stand up and say, "Enough is enough! We are enforcing our victory and taking back ground for God's Kingdom. We are launching a direct attack on the enemy."

We can no longer stand in a defensive stance cowering behind our excuses and fears. We must stand up and take an offensive stance. We must set our feet firmly on God's Word, cladded in the armor of God. We must invite the Holy Spirit to lead, guide, teach and train us with special-forces tactics and strategic insights.

We must go out into the spiritual darkness of night, like stealth bombers, to drop ordinance in strategically calculated locations to destroy enemy strongholds. The bombs are God's presence manifested as Holy Spirit fire and rain that we launch into those regions to redeem, restore, revive and reignite the people of God.

Indeed, worship has the power to do many things. As you will discover in the following chapters, worship can be a powerful weapon we use in our lives to combat the powers of darkness and to take back territory for the Kingdom.

I hope to challenge you to step out of the box, out of the perceived mold of worship. Present your mind and body as a living sacrifice by lifting up your gifts and talents to God as an expression of worship.

Die to self, the selfish desires and the pleasures of this world that constantly try to steal your focus away from God. Yield your whole being over to Him. Render your vulnerability into His hands. Allow the Holy Spirit to teach you and fill you with boldness.

You will never be disappointed. God finds pleasure in your radical, spirit-led and true worship. Within you there is a pure and uninhibited faith waiting to be unleashed through the gifts and talents God has given you.

Let us worship like never before. Let us pray like never before. Let us live lives of holiness like never before. Let us be vessels of His fire and His love.

"My people are destroyed for lack of knowledge."

Isaiah 5:13 NIV

I do not believe anyone has a desire to be held captive, to be destroyed or to remain in exile because of a lack of knowledge. Worship is an important part of unlocking this knowledge, in finding the heartbeat of God and growing closer to Him.

Join me as we embark on a journey to discover how to worship with a true heart, a pure motive and divine purpose; how to become the Holy Spirit-led creative worshipers that God created us to be!

1

THE HEART OF WORSHIP

The time is coming, yes, it is here now, when the true worshipers will worship the Father in spirit and in truth. The Father wants that kind of worshipers.

John 4:23 NLV

In my ministry experiences and travels across the world, I have found very little teaching on worship and the creative expression of movement. There are many people who worship and express themselves creatively throughout the world, but upon asking them what is true God-worship and what does the Bible say about it, not one answer was the same. Many times I was faced with a blank stare or a comment like, "we just do what others do."

If you're new to the topic of worship or someone who has questions about worship in general, regardless of your background, religion, culture or ideas, you'll begin to see that worship is more than just an outward action. Worship begins when our spirit within prompts our soul with an expectancy of experiencing the love, presence and power of God. The outward motions of worship naturally follow suit as we take pleasure in showering our affection on Jesus.

In this first chapter, I want to begin by establishing a good foundation, a clear understanding of the basics of worship, answering the commonly asked *what, who, why, where* and *how* questions.

"How we worship? is one of the big questions that needs answering. We've simply accepted the fact that how we worship is how we've observed others worship, or how "ordinary" worship is conducted in our church services.

Worship is something that we can do whether we are in a church service or going about our daily business.

This is important because true worship opens the door to the supernatural realm and changes the way we see the world, the natural realm. It helps us see through the eyes of God. It adds the super to the natural and empowers us to walk out our purpose and destiny with godly confidence and boldness.

I believe it is imperative that we refuse to be content with "ordinary" worship. Instead, we must insist on experiencing God's presence for ourselves, worshiping God His way, not our way. Our way limits us. His way liberates us. Without a doubt, His way is always the best way.

The Bible has a lot to say about worship, but do we understand worship and do we worship the way God intended? Since we were created to worship, shouldn't we learn to do it the way God intended?

In this chapter, we explore some of the most common questions and issues about worship. What is worship? What is the act and attitude of worship? What is our motive behind our worship?

As we explore these questions, my hope is that you will see the core and foundation of worship in a whole new light. You will discover a powerful new way to connect and commune with God in a personal and intimate way. God will reveal His thoughts about you and who you are as a person founded in Him. You will begin to discover your true identity.

Evangelist Todd White from "Lifestyle Christianity" often says, and I will paraphrase here; once you discover your true identity in Christ you will be set free from what you think about yourself, and from what the world thinks about you.

WHAT IS WORSHIP?

Defining worship is not as easy as one might think.

Personally, when I've been asked "What is worship?" my innermost response is that worship is when I am in complete submission and extreme reverence to the will of God.

Whether answering this question for a new believer, someone who is not yet a believer, and sometimes for mature believers, I realize my response often sounds foreign or complicated.

Many people, whether inside or outside of the Church, also struggle to answer this question. While studying, I stumbled upon the following definition of worship that I liked, and honestly it answers this question quite simply and clearly. It's Warren W. Wiersbe's definition. He's an American pastor, Bible teacher, and prolific writer of Christian literature and theological works.

"Worship is the believer's response of all that they are – mind, emotions, will, body – to what God is and says and does."

In essence, it means that worship is how we respond, in our actions and emotions, to who God is, what He says about us, and what He does for us, His beloved.

There has been quite a large gap between the "teaching" and the "understanding" of this very topic. There are some who have misrepresented true worship, substituting their own ideas and ideologies. Sadly, few teachings answer the question of "What is worship?" Instead, they create more questions and uncertainty.

In my personal journey as a creative worshiper I cannot recall a specific moment when I suddenly *understood* worship. Instead, I understood my worship as a response of submission to, and reverence of God and His amazing love. Worship has always been the one constant in my walk with God and has always been more than enough to empower me to walk out my purpose and destiny daily.

Since worship has always been a personal part of my faith, I hadn't ever considered how to define it or explain it to others. But for me, worship is something powerful and meaningful I want to share with others, so in recent years I began studying extensively and then teaching worship, particularly creative worship.

Through this process, I discovered that a lack of understanding of worship is not only common among regular church-going folk, but sadly it is quite common among church leaders and worship leaders as well.

Most people have just followed the example of others, without questioning it. Instead of seeking out examples in the Bible and the way God intended it to be, they have just accepted the status quo.

ATTITUDE OF WORSHIP

Too often we see worship as something we do, simply an *act*. But to truly understand worship from a Christian perspective we need to recognize that worship is more than just an *act*. The *act* must be accompanied by the right *attitude*.

Taking it one step further, the attitude is what matters most, because the act, or expression, should be a natural product of the right attitude. So, first understanding the *attitude of worship* allows us to better grasp the *act of worship*.

Digging even a little deeper, we should also look at the motive of our worship. The motive is connected to our attitude toward, and during, worship.

Our *attitude* comes from our soul, which includes our emotions, our free will and conscious mind. For the most part, we understand the emotional part of our worship: joy, happiness, peace and love. Our motives drives us to achieve what we desire.

Let's look at the Online Dictionary's definitions for "attitude" and "motive."

> *Attitude* - a settled way of thinking or feeling about someone or something, typically one that is reflected in a person's behavior.

> *Motive* - a reason for doing something, especially one that is hidden or not obvious.

Then there is our free will, which is the ability to make our own choices. God created us with a free will for the very simple reason; that we would have the option of choosing whether or not we want to worship Him. Just like a parent would rather their child choose to love them, so would God rather we choose to love and worship Him. The emphasis lies in the fact that we are free to choose.

God knows how worship benefits you and me, and He wants the best for us. I have no doubt about it. Choices are very powerful and our choices make a clear statement of our intention, without persuasion or influence from someone else.

The conscious mind, where we make choices, is part of our soul. It's where we reason and think. It's through this reasoning or logic we establish an identity, belief structure, awareness and sensitivity toward life. In essence, our conscious mind is our state of being.

I recall as a young girl in South Africa, and growing up in a Christian family, being logical was a big deal to me. I can now see that God had His hand on my life, because my logical thinking and reasoning skills were rooted in biblical principles.

I may not have known the full impact of it back then but now I can see how it opened my soul to the wisdom of God. God's wisdom is a gift and I ask God for His wisdom often, especially when faced with tough decisions.

If we are to look at the whole picture, which includes our emotions, free will, motive and conscious mind, it makes sense that they are interconnected and make up the attitude of our worship.

So, if pure or true worship comes from our soul and requires both the *act* of worship and the *attitude* of worship then it would make sense that we would want our soul to come into submission.

In Matthew Henry's commentary about the book of John, chapter 4 in the Bible, he says that "The spirit or the soul of man, as influenced by the Holy Spirit, must worship God, and have communion with Him."

For this to happen we must bring our body and soul into submission. By doing so we make way for our spirit to step out into the forefront. This is very important to understand because it is when our spirit connects with the Holy Spirit we experience pure and true worship.

If you will, envision this with me for a moment. We are like a trailer that needs to be hooked up to a truck. The trailer symbolizes man, while the truck symbolizes God. To connect the trailer to the truck it requires a trailer coupler and trailer ball. The trailer coupler symbolizes man's spirit, and the trailer ball represents the Holy Spirit. For the trailer to connect to the truck the trailer coupler needs to align and hook onto the trailer ball.

Without this action of connecting, the trailer cannot get anywhere on its own. It requires being connected with the truck to fulfill its designed purpose of hauling stuff back and forth. The truck leads the way and the trailer follows.

We have a preordained purpose and destiny that God uniquely designed for each one of us. It is only when we connect our spirit to the Holy Spirit that we will fulfill our designed purpose. Until then we will get nowhere and feel unfulfilled.

Furthermore, our spirit is the immortal part of our being, whereas our body is the material part. We can see the body but we cannot see the spirit. As a person, we each have a spirit. There are both "dead" and "alive" spirits. The "dead" spirit is found in those who have not yet accepted Jesus Christ as their Lord and Savior, whereas the "alive" spirit is found in those who have. Some like to use the term, born again. It is just a simple term that speaks of the spirit of man that has come to life, or become born again, after accepting Christ as their Savior.

Personally, once I grasped the importance of bringing my soul into submission, I realized that for many years I allowed my fleshly desires and emotions to rule me and it led to my spirit being suppressed. In essence, I pushed my spirit man to the back of the line giving my soul full reign and preference.

Growing up "churched" I have seen and experienced a lot. Since I had not yet fully understood that the *attitude* of worship meant bringing my soul into submission to what God desires in my worship, I struggled to "feel" like I wanted to worship. I would worship out of obligation because I knew it was what we did in church, and that God desired it. But I couldn't stay focused very long. Without the proper knowledge, except for the basics of worship, I didn't find worship interesting or exciting.

As a young child in South Africa, probably around nine or ten years old, I remember how my children's church worship leader encouraged us to sing the words of the songs as though we meant them. Unknowingly, that was where my journey began, where my spirit birthed an intrigue about worship and its purpose. It might have been a simple statement but it made a profound impression on me. The simple act of meaning what we say automatically brings our *attitude* into submission.

Once I understood how to submit my body and soul to God, allowing my spirit to connect with the Holy Spirit in my worship, it became very important to me. As I connected my spirit with the Holy Spirit, I envisioned that connection as an umbilical cord to God. God began to nourish my spirit with exactly what I needed at that given time.

When man's spirit connects with God a beautiful flow of communion begins to take place between our humanity and our Holy God, giving us all that we need to live and thrive.

The dictionary tells us "worship" is reverent honor and homage paid to God or a sacred personage, or to any object regarded as sacred. Synonyms for worship include adore, idolize, esteem worthy, reverence and homage.

This gives us a good definitive foundation, but scripture found in the Bible is an even better place to look for a definition. Interestingly, scripture doesn't provide an explicit definition of worship like a dictionary, but it does provide many examples of worship and more than enough for us to understand worship from God's point of view. We'll find many examples, including praise, thanksgiving, sacrifice, service and obedience.

Let's start with the *who*, the *why*, the *how* and the *where* of worship. Who do we worship? Why do we Worship? Where do we worship? How do we worship?

Who Do We Worship?

Clearly as Christians, we worship God, the God of Abraham, Isaac and Jacob. (Matthew 22:32) God is our creator and ruler over everything. He created all things.

When God gave us the 10 Commandments, He made it clear that He is our God and that only Him should we worship. (Exodus 20:3-4)

Jesus also makes this clear when He tells Satan in the desert that we are to honor and worship the Lord our God only. (Matthew 4:10)

Scripture, again and again, makes it clear "who" we should worship. Clearly, it's the God of the Bible. But many people still have trouble understanding who God really is.

Let's delve a little deeper here and look at the Godhead.

The Godhead is the Trinity; God the Father, God the Son, and God the Holy Spirit. The evidence of the Godhead being three persons can be found in these scriptures:

> When Jesus came up out of the water, the heavens opened. He saw the Spirit of God coming down and resting on Jesus like a dove. A voice was heard from heaven. It said, "This is My much-loved Son. I am very happy with Him."
>
> Matthew 3:16-17 NLV

> Jesus Christ came by water and blood. He did not come by water only, but by water and blood. The Holy Spirit speaks about this and He is truth. There are three Who speak of this in heaven: the Father and the Word and the Holy Spirit. These three are one.
>
> 1 John 5:6-7 NLV

When we worship God, we worship God the Father and God the Son and we do so through God the Holy Spirit. While God the Father and Jesus are in Heaven, the Spirit of God is omnipresent here on Earth. In believers, the Holy Spirit lives within us. He is our vehicle, the channel (the trailer hitch, the umbilical cord) we need to commune in a relationship with God the Father and God the Son, Jesus.

Why Do We Worship?

There are many reasons why we worship. We worship God for who He is, the almighty Creator of all things. We worship in praise and thanksgiving for what God has done, what He is doing and what He has promised He will do. We worship to glorify God and praise Him above all others.

> Let the whole earth sing to the LORD! Each day proclaim the good news that He saves. Publish His glorious deeds among the nations. Tell everyone about the amazing things He does. Great is the LORD! He is most worthy of praise! He is to be feared above all gods. The gods of other nations are mere idols, but the LORD made the heavens! Honor and majesty surround Him; strength and joy fill His dwelling. O nations of the world, recognize the LORD, recognize that the LORD is glorious and strong. Give to the LORD the glory He deserves! Bring your offering and come into His presence. Worship the LORD in all His holy splendor. Let all the earth tremble before Him. The world stands firm and cannot be shaken. Let the heavens be glad, and the earth rejoice! Tell all the nations, "The LORD reigns!"
>
> 1 Chronicles 16:23-31 NLT

Personally, I worship God because I know my worship ushers in divine and on-time moments. In these moments I have received profound revelation, healing and the understanding of how much God truly loves me.

Our worship connects the natural realm with the supernatural realm through the Holy Spirit. A two-way highway of communication with God develops. Any successful and healthy communication requires us to be involved. We cannot expect to build a meaningful relationship with God without doing our part. A relationship takes two. Being involved is the key. It allows us to develop a personal relationship with God.

Our willing involvement is what engages our soul and spirit in worship. It's what transforms a one-sided relationship into a whole relationship. When we're not involved and engaged we alienate ourselves and become spectators instead of partakers.

There is a great reward when we engage. We hear God's heartbeat for us, and we see how He finds pleasure in our surrender to Him. We become so focused on Him and how much He loves us that we automatically shift our focus off our own problems and gaze upon Him in His glory. In these moments we realize why we worship God. All of our problems fade away. When God has our heart, He is able to move heaven and earth for His beloved.

Where Do We Worship?

Worship can take place anywhere and at any time. Worship is not confined to a church building. Worship at church, a conference, a concert or other place may aid in our worship, but worship can take place anywhere; the ballpark, the movie theatre, in the privacy of our home, or in the car.

One of my favorite times to worship is while driving my car. I cherish these times, especially when I am overcome with His love and compassion. I cannot speak for people in other cars as they pass by or sit next to me at a red light. From their viewpoint, however, unable to hear my music, it might be quite fascinating to observe me in worship – having a good ol' time.

Contrary to what some people may think, worship is not an event we attend or observe but rather a lifestyle that we live. It's a part of our relationship with God.

As believers, we are automatically grafted into the family of God, the Body of Christ, when we accept Jesus Christ as our Lord and Savior. Jesus lives inside of us! How cool is that? That means we can take our worship anywhere and everywhere we go.

> Examine yourselves as to whether you are in the faith. Test yourselves. Do you not know yourselves, that Jesus Christ is in you?
>
> 2 Corinthians 13:5 NKJV

If Jesus Christ is in our heart then it doesn't matter where we are when we worship Him because our body is His sanctuary, the temple of God.

> Or do you not know that your body is the temple of the Holy Spirit *who is* in you, whom you have from God, and you are not your own?
>
> 1 Corinthians 6:19 NKJV

How Do We Worship?

Answering the "how" of worship goes hand in hand with our *attitude* in worship. Here in the book of John, we learn more about the "how" as it relates to our *attitude* in worship.

> "God is spirit [*the Source of life, yet invisible to mankind*], and those who worship Him must worship in spirit and truth."
>
> John 4:24 AMP

The word *spirit* in the latter part of this scripture is referring to our own spirit, not the Holy Spirit. It addresses a part of us, our human and natural being.

The word *truth* is made up of two parts, accuracy and genuineness. Accuracy relates to the truth of who God is and what He has done for us. We find this truth in our own experiences with God and in the Word of God.

Genuineness relates to our sincerity, an authentic and true commitment to our godly nature, responding as the person God knows, and in the identity that God has given us. By knowing our true identity in Christ and by engaging in a relationship with Him, we discover our unique purpose and role within the Body of Christ.

It's also important here to address the word *must* in the previous scripture. *Must* means that it is a requirement, a necessity, not an option. To truly know how to worship you *must* do it God's way, which is *in spirit* and *in truth*.

So, if we are to read the above scripture again and paraphrase it to incorporate the definitions above it should sound something like this:

> When we worship God, we must worship Him with our whole being, in the accuracy, genuineness, sincerity and uniqueness of who He created you and me to be in Him, to fulfill our individual purpose and destiny during our time here on earth.

In Matthew 22:37, Jesus commands us to love the LORD our God with all our heart, soul and mind. This is how we worship; by bringing our body and soul into reverent submission, connecting our spirit with the Holy Spirit, believing the truth of who we are in Christ and then following God's lead.

An example of how we worship is a lot like a dance between a married couple. It is the bridegroom that leads his bride in the dance. For it to flow effortlessly and be enjoyable without standing on each other's feet, the bride needs to submit to the bridegroom, connect her rhythm to his and follow his lead.

As believers, the Bible says that we are His bride and Jesus Christ is the bridegroom. Imagine dancing with Christ the bridegroom. If you can imagine dancing with Christ, as His bride, then you can understand worship!

So, at this point we have looked at several aspects of worship, in part answering the question: What is worship? We've learned about the *attitude* of worship. What about the *act* of worship?

John Piper, founder and teacher of www.desiringGod.org, gives a great example of the difference between the *attitude* and the *act* of worship in one short statement. I have paraphrased the statement to clarify the difference.

The *attitude* of worship can be described as the inward feeling whereas the *act* is the outward action that reflects the worth of God.

The *act* of worship is also an expression of our attitude. In the following chapters, we will dive deep into the question: What is the act of worship? This exploration will take you to unexpected places.

Now that we have covered some of the basics, we can begin to see that worship is more than just a one-dimensional act. There is so much more to it - and that is super exciting! The realization that worship is multi-dimensional should spark an excitement in your spirit.

My prayer for you, as we journey together through each chapter of this book, is that you'll not only understand and visualize worship, but you'll also *experience* true worship on a whole new level. As you open your spirit, allow the Holy Spirit to drop nuggets of revelation and truth deep inside your soul.

Revelation and truth are like the flint that will ignite a fire and passion within you. When that happens, you will enter into true God-worship, and your worship will transcend your human limitations.

The revelation of true worship is very important. We must incorporate worship into every aspect of our lives. After all, this short time on earth is our training ground for an eternal life in heaven. Christ has prepared a place for us in heaven with Him. Eternity is going to be absolutely glorious as we worship our Creator. I have a great expectancy in my spirit of the awesomeness of heavenly worship, but I struggle to find the words to describe it. Personally, I don't think those words have been created yet.

> There is more than enough room in my Father's home. If this were not so, would I have told you that I am going to prepare a place for you? When everything is ready, I will come and get you, so that you will always be with me where I am. And you know the way to where I am going."
>
> John 14:2-4 NLT

THE ACT OF WORSHIP

Let's return now to the five earlier points describing how worship can be expressed as praise, thanksgiving, sacrifice, service and obedience. As we look at some of the scriptures that address each *act* or expression, I will include some of my personal experiences in each of these areas.

There is truth in the statement that "worship is a lifestyle" and by adding my reflections I will put it into a real, daily context you can relate to. These examples demonstrate one person's worship, as personal as it can get. It shows that worship is personal, and much more than the musical part of a church service.

Worship as Praise

I bow before Your holy Temple as I worship. I praise Your name for Your unfailing love and faithfulness; for Your promises are backed by all the honor of Your name.

Psalms 138:2 NLT

For me, worship as praise is an expression where all that I want to do is thank God for all that He is, what He has done and continues to do in, and through, my life. I am overcome with thankfulness seeing difficult and challenging circumstances turn around for good. I am filled with joy; a joy that wells up and overflows with pure happiness when I witness firsthand how God answers prayer.

Nothing or no one can taint this joy. I become rooted, immovable and un-swayed by issues I am facing or circumstances that threaten to steal my joy. I am humbled to know that God stops to listen and hear my petitions, my prayers, and answers them in such beautiful ways.

A simple, but impacting, example of an answered prayer as a young child, that boosted my confidence and joy, was when God healed the warts on my fingers. I had three warts on three different fingers. The warts began to bother me, particularly on one finger. It was the one on my right middle finger by the first knuckle. When I would write, it would hurt where the pen or pencil would press on it. I became self-conscious of them when my friends pointed them out.

I decided one night that I would make it a matter of prayer to ask God to heal my hands and remove the warts. Being a child, I wasn't very diligent with my prayers every night, but when I did pray I prayed with a child-like faith. I thanked Him for my healing even though my hands weren't healed yet. I believed God would heal me in His perfect time.

After about two years of believing for my healing I continued to remain hopeful. Then one school morning after doing my morning routine and sitting down to eat breakfast, I noticed the wart that bothered me the most felt oddly smooth and flat. I looked closer and it was GONE! I quickly checked my other fingers and every single one was gone. They weren't just gone, but there wasn't even a trace of them, not even a scar. Excited, I ran to my parents and told them that God had healed me. No more warts!

That was the first time I experienced answered prayer in my personal prayer life. It was such a boost to my confidence. It became evident to me that morning that God doesn't just sit in heaven and watch me but He cares enough about me to heal a few little warts on my fingers. On that day, I experienced the revelation of God's love and faithfulness on a whole new level. God became real to me, not just someone I would imagine or read about.

I am very thankful for this experience. It taught me a valuable life lesson and the power of praise. Now, whenever I experience areas of struggle, or storms in my life, I can simply praise Him knowing how much He cares about me and that He will walk me through it.

Going through storms and struggles are opportunities to worship God in praise. When we praise Him through the storms, a godly character develops and our faith grows stronger.

As we read in the Bible in the book of Colossians, we learn that every time we choose to *worship as praise*, it not only builds our faith, but it boosts our confidence and encourages us to stay strong. Its this strength that allows us to stand in faith and know that God is in control and has our best interests at heart.

> Let your roots grow down into him, and let your lives be built on him. Then your faith will grow strong in the truth you were taught, and you will overflow with thankfulness.
>
> Colossians 2:7 NLT

Praise affects every area of our lives. It affects God and it affects the devil. When there is praise in our life we are giving God control and nullifying the power of the devil's influence. Worship as praise says that God is our source and He is in control. Where there is a lack of praise we open the door for the devil to steal our joy.

Often the way we start our day will determine the rest of our day. Keep this in mind as you begin each day. Choose to praise God when you wake up, even though you don't feel like it.

I'll confess, and my family will tell you, I love my sleep. So there are days that I don't feel like praising God especially after I had a rough night with little sleep. Being a mommy tending to a sick daughter, the sounds of restless dogs or my husband snoring louder than normal, can take its toll. Still, I choose to make a conscious decision to praise Him, especially on these mornings. When I don't I find the rest of my day is filled with frustration, fatigue and feeling low.

Praise as worship not only fills us with joy but it recharges us; it fills us with energy that we would otherwise not have. So let us not just praise God when all things are going right and when things are looking good. Let us praise God when things aren't looking good or feeling so great. That is when we will see how powerful God is amid our storms, as we walk through the valleys.

When we praise Jesus in the moments we feel weak, alone, sad and depressed, we'll experience the supernatural nature of God's love. When we learn to praise Him through the storms, it changes everything.

Worship as Thanksgiving

> I wash my hands in innocence and go around your altar, O LORD, proclaiming thanksgiving aloud, and telling all your wondrous deeds.
>
> Psalms 26:6-7 NLT

I believe thanksgiving is automatically intertwined with praise. When God healed the warts on my fingers I was filled with thanks and gratitude for what He did. As Christians, we cannot have a true heart of gratitude, a heart of thanks, without giving God praise. Thanksgiving unlocks the power of God in our life.

When I look back and I see my own lack of worship in thanksgiving, I wonder if this lack of gratitude was the reason many of my prayers went unanswered. When I prayed, worshiped and petitioned God from a place of desperation, focused on my own needs, I wondered if He even heard me. Even as I reminded God of the promises He made to me, I wondered if He even remembered.

The moment I recognize that I am the one who binds God's hands by not worshiping Him with thanksgiving, I immediately fall to my knees and repent. It is typically when I lose sight of all He has done for me, for who He is, and by staying focused on my own needs that I tie His hands tighter.

Once I repent I begin to thank Him and pour my heart out to Him in gratitude. I thank Him for knowing me before I was conceived, for creating me with a purpose and a destiny, for wanting to have a relationship with me and for loving me when I felt I was unloved. Immediately my focus shifts and I no longer feel the need to seek God's hand for what He could do for me but instead I choose to seek God's face for who He is.

This is an example of a change of heart, a change of attitude. When we choose to prioritize, and press in, seeking an intimate and communal relationship with God, the issues and circumstances of life begin to fade. The hardships we faced before are no longer mountains in our path, but shrink down to molehills that are easy to step over.

When we seek His face, it is the same as seeking His heart. Once God has our gaze we see His heart, what He thinks of us and how much He loves us. We realize that God wants nothing more than to spend time with us, empower us through His Holy Spirit and to live victorious lives of fullness in Him.

Worship as Sacrifice

I know this is something almost every Christian is faced with in life. How do we worship God even when we don't feel like it, when life throws us tough challenges like serious life threatening diagnoses, bankruptcy, or when you just can't see a light at the end of the tunnel?

This is when we need God to step in and rescue a loved one from the snares of addictions or to break their minds free from the lies of the devil. This is when worshiping Jesus is an absolute necessity.

Worship as sacrifice is sacrificing our flesh or worldly natures. It is presenting our idols, our circumstances, our issues on the altar of sacrifice and choosing God above these things. It is submitting ourselves to God to be transformed by His Spirit, not by the world.

> And so, dear brothers and sisters, I plead with you to give your bodies to God because of all He has done for you. Let them be a living and holy sacrifice–the kind He will find acceptable. This is truly the way to worship Him. Don't copy the behavior of this world, but let God transform you into a new person by changing the way you think.
>
> Romans 12:1 NLT

This kind of worship will set us free from the snares of this world and allow us to soar above the storms of life. Just like an eagle flies above the stormy winds using the winds to lift it to soar higher, exerting very little effort, so will worship as sacrifice do that for us in our lives. It will clear our mind, it will remove fear and apprehension from our heart and a transcending peace will result, a peace that surpasses all human understanding. (Philippians 4:7) We will begin to see God's will for our life with clarity.

Worship as sacrifice symbolically takes our flesh and puts it on the altar of sacrifice so that we are free to worship in spirit and in truth. When we worship God in this manner our spirit magnifies God within us.

> I will bless the LORD at all times; His praise shall continually be in my mouth. My soul shall make its boast in the LORD; The humble shall hear of it and be glad. Oh, magnify the LORD with me, And let us exalt His name together. I sought the LORD, and He heard me, And delivered me from all my fears. They looked to Him and were radiant, And their faces were not ashamed. This poor man cried out, and the LORD heard him, And saved him out of all his troubles. The angel of the LORD encamps all around those who fear Him, And delivers them.
>
> Psalm 34:1-7 NKJV

It also magnifies the fruit of the Spirit: love, joy, peace, forbearance, kindness, goodness, faithfulness, gentleness and self-control. (Galatians 5:22-23)

My husband Mike and I have faced some difficult circumstances regarding his business. He invested 19 years of his life in this business, pouring most of the profits back into it. It has been good to him and continues to be good to our little family. But a few years ago, the stress and hardships that come with owning and running a business had brought him to a breaking point. Mike felt like he could no longer carry the weight of the many pressures.

When he started the business, he had expected the hard work, time and money he had invested over the years would eventually provide either a great deal of free time or a financial reward that would give him the freedom to spend as much time with his family as he wanted. Mike realized at this point, this expectation might be lost and it was very possible there would be no such reward. The prospect of starting over at 52, when our daughters are 3 and 5 years old, was heartbreaking.

We have prayed together, petitioned God and have sacrificially worshiped Him regarding what seemed like a hopeless situation. Mike calls it his Isaac moment. It was a Holy Spirit moment when Mike realized the business and the 19 years of reinvesting everything into it had become an idol before God. While God had gently pointed this out to him, this realization terrified him and he immediately felt compelled to repent.

He said "God, I pick you!" Mike wanted to put God first, so he laid it all on the altar and trusted completely in God.

The moment he put his business on the sacrificial altar, immediately something shifted in the supernatural over our family and in our lives, personally. God began to flood us with confirmation after confirmation, through circumstances, words of confirmation and prayer from others. Doors opened and doors closed. Circumstances began to present themselves, revealing the path God has planned for us.

Even through all of this, Mike was still unclear about the timing and path along which God wanted us to move. But we felt God was now clearly evident again in our lives. So we continued to pray. Mike says he wanted a Gideon experience, where God spoke to him and confirmed His word.

Four weeks later, after much toil by Mike to weigh every circumstance, to project every possible option, God spoke to him during the worship service at our church. What's more, only an hour later he recalled numerous points in our pastor's message to confirm, warn and encourage Mike to follow the Holy Spirit's instructions.

Now that we have heard from God, our desires and dreams are beginning to look like they are within reach and the freedom we feel is much more than we expected or even anticipated.

Mike's biggest fear was to move without the instruction of God. As he often said, when the kings of Israel went into battle with the instruction of God, they had victory. But when they did not, the result was destruction and slavery.

Worship as sacrifice is not easy, and at times may seem ridiculous and foolish. You might have seen that in Mike's Isaac experience.

The biblical Isaac experience can be found in Genesis 22 when God told Abraham to sacrifice his only son Isaac. Just as Abraham knew, when we choose

God above everything else, we are making a statement that only God matters and that we trust that He will never leave us or forsake us.

We declare in faith, through our sacrificial worship, that God loves and cares for us more than we can understand, and that He wants the ultimate best for us. You are His, and He will move heaven and earth for you when you willingly put your life and circumstances on the altar of sacrifice.

Worship as Service

> And Jesus answered him, "It is written, 'You shall worship the Lord your God, and him only shall you serve.'"
>
> Luke 4:8 NLT

I first became involved with a local church in Lafayette, Louisiana when we immigrated to the United States in 1997. I was 22 years old and single. My brother and I chose to serve at the church without expecting anything in return by offering to make ourselves available for anything they might need us to do.

My family had not yet been issued work permits. While we waited on the permit process, we had no source of income, and slowly our financial base was dwindling. Yet we trusted in faith that God would provide and we worshiped Him through our service to Him.

It was in those early days after our immigration that I would like to share an example of how I worshiped God through service. A youth pastor from a neighboring town heard that I loved to paint and create. This youth pastor offered me an opportunity to paint the interior walls of their new youth cafe and hangout with 70's retro designs using black light paints.

A friend in my youth group, Chadd, also loved art. He would pick me up early each morning in his little Toyota Tercel hatchback car and we'd drive the 45 minutes to Eunice, Louisiana to paint the youth cafe. We'd leave at the end of the day before the sun would set and we did this for 2 weeks with a deadline set for the grand opening.

The youth pastor said that all he had in the budget was enough funds to cover the cost of our fuel and the paints and brushes. That was enough for us because we were offered an opportunity to express our creativity.

While serving the youth pastor, we were doing what we love and had a heart of excellence while we worked as though we were being paid for it. We enjoyed every minute of the project. I was being fulfilled in being able to create and paint. I often think back to this job with fond memories and of great friendships I made.

Even though I knew of the pressing need of finances, I chose to serve God with my gifts and talents in the meantime until we were issued our work permits. My family was given a promise from God that we were in His will and that we were meant to be where we were at that time.

Through all of this I never once expressed to anyone, or eluded to the fact my family was financially tight. That is why it was a big surprise when we found out that the youth group took up an offering for me and Chadd to thank us for the artwork we did. It humbled me in such a profound way. The offering that would seem minor to most was huge to me because it was God's way of reassuring me that He had me and my family's back.

Phil King, a good friend of ours, shares a great example of how he worshiped God through service. He's a musician, worship leader and teacher. He shares this story in his book *Defending the Purity of Worship*:

> "As a young boy in California I would do all sorts of things that had nothing to do with music just because I wanted to touch God's heart. I would go to our little church founded by my grandfather all alone and do different things like pick up trash, paint walls or clean bathrooms. As I would set out to do those things, with no one else watching, I would purpose in my heart that I was going to do them for the glory of the Lord. As I would pick up trash and clean I would often begin to weep because the Holy Spirit, who knew what I was doing, would come and overshadow me. Picking up trash is where I really fell in love with worshipping the Lord, not by being on a stage."

Worship as Obedience

> "What is more pleasing to the LORD:
>   your burnt offerings and sacrifices
>   or your obedience to his voice?
> Listen! Obedience is better than sacrifice,
>   and submission is better than offering the fat of rams.

> 1 Samuel 15:22 NLT

This act of worship is one that is sadly overlooked way too often. I believe that obedience is the one element in our worship that will unlock God's destiny in our lives. It is imperative we follow the lead of the Holy Spirit as we worship, and obedience opens the door for Him to flow freely through our worship, creative or not.

Most importantly, our obedience places us in exactly the right position for God's will to manifest in and through our life.

So what is God's will for our life? Do you ever wonder if God has a plan for your life? Scripture tells us in the book of Jeremiah:

> For I know the plans I have for you" declares the Lord, "plans to prosper you and not to harm you, plans to give you a hope and a future."

> Jeremiah 29:11 NIV

That is pretty exciting because that scripture alone dispels the idea that God is an angry God who sits in heaven waiting to catch us stepping out of line, ready to punish us accordingly. It also dispels the idea that God is distant and uninvolved in our daily lives.

If we're living a worldly life, even partly, we often believe that Godly obedience confines us, that it hinders our own plans and desires. However, if we seek to live according to God's will, then **obedience does not confine us. Obedience sets us free. It liberates us!**

Its disobedience that binds us up in the chains of anger, resentment, hate, unforgiveness, rebellion, pride, fear and envy.

Both of my daughters, London and Dakota, attend a wonderful Christian school. It is non-denominational and non-church affiliated. The reason my husband and I chose this school was because each teacher has given their life to Jesus Christ and loves the Lord with all their heart.

We know this because we've seen it in action as we have participated in school activities. But we have also seen the evidence of it in our girls. The teachings, whether it is math, science, penmanship, reading, etc. always point back to the Bible and its biblical truths. This grounds our kids in knowing that God is our final authority, and believing the Bible to be His inspired Word.

Since my girls have attended this school it has just reinforced what we as parents have been teaching them at home, especially in terms of obedience. London and Dakota are still young, 6 and 4 years old, but already they understand the difference between making wise and foolish choices, and the consequences thereof.

Just like every parent out there, we face daily challenges with parenting our girls. We have chosen to welcome those challenges because they are perfect opportunities for us to teach them, in love, the value and benefit of obedience.

We believe that successful parenting is not befriending our daughters but providing them with healthy boundaries, and consequences when they overstep those boundaries. My husband and I want only the best for our girls. We can already see the amazing plans that God has for their lives.

We know God wants the same for all of us. Critical to God opening the door to these plans is our obedience to the boundaries, principals and instructions God has laid out in His Word. Obedience does not confine us but rather keeps us on the narrow path to freedom and liberty. It keeps us on the path to God's will in our life.

Obedience also unlocks holiness in our life.

> So you must live as God's obedient children. Don't slip back into your old ways of living to satisfy your own desires. You didn't know any better then. But now you must be holy in everything you do, just as God who chose you is holy. For the Scriptures say, "You must be holy because I am holy."
>
> 1 Peter 1:14-16 NLT

In our day and age modern church services often use lights, shows and entertainment to attract people. The unfortunate consequence is that true worship, worship with a heart of obedience, is sidelined.

This scripture makes it clear why people will choose to ignore holiness. Satisfying our own ideas and desires opposes holiness. When holiness is absent in our worship, the conviction of the Holy Spirit can be too hard to bear. This conviction, and the emptiness of ordinary worship, lead people to disengage. They often resign to be entertained and to follow familiar routines instead of responding to the conviction of the Holy Spirit with holiness.

While a lack of holiness can be detrimental to worship, we must also watch out for false holiness. False holiness is when one conducts themselves in a holy manner, but lacks the sincerity and devotion to obeying God.

An example of false holiness is when someone chooses to sacrifice the flesh by fasting or abstaining from social media, food, entertainment or television for a period, except it is not done in obedience and in submission to God through prayer and supplication. It ends up being a waste of time and a worthless sacrifice.

Both false holiness and a lack of holiness will negatively impact our spiritual life and our relationship with Jesus. They are dangerous because the more we engage this way, the more we sear our heart and spirit, and the more insensitive we become to the Holy Spirit.

This often happens and we don't even realize it. With good intentions, we're going through the motions. But we fail to submit ourselves in obedience.

So how do we worship God with obedience? We simply submit our body as a living sacrifice. We do this by laying down our own desires and agendas at His feet. We look up to Him with our hearts and souls wide open. We welcome the Holy Spirit into our worship and follow His lead. In our everyday lives, we walk with Him into holiness.

CONCLUSION

Obedience was the spark that ignited the fire and passion for more of Him in my life. It birthed a desire in my heart to grow more intimate in my relationship with the Father. It created a desire in me to get to know Him for who He is and not for what He could do for me.

Worship comes from the inside out, not the outside in. By starting with the inward expression of our worship we will have the opportunities to learn and make the necessary changes to align ourselves to His Word. We'll be able to prepare our spirit to become sensitive to the Holy Spirit again. Our outward expression of worship will naturally flow from our heart and soul and it will testify of the goodness and mercy of God and His glory in our lives.

After reading this first chapter it should be obvious there is so much more to worship than singing a few songs in a church service. It is truly multi-dimensional.

My prayer is that as you read through each of the following chapters you will find your place and purpose as a true worshiper of God. I pray that you will be set free and step out in boldness as God takes you on an exciting journey through creative expression, through which He does His amazing work in you and in your life. Through it all, I pray that you will get the revelation of who God is and who you are in Him.

> "We should not be concerned about working for God until we have learned the delight of worshipping Him. A worshipper can work with eternal quality in his work, but a worker who does not worship is only piling up wood and hay and stubble." -- A.W. Tozer

2

THE POSTURE OF GOD-WORSHIP
How True God-Worship Changes Everything

Since we are receiving a Kingdom that is unshakable, let us be thankful and please God by worshiping him with holy fear and awe.

Hebrews 12:28 NLT

At this point, you may be asking yourself: "Is this worship thing really for me? What will it do for me? Will it change anything? Will it change me?"

The answers are yes, yes, yes and yes! Much of what I write here is to help you understand the importance and purpose of worship. It's to help you learn how to enjoy worship while you are here on earth. It's through worship we experience a taste of heaven on earth. As you learn to enjoy worship and delight in all of its benefits, worship will become something you crave.

Worship is similar in principal to the tithe principle: Without an investment there is no reward. To experience the benefits of your worship, you must do your part. You must make an investment.

When Mike, my husband, and I were dating, I explained the principal of the tithe to him. Mike grabbed hold of the principle and put it into action right away. At the time of that discussion, he was in a season of financial difficulty. An employee had stolen a large amount of money from his company. It put him under a very heavy financial strain.

He committed to try this tithing thing, regardless what his bank account looked like. After a year of faithfully tithing, all his financial obligations were met *and* he was able to pay off all of his credit card debt. Mike would never have been debt free in one year if he hadn't acted on the principals of the tithe.

Worship is much the same. Until we take the principles of worship and apply them to our lives and engage in worship with all our heart, we will not experience the glorious benefits of worship.

As we explore the following questions, I want you to open your mind and spirit to the Holy Spirit. Invite Him to answer these questions for you and give you revelation. Ultimately, our best teacher is the Holy Spirit. He empowers us with knowledge and reveals our purpose and destiny.

WHAT DOES WORSHIP DO FOR OUR CHARACTER?

Worship builds godly character in us, and moves us away from captivity; the bondage and hold of sin. As we worship, we honor and magnify God. This edifies and strengthens us. It builds a Christ-like character within us.

There is a principle many in the secular world use to achieve success; we become like those we admire and those on who we focus. Developing a Christ-like character comes from focusing on Christ and embracing His ways.

When we worship Jesus, it focuses us on His character traits; forgiveness, tenderness, justice, righteousness, purity, kindness and love. As we worship, these become our character traits, traits that prepare us for eternal life in heaven with God.

> Set your mind and keep focused habitually on the things above [*the heavenly things*], not on things that are on the earth [*which have only temporal value*].
>
> Colossians 3:2 AMP

WHAT DOES CORPORATE WORSHIP DO FOR US?

Worship in a church service is referred to as corporate worship. Corporate worship is when we gather and worship together. It allows the body of Christ to commune with one another. It sparks the spiritual fire of God in our hearts as we unify in worship.

Our unity in corporate worship is the key that stokes and maintains the spiritual fire that burns in our spirit. This spiritual fire consumes all the cares and worries of the past, present and future. Therefore, corporate worship restores, revives, refines and reignites us.

The devil wants to isolate and disengage us from corporate worship in order to quench our spiritual fire. Isolation makes us vulnerable and an easy target for the demonic influences and attacks the devil uses to rob us of our hope, joy and peace.

There's a TV show on the History channel called Alone. It's about survival and being completely isolated from human contact. The biggest struggle contestants experience is not hunger, the environment, building a shelter, or the fear of wild animals. The biggest struggle is the loneliness, being isolated with no one to talk to.

Having watched a few seasons of this show, I have a renewed appreciation of my relationships with family and friends. When I observe the effects of the isolation and loneliness on the contestants, I can see the blessings of these relationships. This scripture in the book of Genesis comes to mind:

> Later the LORD God said, "It is not good for man to be alone. I will make for him a companion that is a suitable match for him.
>
> Genesis 2:18 ISV

God created us to be communal in nature. So, when we are isolated, withdrawn and alone it will lead us down a road to despair.

In today's culture, anxiety and depression are at record highs. When we withdraw into isolation we become vulnerable and unprotected from the wiles of the enemy. Isolation is the perfect environment for the devil to knock on the door of our mind. When we answer, it gives the devil permission to access and influence our mind and wreak havoc on our emotions.

The devil loves to mess with our emotions. Emotions are powerful, and when we start believing and relying on our emotions, we walk straight into a trap of feeling worthless, rejected and unsuitable for society. These lies imprison us. They isolate us.

Seeking relief, some sort of refuge, in many cases these emotions lead us into alcohol and drug addiction, or worse.

In the book of Proverbs we see that Solomon points out that isolation keeps us from embracing wisdom in our life.

> A man who isolates himself seeks his own desire; He rages against all wise judgment.
>
> Proverbs 18:1 NKJV

So where should we turn when we find ourselves isolated and hopeless? God's wisdom! God's wisdom is far superior to man's wisdom and when we embrace His wisdom we ultimately embrace the source of perfect infinite knowledge and understanding.

> "My thoughts are nothing like your thoughts," says the Lord. "And my ways are far beyond anything you could imagine. For just as the heavens are higher than the earth, so my ways are higher than your ways and my thoughts higher than your thoughts.
>
> Isaiah 55:8-9 NLT

God is the source of all good things, and within His goodness is the absence of pain, hurt, sadness, confusion, trouble, poverty, fear, hopelessness, sorrow and despair.

Gathering together in corporate worship brings the Word of God, prayer and fellowship together in a cohesive manner, unifying us in one heart. It pulls a person out of isolation. It creates an environment of accountability. It helps us overcome obstacles. It encourages us. It motivates us to try harder and challenges us to live lives that reflect Christ.

There are so many scriptures in the Bible that talk about the benefits of gathering together. Below are three of the major benefits of corporate worship.

A Favorable Environment

A favorable environment allows God's Holy Spirit the freedom to set people free, offer salvation for the lost and heal the sick. (Matthew 18:20)

A Supportive Environment

A supportive environment provides those who face tough challenges with a support structure to encourage them and to help them walk through it and not withdraw into isolation. Studies have found that a good support structure in life will not only help a person overcome but will also make them stronger. (Hebrews 10:25)

A Teachable Environment

A teachable environment equips us with keys and tools to be trained in the ways of the Lord. (Colossians 3:16) It is clear we are in the middle of a spiritual battle between good and evil. It is not only evident when we read the Bible from beginning to end, but if we look at the condition of society today, its chaos! Being equipped with spiritual weapons and strategies is very important.

Just as a soldier needs to be taught, equipped and trained, so do we need the spiritual training on how to use what God provides as weapons: truth, righteousness, peace, faith, salvation, the Word, prayer and God-worship. Corporate worship creates a unified victorious voice that will send the devil a unified message; "We are untouchable. Devil you must flee. You are defeated!"

The choice is up to us whether we will walk in the victorious power of God and enforce the victory we have daily. In worship, we will never have to fight life's battles alone. God never said that once we become a child of God through salvation we would not face any battles. What He did say is that we are now in possession of His power within us through Jesus Christ to be overcomers, victorious and more than conquerors.

God-worship is warfare, a powerful way to fight these battles!

WHAT IS GOD-WORSHIP?

I beseech you therefore, brethren, by the mercies of God, that you present your bodies a living sacrifice, holy, acceptable to God, which is your reasonable service. And do not be conformed to this world, but be transformed by the renewing of your mind, that you may prove what is that good and acceptable and perfect will of God.

Romans 12:1-2 NKJV

In short, God-worship is presenting our life to God as a living sacrifice. It is a life that no longer belongs to us. It is engaging and embracing the heart of Jesus that in turn reflects His character. God-worship produces a humble heart, a heart of a servant. God-worship is, in essence, the attitude of our heart toward God in worship.

Knowing the character traits of a servant of God broadens our understanding of the impact and benefit God-worship will have on us. Throughout the Bible we find descriptions of the character of God's faithful servants.

Some examples of these character traits are: a motivation to please God and not man; having a selfless heart; putting others first; helping the least of those without seeking recognition; being a diligent worker without complaining; unafraid of hard work; observant to the needs of others and willing to help; being faithful and trustworthy.

God-worship develops these character traits. The only requirement is that we surrender our heart to Jesus as we enter the posture of God-worship. He will do the rest.

What is the Posture of God-Worship? How Do We Achieve It?

A posture of God-worship is a worship that abides by three things: order, purpose and action. To achieve the posture of God-worship, we simply apply these to our worship, step by step.

Order - The first step that brings order in our worship is when we behold God. We step out in faith and turn our face away from man and engage the Lord, face to face, focused on Him. Keeping our eyes fixed on Him opens our heart for a divine exchange between the worshiper and God. By shifting our focus off man and our agendas and fixing it on Jesus we declare that God is at the head of our lives and that He is the subject of our worship. This action automatically unlocks God's supernatural order in our lives.

Purpose - Purpose is birthed after order is embodied in our heart and life. Purpose is an inward response to God's heart toward us. When we are engaged in a divine exchange with Jesus, He tells us how much He loves us, how He desires we live prosperous lives and to receive what He has planned for us. As He pours His heart into our life, we are filled with purpose, the purpose He created us for. Knowing God's intention for our individual lives gives us direction. Once we have purpose and direction we are propelled into the next step, action.

Action – Action becomes the result of our purpose realized. God plants direction in our hearts. Action is an outward response to our purpose revealed in our heart. What that means is that when there is an inward revelation, or emotional response to God's love we respond with an outward expression of adoration and reverence. For some people the outward expression may manifest as creative worship. Our action is the desire to be obedient to God's call and commission to advance His Kingdom on this earth.

These three steps embody God-worship. They unlock and open the door for God's perfect will to manifest in and through our lives.

What Are the Dynamics of God-Worship? How Do We Benefit Personally?

When we shift our focus upward toward Father God it automatically raises our line of eyesight above our circumstances. We begin to view our circumstances from a different perspective, a heavenly perspective.

As our natural line of sight is raised we are brought into the supernatural presence of the Lord. It is healthy to have this viewpoint because it allows us to build a trusting relationship with God; a relationship through which we can ask Him what He would have us do and embrace His wisdom. Worshiping in this posture, beholding Him, prepares us for a supernatural encounter with God.

Why would we want to have a supernatural encounter? It gives us a taste of heaven. In true God-worship, the natural and the supernatural come together. Heaven and earth come together.

We don't have to die to experience heaven. God-worship brings the super into our natural expression of worship. The supernatural reveals a glimpse into what heaven is like. I love the supernatural realm and how God-worship empowers us to walk in the confidence that we, His beloved, will one day be transformed by His glory into His likeness.

Imagine for just a moment that God gave us a glimpse of His glory and holiness just like Isaiah experienced when God called him to be a prophet. Isaiah 6 describes the vision Isaiah had of Jehovah God in His temple, the most holy place. He saw the Lord sitting on His throne, the train of His robe filling the temple and the angels crying holy, holy, holy. Don't you think you would immediately fall to your knees in holy reverence and feel the pressing desire to live a holy life?

Not only did Isaiah have this glorious vision, but this experience also simplified his purpose and destiny. He willingly accepted the commission to live a life of holiness, to go and tell God's people the truth and to serve as God's messenger.

After we have gazed upon God's glory and given Him permission to bring His order into our life, our purpose is revealed with simplicity and clarity. Personally, these times of worship are the most life changing experiences I have had. God would speak to me during my worship through visions.

These visions have prompted me to make the necessary changes in my heart and life. Sometimes the change is to better myself as a person, or to teach me how to be more sensitive to the convictions of the Holy Spirit and obey His leading. Other times God has given me revelation and answers for situations or questions, that under normal circumstances, I would not get.

Many times, the difficult circumstances in life are due to a lack of knowledge, or foolish decisions, because our emotions dictate our choices instead of trusting the leading of the Holy Spirit. The Holy Spirit will always lead us to make wise choices. This godly wisdom reveals our *purpose*, and leads us to our *destiny*.

After godly *order* is restored and our *purpose* revealed we would be propelled into *action*. Just as with Isaiah, once he saw Jehovah's throne room, understood and accepted his purpose, he responded without hesitation to the voice of the Lord.

> Then I heard the voice of the Lord saying, "Whom shall I send? And who will go for us?" And I said, "Here am I. Send me!"
>
> Isaiah 6:8 NKJV

Isaiah is a great biblical example of how a true encounter with God transforms us through the posture of God-worship. Not only will it cause us to change from the inside out, but it will spark a passion and desire within us to fulfill God's will and destiny for our life.

In short, God-worship restores godly *order* in our life that simplifies our *purpose* and propels us into *action* with passion to advance His will in, and through, our individual lives.

What Does God-Worship Do For You In Heaven & Eternity?

Once we are in heaven we are no longer under any curse or earthly limitations. There will be no more tears, sorrow or death. Everything will be made new. That is super exciting.

Still, for many of us, heaven is a place we cannot quite describe or know a whole lot about. In fact, this question alone could have a whole book dedicated to it altogether. The scriptures are sometimes a little hard to comprehend, especially in the book of Revelation when it describes heaven.

Typically, when a person doesn't understand heaven and an eternity of worshiping God they feel like they are at a disadvantage. So, their view tends to lean toward a narrow-minded perspective. Alternately, when there is a broader understanding, our view of heaven and an eternity of worship will sound exhilarating.

Initially, I had this narrow-minded perspective. But then I began engaging in the posture of God-worship. That was when I started to experience His presence and the revelation of heaven became more real to me. I started to develop a hunger for more understanding through His Word and worship.

A scripture that jumped off the page and hit me in my spirit begged a question that birthed a curiosity of what worship in heaven must look like.

> Jesus replied, "I tell you, if these [*people*] keep silent, the stones will cry out [*in praise*]!"
>
> Luke 19:40 AMP

This is where Jesus told the Pharisees that even the rocks would cry out if man were silent. So, if the rocks on this earth will cry out in worship to God, they must know something we don't. Through God-worship we must let our spirit begin to anticipate how glorious worship will be in heaven, when we are in the throne room of Jehovah, the most holy place.

In my opinion, many believers in the body of Christ are at a disadvantage regarding their initial understanding of God-worship. Their understanding is driven by what they see or have experienced in their churches. Sadly, most churchgoers associate boredom with attending church and participating in worship.

This line of thought might lead one to wonder: "Are there churches in heaven?" and "Will there be churches on earth once the earth is re-created post Armageddon?" We see in the book of Revelation a description about the New Jerusalem and how churches, as we know them on earth, will not be present in heaven.

> But I saw no temple in it, for the Lord God Almighty and the Lamb are its temple.
>
> Revelation 21:22 NKJV

The New Jerusalem is described as the Tabernacle of God, the Heavenly Jerusalem, the Holy City, and the City of God. It is also described as God's Heavenly City on the re-created earth. The book of Revelation, Chapter 21 describes the New Jerusalem beautifully.

If there are no churches in heaven and eternity with worship services, programs, prayer meetings, youth gatherings, etc. how will we engage in worship in heaven? Will we be on our face continually at the feet of Jesus Christ worshiping Him?

> Now our knowledge is partial and incomplete, and even the gift of prophecy reveals only part of the whole picture!
>
> 1 Corinthians 13:9 NLT

Since we only "know in part," and the scriptures allow us just a glimpse of the big picture, let us explore what we do know. Not only will we worship Christ with our face at His feet singing, holy, holy, holy, but our worship will be extended in fellowship, serving, learning, gathering at feasts, eating and drinking and living in heavenly dwelling places.

If we associate boredom with church and worship, then the idea of an eternity of worship might not sound very appealing or enticing. This view of worship doesn't create a desire for worship. That is why it is so important we have a clear understanding about the revelation of God-worship.

When we are told that we will worship God for the rest of our days, the thought of spending an eternity as a worshiper should cause our heart to leap with joy.

We will also gather together for feasts and celebrate with Christ. Now that should excite you knowing that we will be feasting in heaven.

> Assuredly, I say to you, I will no longer drink of the fruit of the vine until that day when I drink it new in the kingdom of God.
>
> Mark 14:25 NKJV

> Now when one of those who sat at the table with Him heard these things, he said to Him, "Blessed is he who shall eat bread in the kingdom of God!"
>
> Luke 14:15 NKJV

I have lived in Lafayette, Louisiana for almost two decades. After living within the Cajun culture my dad would often say that people live to eat, rather than eat to live. It's true! The food is so good and it seems that there are festivals year round. It is easy to fall in love with the food and culture. Personally, the sound of feasting in heaven with Christ is one that excites me.

You may have heard that heaven is paradise. Take a moment to think what the word paradise means to you. When we hear the word paradise we tend to picture a beautiful place, being served as royalty, perfect weather, and perfect circumstances overflowing with beauty and bounty.

> "Eye has not seen, nor ear heard, nor have entered into the heart of man the things which God has prepared for those who love Him."
>
> 1 Corinthians 2:9 NKJV

Paul clarifies here that no manner of human ability or methods will allow us to know what God has prepared for us. Nothing in science or nature on this earth can be used as a reference to describe heaven. It is only until we enter the spiritual realm through God-worship that we begin to get a glimpse, or a taste of what is to come. God-worship is like our earthly window into heaven.

God-worship is an important key that can take a once narrow minded perspective and broaden it. Having a narrow or limited perspective confined by our human ideologies, processes and reasoning prevents us from seeing how much God loves us. It prevents us from seeing what heaven is truly like.

> And may you have the power to understand, as all God's people should, how wide, how long, how high, and how deep his love is. May you experience the love of Christ, though it is too great to understand fully. Then you will be made complete with all the fullness of life and power that comes from God.
>
> Ephesians 3:18-19 NLT

Trying to fully understand heaven with our human mind can be daunting. Thankfully, through God-worship, we can see and experience a whole new level of revelation and understanding that would otherwise not be available to us.

Not only will we be living in paradise enjoying a sin-free life without fleshly temptations, but we will also enjoy a full and unbroken daily fellowship with Christ. How glorious our times will be as we assemble with the multitudes to worship Him in unity crying holy, holy, holy as we are elevated into higher and higher heights of praise. I can't wait, can you?

WHY WORSHIP IS FOR YOU

As believers, we are part of God's big plan, and worship is for all believers of God. Worship is where the life of God is present and evident. God-worship is what will empower and equip us. The posture of God-worship is adjusting our focus onto the source of everything, God.

To live an effective life on this earth we must worship. It should not be an option because we have been created to worship. Ignoring or neglecting what we have been created to do cripples us.

I strongly believe that God is breathing life into the valley of dry bones again, awakening the sleeping giants, calling the prodigals home and convicting the hearts of the lost. There is a hidden movement emerging that has been behind the scenes for far too long.

It has become evident that God is blowing a fresh new fire of His holiness into the hearts of a nameless and faceless people who want nothing to do with recognition, titles, acknowledgment or promotion. They just want God and nothing else! They live, eat and breathe His Word. They are passionate about God.

The condition of their hearts and the motives of people have been sick for a long time. But through God-worship and the Holy Spirit, a revival is taking place in the hearts of man. This revival is setting people free from their perceived thoughts about themselves, giving them a godly purpose and birthing a passion for more of Him and for calling home the lost.

Yes, worship is for you! I say that because God-worship is what will empower and equip you and include you in this emerging unified holy army.

This unified holy army consists of people like you and me, our neighbors and our family members. A holy righteousness is growing and we can see the evidence of it just by looking around us. This holy army is sick and tired of political correctness inside and outside of the church. They are tired of a watered down gospel where the message of the cross is no longer preached and the power is taken out of the Blood of Jesus.

They are tired of being walked over like doormats and shushed into silence just because they are Christians. They will not bow down to the belief systems of others. They are tired of leaders in the church who say one thing and do another, having one foot in the church while living like there is no God outside of the church.

They are tired of the biblical role of men and women being reversed and diminished, resulting in gender confusion and their identities robbed through perverted sexuality. They are tired of the inclusion of sin that has entered every aspect of life and then reasoned away to suit and fit a perceived and deceived truth.

They are tired of the attack on prayer because they know that prayer is the key to untying God's hands to accomplish His will. They are tired of an educational system that is used to brain wash and indoctrinate our youth instead of educate them to prosper and abound in life.

Lastly, they are tired of the rejection of the Holy Spirit in our churches. He has been kicked out to the curb because the truth and conviction that He brings makes people uncomfortable.

CONCLUSION

This glorious awakening is moving people to action. They are taking a stand and saying, ENOUGH IS ENOUGH! Let us pick up our shield of faith and sword of truth. Let us clad oneself in the armor of God. Let us enforce the victory over the dark forces of this world.

Such love has no fear, because perfect love expels all fear.

1 John 4:18 NLT

Our greatest weapon in this fight against the ruler of this world, Satan and his demons is LOVE. God is Love. As we worship Jesus in the posture of God-worship with extreme submission and extravagant adoration, our love and passion for Him will grow in ways we never knew possible. As a result, our most powerful weapon, worship, will be used correctly and effectively.

It is this passionate love for God that will become so contagious we will not be able to contain it. His perfect love will trump all fear and insecurity. It will empower us to walk with fearless confidence and godly boldness. This perfect love will enrapture us and set us on the narrow path, which frees and liberates us. This is the way God intended us to do battle.

31

The next chapter introduces creative worship. There we will discover how the Holy Spirit empowers us through our gifts and talents to become a victorious warrior in the army of God.

You are God's living canvas, His unfinished masterpiece. We should present our lives to Him as a blank canvas. We should put the brush in the hand of the Holy Spirit and let Him create a powerful and glorious masterpiece as we worship Jesus, as who God created us to be, and in true God-worship.

> For we are God's masterpiece. He has created us anew in Christ Jesus, so we can do the good things he planned for us long ago.
>
> Ephesians 2:10 NLT

You are God's living canvas, His unfinished masterpiece.

3

A LIVING CANVAS

Our Gifts & Talents Empower Our Creative Worship

These gifts help His people work well for Him. And then the church which is the body of Christ will be made strong.

Ephesians 4:12 NLV

What are my gifts and talents? Have you ever asked yourself that question? Growing up I didn't really know what my gifts and talents were. It seemed like I was good at anything I put my mind to.

When asked that question by others, I stood there with a mouth full of teeth, unable to give an answer. Only later in my adult years did I come to know how to answer that question.

Today, I wonder if I would have been more likely to recognize my gift if that question had been "What is your passion?" or "What drives you and fulfills you?" Could I have begun using my gifts sooner to advance God's Kingdom, instead of my own ego, had the question been framed differently?

Uniquely created by God, each of us has been given divine gifts and talents. God revealed mine to me through worship. One of my gifts is the ability to understand and move to the cadence and rhythms in music as an interpretative dancer. My mother said that before I could walk I was dancing.

Music has had, and still has, such a powerful influence in my life. It is part of every aspect of it. That is why I am very careful what music I listen to because of how it impacts my being.

In today's day and age, we are faced with many challenges; attractive distractions that entice our flesh, our human nature.

> For those who live according to the flesh set their minds on the things of the flesh, but those who live according to the Spirit, the things of the Spirit.
>
> Romans 8:5 NKJV

It is very easy to fall victim to these distractions and worldly traps, where our divine talents are misplaced and misused. God created us to serve Him, to worship Him, to have relationship with Him and to glorify Him. ***Our gifts are part of the person He created us to be, and were given to us to fulfill His plans and purposes for us.***

Yet, many of us fall away from His plans and purposes, and our gifts are used to serve the world and ourselves! We squander our gifts and talents in places that do not bring glory to God. We become bound in the grips of fear and insecurity, and our gifts and talents become bound as well.

For the Church, the body of believers, the purpose of our gifts and talents is to bring glory and honor to God. When this happens, our lives are empowered and God fills us with His peace, confidence and boldness. There is no room for fear and insecurity. If we are to experience this level of empowerment, we must be wholly and completely surrendered to the Holy Spirit, the Spirit of God.

I want to take a moment here to focus on those who struggle with fear and insecurity, which is most of us. Fear is one of the traps the enemy loves to use because it keeps the believer from living a fulfilled and prosperous life with confidence and boldness.

> Have I not commanded you? Be strong and of good courage; do not be afraid, nor be dismayed, for the Lord your God *is* with you wherever you go."
>
> Joshua 1:9 NKJV

We should walk in confidence, believing what God says about us, yet many see this kind of confidence as arrogance. It is not. We should walk in humility, but many believe that means we should be timid, weak and fearful. It does not.

These false beliefs are pure deception and blatant lies! Believing these lies ensures the devil's continued reign and power on this planet, and it ensures that we will never fulfill God's plans and purposes for our lives.

I love how Steve Thompson, an author, speaker, prophetic minister and business owner, who also happens to be one of my favorite teachers, breaks down fear.

He says "Fear is not a character flaw or weakness. Fear is sin."

This is not a criticism of people who struggle with fear, but rather it is a revelation of what fear really is. You see, fear cripples a person and can make them physically and mentally sick. Fear is a tactic the devil uses to steal our focus and relationship with God. It blinds us to the truth of our intended purpose and destiny God has set before us.

So, how do we overcome fear and insecurity and be set free from these lies of false humility? The answer is love. God's perfect love is the antidote to fear.

> Love has been perfected among us in this: that we may have boldness in the day of judgment; because as He is, so are we in this world. There is no fear in love; but perfect love casts out fear, because fear involves torment. But he who fears has not been made perfect in love.
>
> 1 John 4:17-18 NKJV

God's love empowers us. When we are in love, our focus is on the very one we are in love with. We will do anything for that person. When we worship in spirit and truth it creates the perfect environment for us to fall madly in love with Jesus Christ. When we shower our affections on Him, all our wants and desires come into alignment with His, and those wants and desires will be added to us. (Matthew 6:33)

Personally, my want and desire is, and always has been, **to dance freely and creatively all the days of my life**. It is the very thing that makes me feel alive. Until I fell madly in love with Jesus, the revelation of this and its purpose never made sense to me.

Today, we have a generation of people who have grown up in a culture that believe artistic talent is only found among celebrities and famous people. This culture measures greatness and success by comparing themselves to these people. Sadly, it's their focus on these very idols that have created such a toxic creative culture.

C.S. Lewis, a famous British novelist and Christian apologist explains that in order to turn a bad culture into a good culture it is important that we recognize that artistic talent is a gift from God and that developing our talents as a gift to God is the only way we can create a good culture.

We are bombarded with idols everywhere, through TV and social media: music idols, sports heroes, movie stars, politicians and even religion. It seems that human nature has a need to idolize something or someone. Instead of seeking God who is the author of our individual identities, we seek to validate ourselves through an external identity. This idol worship occurs when there is a void in our life and we try to fill it with any thing other than God.

What is an idol really? It is someone, some thing or an ideology that occupies the place of God in our life. Human nature seeks validation. Idols are what people use to give himself or herself an identity, meaning, value, purpose, love, significance or security. (Exodus 20:4-6)

How does one recognize if there is an idol in one's life? It is quite simple. Ask the

Holy Spirit to reveal it to you. The Holy Spirit is our revelator and His purpose is to help us discern the difference between truth and lies. The Holy Spirit also brings conviction.

Conviction does not translate to condemnation. Condemnation is from the devil and its intent is to break our spirit, tear us down and destroy us. Conviction is godly correction. It is where God says, "This is not right. Come to Me. Let Me help you."

Holy Spirit conviction leads to revelation and repentance. Repentance leads to a change in behavior, which is correction. When we allow the Holy Spirit to reveal idols in our life, things that occupy our time or steal our focus from God, it is through conviction that He brings it to our attention, urges us to repent, to turn away from it and to give our attention back to God.

Personally, food became an idol at one point in my life. This idol stemmed from having a need to exert control over something that made me feel good about myself. Although, the more I focused on food the worse the struggle and fight for control got and eventually I lost control and I ended up with bulimia.

I began to worship food. This food worship was rooted in insecurity and self-condemnation. I found myself constantly comparing my body to fellow dancers. This act turned into a form of false worship.

My husband Mike offers another example. His business had become an idol. Mike says the Holy Spirit finally hit him over the head with it. In a moment of conviction, he realized he had convinced himself that God would reward the many years he spent building his business. He even sought out and found scripture to support his idea of sowing and reaping.

Mike had given the business over to God, but he was holding on to the expectation of a certain reward. Therefore, the business and the expected reward had become an idol! He let his worldly view, one that had been created before he was born again, blind him to this reality. As soon as he gave up this idol, it was amazing how the Holy Spirit quickly filled the void. He was instantly freed of the toil and torment he had been struggling with for many years.

He didn't give up his business. He simply returned it to God, and prayed for God's forgiveness and for His will. He accepted that his reward would be serving God through his business, rather than expecting a reward from his service to the business.

Idol worship can be avoided or corrected when we recognize that God created us to worship Him. That means when we are in good working order, we are not prone to false worship.

Gifts and talents can also become idols. There are many attractive vices that can open the door to idolizing our own gifts and talents. Whatever our gifts and talents are, it is imperative that we recognize God gave them to us for a purpose; to fulfill the plans and purposes He has for our lives and to glorify and honor Him. The moment we lose sight of this we begin to glorify and honor ourselves.

Using our gifts and talents in God-worship will always bring glory and honor to Him. Our gifts and talents become the channel or path through which our God-worship reaches and connects with the heart of God. When others watch our lives, or observe us as we worship, their focus should automatically be shifted away from us and our abilities. Their attention should be redirected to the One we are worshiping.

Simply said, our lives and our worship should point to God. It should glorify Him. It should lead others to Him, the source of our gifts and talents.

God takes worship very seriously. God is a jealous God. When we allow the Holy Spirit to live and dwell within us, He will help us. He will reveal the idols that occupy the void and steal our focus from the One who created us. God not only *created* us to worship but He also *called* us to do the same.

God Created Us to Worship Him

There is something so pure and beautiful about true God-worship. The revelation of knowing that we have been created to worship has completely revolutionized my view of creative and interpretive worship.

My husband, Mike explained it once so simply. When we use our imagination, we are in essence tapping into our creative nature. Our imagination gives us the ability to create. We serve a creative God. So, it would make sense that He created us with a creative nature. Our imagination is limitless. It is fear and insecurity that limit our imagination and imprisons our creativity.

Worship and serve him with your whole heart and a willing mind.
For the Lord sees every heart and knows every plan and thought.

1 Chronicles 28:9 NLT

God created man so that we could have a relationship with Him. He also uniquely created each of us with gifts and talents to serve Him in this world and throughout eternity. Our God-worship through our gifts and talents is how we begin to develop and grow in a personal relationship with Him.

Personally, in times of intimate worship I free my imagination and I begin to envision myself dancing with Jesus, waltzing across a heavenly dance floor like a little child. Then there are times I see myself without any earthly limitations spinning, twirling, leaping and flying with the angels.

The joy and love in my heart explodes in my chest and I am overcome with extravagant adoration and extreme submission to God. Words cannot truly express how life altering and transforming these times of worship are for me.

Worship becomes like an addiction and I need to satisfy and fill my spirit with His Spirit. I cannot wait for the next opportunity to enter into true God-worship.

Nothing in this world can come close to satisfying these times of worship.

If we look at the book of John, we can see that Jesus reveals Himself to a Samaritan woman at the well, and He gives her a personal lesson about worship and the kind of worship God seeks.

> Jesus replied, "Believe me, dear woman, the time is coming when it will no longer matter whether you worship the Father on this mountain or in Jerusalem. You Samaritans know very little about the one you worship, while we Jews know all about him, for salvation comes through the Jews. But the time is coming—indeed it's here now—when true worshipers will worship the Father in spirit and in truth. The Father is looking for those who will worship him that way. For God is Spirit, so those who worship him must worship in spirit and in truth."
>
> John 4:21-24 NLT

God created us with a void that only He can fill. Jesus also speaks to the woman about the "living water," earlier in John 4:10. He explains this living water flows from God to satisfy a spiritual thirst, or said another way, to fill a spiritual void.

In my case, this living water is what fills and satisfies me, refreshes and invigorates me and gives me purpose.

Worship is one way we can draw living water from the well that is God. Worship allows us to go to the well and drink the living water. When we do, something amazing happens. We begin to fully comprehend and understand our true identity, meaning, value, purpose, love, significance and security.

God Called Us to Worship

If there is one figure in the Bible that best represents how God created man to worship, we can look to King David. He offers the greatest example of true worship. God called him, "a man after my own heart." (Acts 13:22) Samuel even testified to it:

> ...for the Lord has sought out a man after his own heart...
>
> 1 Samuel 13:14 NLT

David was a tremendously gifted and skilled musician. His skill with the harp was the only thing that calmed King Saul. David also wrote an enormous part of the book of Psalms. The engagement of David's heart with God's heart is seen in his writing. There was a pure and transparent passion that exuded his very being. All he desired was for more of God and to continue growing deeper in his passionate relationship with God. His poetry and song writing are still widely used in today's worship songs.

Before the rule of King David, worship was primarily viewed and expressed as prayers and sacrifices. Thankfully King David was sensitive to God and understood the power of pure and true God-worship. His heart was so full of love for God that his inner worship overflowed into his outward worship.

We could say that his worship was on the cutting edge. As King, seated in a place of influence over the nation of Israel, God used David to revolutionize worship. He was not ashamed of God or how he felt about God.

Here in the book of Psalms, we can see how God has not only created us for worship but how He has also called us to worship Him. We are called to use our gifts and talents as worship in this summoning below.

> Bring gifts and celebrate,
> Bow before the beauty of God,
> Then to your knees—everyone worship!

Psalm 96:8-9 MSG

All the earth, including nature will bow down to Him.

> All the earth shall worship You
> And sing praises to You;
> They shall sing praises to Your name."

Psalm 66:4 NKJV

Have you ever wondered what the leaves on the trees, blades of grass, birds and rocks will do the moment God makes His presence known when He returns?

No thing will be able to contain the extravagant adoration of God's magnificence and glory. The leaves will clap with joy, the blades of grass will quiver with praise, the birds will unify in glorious song and flight and the rocks will cry out. And that is just the beginning. All of creation will bow down and cry holy, holy, holy is He the Lord God Almighty! Holy is His wonderful name!

Once we understand and operate in the revelation that we have been *created* and we have been *called* to worship God through our gifts and talents we will no longer walk in fear and insecurity. We will walk in confidence and boldness.

At this point we have established: God is our creator. He created us in His image and likeness. He created us to worship. He has given us gifts and talents. And He has given us a creative nature.

Considering all of these things God has given us, it's easy to extend this godly nature to worship, creative worship!

How True God-Worship Can Also Be Creative Worship

Is creative worship biblical? How does creative worship benefit believers? These are questions I asked myself as I began teaching creative worship many years ago.

God-worship becomes creative worship when our worship is expressed through our creative gifts and talents. Creative worship comes through song to some and through musical instruments to others. We are all familiar with this kind of creative worship.

But I believe there are many people with various other creative talents and gifts who can use these talents in their worship. Personally, mine are through dance and flags.

But whether or not we worship creatively with our gifts and talents, the goal must be the same. We must honor God in extravagant love and extreme submission. This must be the true intent and motive of our worship.

Here in the book of Psalms we can see the different ways one's gifts and talents can be offered to God as a creative expression of worship.

> Praise Him with a blast of the ram's horn; praise Him with the lyre and harp! Praise Him with the tambourine and dancing; praise Him with strings and flutes! Praise Him with a clash of cymbals; praise Him with loud clanging cymbals. Let everything that breathes sing praises to the Lord! Praise the Lord!
>
> Psalm 150:3-6 NLT

Creative worship is biblical. In Genesis 35, we read how Moses instructs the building of the temple according to God's appointments of Bezalel. Not only did God choose them, but He also equipped them with skills, intelligence, knowledge and creativity through the Holy Spirit.

> Then Moses said to the people of Israel, "See, the Lord has called by name Bezalel the son of Uri, son of Hur, of the tribe of Judah; and he has filled him with the Spirit of God, with skill, with intelligence, with knowledge, and with all craftsmanship, to devise artistic designs, to work in gold and silver and bronze, in cutting stones for setting, and in carving wood, for work in every skilled craft.
>
> Exodus 35:30-33 ESV

I think this is the best way to describe how God-worship becomes creative worship in my life. When I tap into God's presence during true God-worship the inward filling of God's Spirit begins to well up within my spirit. The overflowing that results is an explosion of outward expression. This outward expression is released through a variety of creative or interpretive expressions in dance and with flags. I find the more I open my spirit to God's Spirit, the less I hear my mind trying to reason with what I am doing, and I don't limit God.

Breaking it down into an even more basic form, worship is a form of communication, very much like prayer. This communication can be both verbal and non-verbal. Creative worship, or creative interpretation or expression, is the part of our worship that consists mostly of outward non-verbal communication.

In essence, worship is a language that becomes a conversation between you and God in which you share your inner thoughts and heart's desires. This conversation consists of thoughts, emotions, words and movement.

We were made in the image of a creative God who dwells within us. It would make sense that we are created with a desire to create also. So why wouldn't our worship be creative? If we look at the people around us, friends, family, and co-workers, we can see their desire to create. It's evident in the way our children play.

God created us with an innate creativity, unique to our identity in Him. These creative communications can be expressed in many ways. Certainly, worship is one of those ways.

As a dancer, I use my body to communicate a non-verbal message through interpretive movement. As a prophetic painter, my husband Mike communicates through the strokes of his paintbrush on the canvas. A drummer communicates through rhythms and beats, and so on. These are creative expressions of worship.

We can speak without uttering a single word. Through our own experiences, we know that one's posture, tone of voice or facial expression provide a powerful means of communication. It is often this non-verbal communication that speaks louder and is trusted more than words.

Dance, music and the arts can be very powerful and empowering experiences. Therefore, we must recognize its power to influence. We must be careful how we use these creative expressions and how we are personally affected by it.

In the same way that creative expression is used for God-worship, it can also be used as false worship. In fact, if we look around us, most of what we see in the world is creative expression used as false worship.

Satan recognizes the power of creative expression. In today's culture, he has hijacked the creative arts. He has capitalized on the power of creativity and how it captivates the mind and soul of people. Through music and the arts, he has targeted the inner thoughts and imaginations of a person's mind. He understands that once he has gained a foothold in our mind, he can affect, influence or control our behavior, as well as our creative gifts.

If we look closely at our culture today, we can see that idols, such as the desire of fame, money, influence and stature lead creative people into destruction. How does this happen? It is when our gifts and talents are used to lead audiences into sinful living and idol worship.

Our gifts and talents are given to us by God to glorify Him. We must guard our hearts so that our gifts and talents are used to help one another, which means our gifts and talents should always point to God.

God has given each of you a gift. Use it to help each other. This will show God's loving-favor.

1 Peter 4:10 NLV

There is good news. Satan cannot create, he can only pervert or twist. In Ezekiel we see that even though Satan, the fallen archangel Lucifer, was amazing to behold he was never able to create anything, not one thing. All he had was powerful influence when he allowed evil to enter his mind and pride to take root in his heart. (Ezekiel 28:12-14)

Satan, the fallen archangel Lucifer, who now resides in the earth, is still unable to create anything. The only ability he has is to influence our minds and hearts if we give him access. He uses those he can influence to create.

One of the ways he does this is by leading us to believe we need to follow the example of Hollywood, or other secular institutions, using their methods of creativity or outward expression. This influence leads us to falsely believe that if we want to attract people to our church worship services, we must employ the same things that excite people at a pop music concert.

For example, many churches have gleaned from Hollywood's example by theatrically structuring their services to draw people into their meetings. Spectacular lights, fog machines, cameras, and state of the art sound systems create incredible experiences. But often these theatrics overshadow what should be the focus of worship: God's Holy presence and His glorification.

In the book of Romans, it is clear that we are not to imitate the world.

Don't copy the behavior and customs of this world, but let God transform you into a new person by changing the way you think. Then you will learn to know God's will for you, which is good and pleasing and perfect.

Romans 12:2 NLT

It is in spirit-led creative worship we discover God's will is for us. The scripture says that it is not only good and pleasing, but it is perfection.

Don't get me wrong. Creating an incredible worship environment is not "of the devil." But it must not produce or lead to a counterfeit experience. The outward expression of creative worship (music, dance, song, visual effects) must point to God, not distract from God. The focus must be a godly one in which we engage the Holy Spirit in true God-worship to glorify Him and Him alone.

Even though I love special effects, lights, state of the art sound systems with a kicking bass and surround sound, I must stop for a moment and ask the question, "Do I really need those things to enter into true God-worship"? The answer is a resounding NO. All God wants is my heart and I want His.

So, whether I am in a fully equipped church with all the bells and whistles, or I'm in the privacy of my home, it shouldn't matter. My worship should still attract the face and heart of God as I am enraptured by His majesty in true God-worship. My worship, through my gifts and talents, are my gift to God. I want to be transformed by Him and not by this world.

> Christian brothers, I ask you from my heart to give your bodies to God because of His loving-kindness to us. Let your bodies be a living and holy gift given to God. He is pleased with this kind of gift. This is the true worship that you should give Him.
>
> Romans 12:1 NLV

How Do We Restore the Arts Back to God in Worship?

You and I have a great opportunity to be instrumental in restoring the arts back to God in worship. The only way this can happen is through you and me. This is how God chooses to work, in and through us, empowering us with all we need to fulfill and carry out His will and purpose in this world.

What is God's will and purpose for man? God reveals it, in part, here in Genesis.

> Then God blessed them, and God said to them, "Be fruitful and multiply; fill the earth and subdue it; have dominion over the fish of the sea, over the birds of the air, and over every living thing that moves on the earth."
>
> Genesis 1:28 NKJV

He wants us to live lives that are full, happy, healthy, and prosperous and to take territory to expand God's Kingdom while on this earth, without giving the devil room, influence or power.

IDENTITY

Before we tackle the question of "How do we restore the arts back to God," we must first understand our true identity. Our identity is not found in our gift or talent. Our identity is found in the giver of our gifts and talents, Christ Jesus.

In order to live empowered lives through our gifts and talents we need to have a solid understanding of our identity in Christ Jesus. Our identity is found in Jesus Christ alone. Believers are not called Christians by mistake. The word Christian is a Greek word that means 'little Christ'. If our identity is found in Jesus Christ then we should be imitators of Him.

We explore identity in much greater detail in the next chapter. But it is important to emphasize here the foundation of our worship and service to God is our true identity in Christ. Understanding our identity frees us to fully tap into our gift or talent. It allows the Holy Spirit to flow and create through us as we offer up our gifts or talents as an expression of worship.

The result is true God-worship and this kind of worship effectively restores the arts back to God, where it rightly belongs.

Now, let us return to the question, "How do we restore the arts back to God in worship." Let's start with the word restore. It suggests that something must have been taken away or stolen.

The creative arts were originally used to bring glory and honor to God. However, due to the sinful nature of man, Satan has influence over our minds, including our ideas, imagination, thoughts, feelings and emotions, and even the way we respond or react to things.

This is also true regarding the creative arts. As the former worship leader in Heaven, Satan understood the power of creative expression. Once God threw him out of Heaven, he began to taint and defile the arts, using it for his own purposes and glory here on the earth.

One of the most destructive ways Satan can affect us is to cancel or delay the fulfillment of God's purposes and will in our lives by getting us to focus on ourselves. How does Satan accomplish this? Well, he uses music and the arts as tools to bring glory to oneself. Through greed, egotism and self-glorification Satan has successfully deceived and led man into sinful living.

Satan has perverted creative expression, robbing God's people of a powerful and essential means to worship and glorify God. This is not to say that Satan uses all music and creative expression for his own purposes. But if we look at the secular world and how music and the arts are used to draw man into darkness, it's easy to see the truth in this.

When this happens, our focus is no longer on God. Instead it is fixed on our gifts, talents and abilities. All praise, honor and recognition are now showered on our gifts and man instead of on God, the giver of our very gifts, talents and abilities.

Warren W. Wiersbe, an American pastor, Bible teacher, and prolific writer of Christian literature and theological works, hits the nail on the head with this quote saying:

> "In our universe there is God and there are people and things. We were made so that we should worship God, love people and use things. However, if we worship ourselves, we will ignore God, start loving things and begin to use people."

To restore and return the arts to its original and intended purpose, to glorify God, we must stop fixating on ourselves and shift our focus onto Jesus, because this is what pleases God. We cannot focus on two things at once. It is impossible. We either focus on Christ Jesus or we focus on ourselves.

We read here in the book of Philippians that if we, in our imperfect human ways, keep focusing on Christ Jesus and giving Him our all, we will win the race and receive the crown of God's upward call.

> Not that I have already obtained all this, or have already arrived at my goal, but I press on to take hold of that for which Christ Jesus took hold of me. Brothers and sisters, I do not consider myself yet to have taken hold of it. But one thing I do: Forgetting what is behind and straining toward what is ahead, I press on toward the goal to win the prize for which God has called me heavenward in Christ Jesus.
>
> Philippians 3:12-14 NIV

Our focus cannot be horizontally set, looking to man. Instead we should set our focus on a vertical plain. This brings us into the posture of God-worship where our focus is upward and set on Christ Jesus.

When we do this, the natural order of God will begin to manifest in our lives. This allows God to reveal our individual purpose, which then propels us into action to advance God's Kingdom.

All this occurs with a simple shift in focus. Our focus is where our heart is. And where our heart is, our future awaits.

So, how do we successfully restore the arts back to God? It's simple. We restore music and the arts back to God by assuming the posture of God-worship. We use our God-given gifts and talents to glorify God. We allow His Holy Spirit to lead us in His transforming creative expression.

How Are We Empowered Through Our Gifts & Talents?

Our gifts and talents have a two-fold purpose in worship: to glorify God and to help others.

First, by presenting our gifts and talents back to God, we express our love for Him. Our gifts and talents glorify Him. We can see how this translates to our children and how they express their love for us as parents. When my daughter is finished with her drawings, she ends up tugging at my pants leg saying, "Mommy, mommy, look what I drew for you!"

It is in our nature, to express our love through the creative gifts and talents God has given us.

Secondly, our gifts impact and empower the lives of others. For example, my husband Mike is very gifted with design and digital marketing. He used his gifts to create a professional web presence and cutting-edge design for a friend, who is also a powerful worship leader and man of God. He did this in service to God, creating something he knew would be used to advance God's Kingdom on this earth and give glory to God.

Someone once explained the difference between a gift and a present. A gift is generally more valuable than a present and passes from the rich to the poor. This makes sense when we recognize the value of our gifts and from whom they came.

> God has given each of you a gift from his great variety of spiritual gifts. Use them well to serve one another. Do you have the gift of speaking? Then speak as though God himself were speaking through you. Do you have the gift of helping others? Do it with all the strength and energy that God supplies. Then everything you do will bring glory to God through Jesus Christ. All glory and power to him forever and ever! Amen.
>
> 1 Peter 4:10-11 NLT

We can also look at the difference between a gift and a present in terms of intent of the heart. A present is often something the giver wants to give the receiver. A gift is something the giver knows the receiver wants or needs. When we offer our gifts to God and others, we give to them something we know they want or need.

Ultimately, our creative gifts, like spiritual gifts, give us joy as we offer them to others. It's so important to remember that God has given them to us, to please Him, and for the benefit of others.

This idea can be demonstrated in a notable quote from Eleanor Powell:

> "What we are is God's gift to us. What we become is our gift to God."

Interestingly, Eleanor was a famous dancer and actress in the late 1930s and early 1940s. She danced with the greatest of partners, including Fred Astaire. But when frequently asked who was her favorite dance partner, she always answered, "God."

Eleanor's creative talents and gifts may have pleased and inspired many audiences, but clearly her sentiments reflected that her dancing was intended to please God.

CONCLUSION

I want to conclude with this quote from Nancy Leigh DeMoss, a Christian radio host and author. It is an encouragement and a constant reminder to us that God is not looking for those who are able, but those who are available.

> Don't assume you have to be extraordinary to be used by God. You don't have to have exceptional gifts, talents, abilities, or connections. God specializes in using ordinary people whose limitations and weaknesses make them ideal showcases for His greatness and glory.

God can achieve anything with the *available*, who are wholly and completely surrendered to Him.

Are you available?

4

YOU DON'T ESCAPE GOD'S NOTICE

Your Identity is Key to Fulfilling God's Plans & Purpose

> But the Lord said to Samuel, "Don't judge by his appearance or height, for I have rejected him. The Lord doesn't see things the way you see them. People judge by outward appearance, but the Lord looks at the heart."
>
> 1 Samuel 16:7 NLT

In this chapter we will look at the heart and explore the importance of our identity in Christ, the identity that God has given us.

We'll delve into the value of a given name and reputation. If asked, "Who do you believe you are and what do you believe your plan and purpose is in the body of Christ," would you be able to answer that question with confidence? Would you be able to describe who you are, the real you, when no one else is looking?

According to a 2015 nation-wide Barna study, 62% of Americans indicated faith does not impact their identity in any significant way. In my experience as part of the creative community, I believe this percentage is significantly higher among creative people.

This translates to the Church, the body of Christ, as well. It means that a large percentage of Christians base their identity on something or someone other than Christ.

Understanding our true identity is foundational. Until we understand and embrace our true identity in Christ, from within our heart, we cannot unlock our divine purpose and destiny, not as individuals, not as a corporate body.

Our identity is established in Jesus Christ, and it manifests in-and-through our gifts and talents. Together, our identity in Christ and our God-given gifts and talents provide the means through which we accomplish the plans and purposes of God in our lives.

When we don't know our true identity and where it comes from, we look for other ways to affirm and confirm our identity, apart from God.

When we look to the world as the source of our identity, what others think of us, we seek affirmation from the world. We measure ourselves according to what others believe. It is just the nature of mankind to seek fulfillment of this need for approval.

But what if instead we measured ourselves by what God thought of us? What if we looked at ourselves and saw what God saw? Our true identity is exactly that: We are who God says we are and we can do what God says we can do!

Knowing our true identity will save us from a life of striving to fulfill our dreams and visions in our own strength. It will steady and shield us from the whims and fashions of an ever-changing world of contradiction. It will rescue us from the rejection and smothering opinions of man.

When your identity is established and grounded in Christ it brings those once out-of-reach dreams and visions within reach.

Trust me, I've been there, done that, got the T-shirt too many times. This is especially true among creative people who are looking for a place to fit in within the Christian Church.

Creative people are very expressive by nature. If a creative person doesn't have an outlet to release their creativity, using their gifts and talents in the safety and acceptance of the body of Christ, they will likely go elsewhere.

This is not to say creative people are more important than those who don't feel like they are artists or creative types. Creative people that don't fit into the traditional artist roles are simply more prone to be criticized, offended or pushed aside. That is why I believe that creative people must focus on finding their identity in Christ first, before they pursue a creative role in the Church.

It is imperative that a creative person knows who they are at their core by being grounded in God's Word and in Christ Jesus. This will not only protect them from being hurt by the Church and Christians, but it will give them a boldness, confidence and gracious understanding when criticism comes from within the Church or from Christian leadership. It is often said that people will criticize something they do not understand or fear. That is often the case here.

It has been in my personal times of worship that I have sounded like a stuck record, complaining to God, questioning Him about everything. I even questioned

Him about why He put all these big and amazing dreams and visions in my heart for my life and ministry. No matter how hard I tried to make it happen, I felt I was far from ever seeing any of it come to fruition.

Thankfully, God is all-knowing and all-powerful. He knows me better than I know myself. He started right at the beginning. He took me right back to the basics, the very foundation of His Word, the Bible. He started me down a path of finding myself and showing me where my roots began. I realized that understanding my identity was paramount to getting me to where I believed God was taking me.

My identity is not found in my gifts and talents, but my identity is found in Jesus Christ.

No successful leader succeeds in life without the confidence of knowing who they are, being really good at the basics, and understanding the importance of a solid foundation. The bigger the foundation, the taller the tower can be built. The deeper the roots, the taller the tree can grow. A strong wind will never uproot a tree with strong roots and a solid foundation.

If you're thinking, "Well, I don't really know who I am in Christ," don't feel bad. I'm about to help you with that!

Today, most people have no idea who they are in Christ. Many of our churches have failed in this area of teaching. In too many churches today, in an effort to draw members and increase attendance, entertainment has become the focus of services, and the Holy Spirit has been kicked out.

There is no longer a desire for the manifest presence of the Lord God Almighty. This has led to a decline in the power of the Church and the human condition, resulting in depression, hurt and confusion among God's people. At the center of this is a lack of understanding our true identity in Christ.

Depression is at an all-time high. More people than ever are dependent on pharmaceutical drugs, keeping their emotions dull and tainted. Confusion has taken root and infected the minds of people, leading them to embrace all kinds of twisted and perverted doctrines. Social norms have uprooted biblical truths in the name of tolerance and inclusion, establishing lies as truth, even targeting the very identity of a person's gender and sexuality.

Pride has been around since the beginning of time when Lucifer was kicked out of heaven. He wanted to be God, not a servant of God. We can see this same pride running rampant through our churches. People who think they are gods lord over others to further their own agenda. They form cults or false doctrines that take the absolute true Word of God out of context and twist it.

Also undermining the power of our churches is the competitive nature of many churches. Many vie for stature as the *best, biggest* or *coolest* church, instead of working together in unity to make an impact in their local communities, to change lives and help those in need.

In many communities, the size and growth of church membership have become more important measures than the manifest Holy presence of the Lord God

Almighty. When church activities involve food they are better attended than prayer meetings to seek God's face and hunger for His Holy presence.

Don't get me wrong. Activities in the church are not a bad thing. I attend them too. And having food is a perk! But my question is this: What has happened to the pure motive, the intent and hunger of the heart for the presence of God and His glory?

Thankfully, we serve a God who has a plan and purpose for all of us, despite our shortcomings. That is why it is so very important to know who we are in Christ and our purpose in accomplishing His plan.

I have great news for you! YOU are perfectly created for such a time as this! Don't let anyone ever make you believe you are a mistake or were born in the wrong era, or that you are insignificant in the plans and purposes of God.

> Yet God has made everything beautiful for its own time. He has planted eternity in the human heart, but even so, people cannot see the whole scope of God's work from beginning to end.
>
> Ecclesiastes 3:11 NLT

> "For we are God's masterpiece. He has created us anew in Christ Jesus, so we can do the good things he planned for us long ago."
>
> Ephesians 2:10 NLT

So, let us start at the beginning.

GOD KNEW YOU BEFORE YOU KNEW YOU

It was in God's plan when He created man to have a relationship with Him. Unlike all the animals, God's plan in creating man was to reflect His own character and create each of us to be like Him: gracious, kind, patient, loving, truthful, compassionate, forgiving and just.

> When God created mankind, he made them in the likeness of God.
>
> Genesis 5:1 NIV

God desires to have a relationship with us! The scripture from Jeremiah below makes that clear. I like to look at it this way; God so desired to have a relationship with me that He couldn't wait until I was born. So He made it His prerogative to know me even before I was conceived, even before I knew myself. He knew me even before my parents met me. Not only did He know me, but He set me apart with my own unique purpose and destiny, one that only I can fulfill on this earth.

Before I formed you in the womb I knew you, before you were
born I set you apart;

Jeremiah 1:5 NIV

There is plenty of evidence of our importance to God in His Word. In Psalm
139:13, Ephesians 1:4, and Isaiah 64:8 scripture reveals the elaborate, careful and
purposeful plan God made for man.

Think about this for a second. There are about 100 million sperm present at
conception. That means there are 100 million sperm on a mission to be the 'one' to
penetrate the egg. The amazing news is that you were predestined before the very
foundation of this world to be the **one** to penetrate the egg.

God purposed you to be the **one,** and that was God's design; for you to make it
into the egg with ease amid millions of others. Nothing in this life happens by
chance. God attends to every detail. You are that important to God.

At the point of conception, we have not yet experienced death, rejection,
disappointment, abandonment, or even what our mom and dad has walked
through in life. We know nothing except the absolute truth of God; that we have
just come from God, the author of life and goodness to fulfill our predestined
purpose on earth.

GOD HAS A PLAN AND PURPOSE FOR YOUR LIFE

Your eyes saw my substance, being yet unformed. And in Your
book they all were written, the days fashioned for me, when as
yet there were none of them.

Psalm 139:16 NKJV

Regardless of how you were conceived, whether your parents were married or
not, and regardless of any other circumstances, none of that matters and it has no
effect on the plan and purpose God had already predestined for your life.

Your parents are merely the channels through which God brought you into this
world to walk out your plan and purpose. You must understand that God is the
author and finisher of your life, your eternal life. (Hebrews 12:2) God knit you
together in your mother's womb with a plan and purpose, even before your mom
ever knew she was pregnant.(Psalm 139:13)

As a mother of two precious daughters, Mike and I knew that God knit our girls
together in my womb with a predestined plan and purpose. We went to God in
prayer and asked Him to reveal to us His plan and purpose for them, so that we
could raise and guide them in the knowledge of it.

Your parents may not have known this. They may not have asked God, as Mike
& I did. But that does not negate that God is still the author of life. You are the
precious life God created. God predestined you with a plan and purpose. You were

fearfully and wonderfully made as we read in Psalm 139:14.

It's never too late to discover what God has planned for your life. You can still ask Him to reveal His plan and purpose for you. Whatever your age, whatever's in your past, God is ready to help you fulfill the plan He has for your future.

In Jeremiah 29:11, the Lord God says that He knows all your thoughts. What's more interesting the scripture reveals He even has thoughts about you, thoughts of peace and not of evil, to give you a future and a hope.

In Deuteronomy 30:9 God says that your life will be one to prosper and that He delights in you. God delights in you, His creation, and He desires for each and every one of us to live a full and abundant life.

GOD IS WATCHING

God loves and values you and He has saved you through Jesus. Through Jesus' crucifixion and resurrection, God gave us eternal life. Not only is God watching, but He's watching over you.

God is not like a man with a stick sitting on His throne waiting for us to fail or to do something wrong so that He can strike us down. No! God is a good and loving God. God is love, the author of love and He loves you, deeply!

> Are not five sparrows sold for two copper coins? And not one of them is forgotten before God. But the very hairs of your head are all numbered. Do not fear therefore; you are of more value than many sparrows.
>
> Luke 12:6-7 NKJV

It is the devil and his demons' that come to steal, kill and destroy man. It is he and his minions who find pleasure in twisting and perverting the truth of God's creation. It is Satan who sows confusion and leads people into sin.

You can't turn on the television, scroll through social media, or page through magazines and newspapers without seeing the evidence of a world in crisis, identity crisis. Satan has targeted the very identity of people, undermining the truth and very foundation of who we are, who we were created to be.

In New York City alone its citizens can choose between 31 gender identities. A simple truth has been perverted. God created man and woman, and it's a lie of the devil to suggest otherwise.

> So God created mankind in his own image, in the image of God he created them; male and female he created them.
>
> Genesis 1:27 NIV

When a person struggles to understand who they are at very core of their identity and chooses to believe the lies of the devil it produces the bitter fruit of sadness, insecurity, depression, deception and confusion.

A recent study by the Anderson School of UCLA in 2016 found the national suicide rate among the transgender community is significantly higher than those who have been raised in poverty or have been bullied. The transgender suicide rate is 40% versus 4% in what is termed 'normal' suicide rates.

Racism and poverty are found to have very little impact on the "normal" suicide rate. In fact, the suicide rates in the black community are significantly lower than the white community, and third-world countries have a significantly lower suicide rate than first-world countries.

The impact of racism and poverty are the result of the devil's work and they affect us, but we must not let them define who we are.

Gender confusion is also the work of the devil, another lie designed to undermine our true identity in Christ. Assigning people to a false identity, classifying them by worldly characteristics, and then pitting them against one another, is a trap set by the enemy known as identity politics.

When we fall victim to the lies of the enemy, we are opening up our hearts and minds to the enemy. Confusion, about our identity or any of God's truths, makes us vulnerable to the wiles of the enemy, who wants nothing more than to steal, kill and destroy mankind. If you were born a man, and the devil can make you believe you are a woman, then he can deceive you about anything, can't he?

Personally, I believe that when a person finds their true identity, who they are in Christ, and believes what God says and thinks about them, it not only sets them free but transforms them into the likeness of who God created them to be. It resets the course of their life to the original plan and purpose that was predestined by God.

God came that we may have life and have it abundantly with purpose and destiny. God sent His son Jesus to this world to save us through His death on the cross and His resurrection three days later. (John 10:10-11 & John 3:16-17)

God loves us so much. And when we realize and accept the enormity of His love for us, it will not only liberate us but it will protect us from the prowling devil.

GOD IS WAITING

God not only has a plan and purpose for your time on earth, but He has gone beyond that and prepared an eternal place for you in heaven. You see, God's commitment is for the long haul. He desires an eternal relationship with His children. The love He has for us is so vast that even in our wildest imagination we are not able to fathom what God has awaiting us in heaven, our eternal home.

> "No eye has ever seen or no ear has ever heard or no mind has ever thought of the wonderful things God has made ready for those who love Him."
>
> 1 Corinthians 2:9 NLV

After His resurrection, and before Jesus ascended into heaven, in John 14:1-4

He told His disciples He needed to go ahead of them to prepare a place for them. He encouraged them not to worry and to not let their hearts be troubled. He told them to trust and believe in God, that He has prepared a place for His children to spend eternity with Him.

Personally, at a very young age I had a very deep love for God. It was a love I couldn't describe with words. Beyond words, it was how this deep love manifested in my life that served as the key to discovering my identity in Christ.

This deep child-like love gave me a sure sense of security. If others said things about me that were contrary to what I knew God said about me, I would not accept it and wouldn't let it shape my identity. This love gave me comfort and peace as I laid in my bed in the dark of night knowing that there was no reason to fear because God lives in me and He would never harm me.

Just these two things alone, being secure in who I was and not allowing fear to enter my heart began to build a godly confidence in me as a person. I began to discover my strengths and grew confident in them.

Along my path, my parents have always been faithful supporters who have stood beside me with wise counsel whenever I needed or asked for it, even today. Now that I have my own family, my husband is my greatest supporter and cheerleader.

Even greater, we have a God that supports us. He gives us wise counsel and leads us to fulfill His plan and purpose. But He requires our participation. We must simply trust and love Him. We must follow Him!

You may not have been raised in the optimum environment, a two-parent home surrendered to God and living in His ways, but that does not negate or cancel your divine plan and purpose.

A great example is my husband Mike. For much of his latter childhood his grandmother raised him. His mother and father divorced early on. He lived through two more divorces before he finally went to live with his "granny." It may not have been until in his later 40's, but he finally found his way to God and is now living out God's plan and purpose for his life.

Whatever your case, you must remember: You have a heavenly Father, who is greater than any other, who provides for your every need, and He delights in you.

Consider David's prayer in Psalm 27:10 AMPC: "Although my father and mother have forsaken me, yet the Lord will take me up [*Adopt me as His Child*].

Regardless of your life's circumstances, it is not too late for you to live out God's plan and purpose for your life. God awaits you. Simply ask and He will answer.

GOD CALLS YOU BY NAME

At some point in my life I wondered, "Is a name important? Why is a name even necessary?" Through prayer and study I found the answer. I believe there is power in one's given name. A name not only differentiates one person from another but it speaks of a person's identity and character.

But now, thus says the Lord, who created you, O Jacob, and He who formed you, O Israel: "Fear not, for I have redeemed you; I have called you by your name; You are Mine.

Isaiah 43:1 NKJV

If God knows my given name, then do I know my name? When the Lord says, He knows you, that goes deeper than just knowing of you or just knowing your name.

"I am the Good Shepherd. I know My sheep and My sheep know Me. I know My Father as My Father knows Me. I give My life for the sheep.

John 10:14-15 NLV

God knows us far better than anyone could ever know us. He created us and gave us His identity. He also created us uniquely, with special gifts and talents, so that we would be equipped to live a life according to His plans and purposes for us.

IDENTITY PRODUCES REPUTATION

Even a child is known by his actions, whether his deeds are pure and right.

Proverbs 20:11 ISV

Your reputation, what you're known for, becomes part of the framework of your identity. The scripture above suggests that even a child has a reputation.

Anyone who has children in school can identify with this point. As a parent, we soon learn of the reputations of our children's classmates. We want to know which kids might be a positive influence, and which might be a negative influence. As a parent with a four-year-old and a six-year-old in school, I can testify to this. I can also tell you that it leads me to wonder about the reputation of my own children.

Whether we like it or not, our actions, how they are perceived by others, and what others say about us establish our reputation. But it should not establish our identity. Unfortunately, many people incorporate their worldly reputation into their identity, whether it's good or bad.

When the reputation is bad, they find it difficult to escape it and they become a slave to what others think and say about them. Their identity assumes that reputation and they often become who other people say they are.

On the other hand, many people spend a lifetime carefully building their reputation to achieve personal goals. This is very common in business circles, the workplace and even in the Church.

However, just as with a bad reputation, as these people carefully work to craft an identity and reputation they hope produces the outcomes they want, they are still enslaved to what others think and say about them.

The problem is that reputations and identities built on what other people think and say are false identities. They are built on worldly deeds, are subject to the interpretations and opinions of others, and are intent on pleasing others.

Worldly reputations and identities are harmful to our relationship with God. They provide no spiritual fruit. They set themselves against the identity God has given us. When our identity is from the world, it leads us away from the plans and purposes of God.

Instead of seeking to build a worldly reputation and a worldly identity, we must seek to build a godly reputation. Our identity should be in Christ, not the world. You are who God says you are, not who Nancy in accounting says you are. You are who God says you are, not who Joe the CEO says you are.

We may live in the world, and we should not ignore how the world views us. But, as a Christian, you are not of this world. You have been born again. You are a new being, set apart from the world.

> Therefore, if anyone is in Christ, he is a new creation; old things
> have passed away; behold, all things have become anew.
>
> 2 Corinthians 5:17 NKJV

When you committed your life to Jesus and became a Christian, your old reputation ceased. With your old identity dead, all things became anew, including your reputation and identity. Having been born again, you are no longer an enemy of God and under the curse of Adam.

The curse of man happened when Adam and Eve ate of the forbidden fruit. They were cast out of paradise, the Garden of Eden and into the world, and became subject to the false identity and reputation of fallen man.

But then…Jesus! When we become believers, we become the sons and daughters of God. (John 3:16)

In Romans 11 it says that believers are grafted into the family of God. We become descendants of Abraham and David. We become part of the bloodline of Jesus. This is our identity! We are the bloodline of Jesus. When we accept Jesus as Lord and Savior, we are redeemed and our Father in heaven receives us as He does His very own Son, Jesus!

As amazing as that is, it gets even better! When we receive the Holy Spirit, God lives and dwells in us and makes available to us all the power and wisdom Jesus had when He was here on earth. This is the foundation of your reputation. God created you, He has plans for you and He has equipped you to achieve those plans.

The main point is this: We serve an almighty loving God, who has good plans for us. If we want a relationship with Him, if we are to lift up our prayers to Him, if we are to praise Him and worship Him, we must understand that our reputation is built on our identity in Christ.

In scripture we find several instances of when God transformed someone, changing their reputation and identity. In some cases, He also changed their names. Here are some biblical examples of when God changed the names of people to establish a new identity. He transformed them to fulfill His plan and purpose for their lives.

When God changed the names of Jacob, Abram and Sarai, not only did they get a name change, but their reputation changed also.

- Jacob the *supplanter*, which means to *trip up or overthrow* was changed to *Israel the prevailer*.
- Abram the *exalted father* was changed to Abraham the *father of nations*.
- Sarai *my princess* was changed to Sarah the *Princess*.

When their names changed, God caused their former reputations to cease. I believe the name change was part of the transformation, but it was the transformation that mattered most.

Following the transformation were changes in behavior and deeds. The transformation led these people into God's calling and to accomplish His plans and purposes. Fulfilling the plans and purposes of God established their reputations.

It's a process. God transforms us. God changes our identity. God equips us. God sends us to fulfill His plans and purposes. God tells us what He thinks of us.

Jacob, Abram and Sarai did not escape God's notice back then, and neither have you. We might feel like we are unqualified or even unable to fulfill our plan and purpose. Because of pain, sorrow, loss, or hopelessness in our lives, we might feel we were robbed of our plan and purpose.

It may be because of your reputation, your family's reputation, or other things that you feel unworthy or unqualified to receive what God has for you. Do not believe it! There is great news and the solution is an easy one. Go straight to God; give Him your whole heart. Let Him transform you. Let Him tell you who you are. Ask Him to equip you and ask Him to make plain the plans and purposes He has for your life. This is how you will begin to establish your **eternal reputation**.

Our true identity is in Jesus Christ. He paid a price for us with His life. He will not withhold from you your plan and purpose, and He will give you what you need to accomplish it.

> Most assuredly, I say to you, he who believes in Me, the works that I do he will do also; and greater works than these he will do, because I go to My Father.
>
> John 14:12 NKJV

When we take hold of what God says about us in His word, accept it and believe it as truth and act on it by applying it to our lives, we are set free from ourselves. Our identity will lead to our divine destiny.

God says that you are His own (Philippians 3:12), His chosen (1 Peter 2:9), and His masterpiece (Ephesians 2:10) just to name a few.

IDENTITY PROTECTION PLAN

Identity theft has become a big problem in the technology age. The frequency and ease with which criminals can steal important personal information has spurned an entire industry. If not safeguarded, they dig around in your email, online accounts, computers and even your mail until they find a way to steal your identity.

In the same way, the enemy comes to destroy believers, targeting our very identity. His strategy is to find weaknesses, attack them and build strongholds around them until he has defeated us.

This is why God tells us to resist the enemy and his schemes. I love how the Eugene H. Peterson translation says it.

> So let God work his will in you. Yell a loud no to the Devil and watch him scamper. Say a quiet yes to God and he'll be there in no time. Quit dabbling in sin. Purify your inner life. Quit playing the field. Hit bottom, and cry your eyes out. The fun and games are over. Get serious, really serious. Get down on your knees before the Master; it's the only way you'll get on your feet.
>
> James 4:7 MSG

CONCLUSION

There is a real war going on for our souls and our identity. The devil was defeated long ago. Even though he still prowls the earth, looking to destroy us, we must still defeat him daily by reminding him of his defeat and by walking in the promises and principals of God's word.

We are equipped to fight this battle. God provided us with the *Armor of God* as described in the book of Ephesians 6:10-20.

We have never, and will never escape God's notice. His love for us is far too great. There is nothing that He will not do for us when we surrender our heart to Him. The truth is that we, as Christians live in this world, but we are not of this world. Our identity is, and should remain in Jesus Christ.

Remember, you are who God says you are! Forget about who the world (devil) says you are. God is with you. You are His.

God knew you before the laying of the very foundations of this world. He created you uniquely, with gifts and talents, so you can do what He says you can do. He authored His purpose and plans in your life before you were born. He has called you by name. He knows your deepest desires. He knows your heart.

Cast off your worldly identity. Forget your worldly reputation. Put on your godly identity, your identity in Christ and begin to establish your eternal reputation.

As you assume your godly identity it will unlock the plans and purposes for your life. It activates your gifts and talents. It empowers you to accomplish the plans and purposes God has for your life.

5

GOD CREATED YOU TO FIT IN

Our own body has many parts. When all these many parts are put together, they are only one body. The body of Christ is like this. It is the same way with us. Jews or those who are not Jews, men who are owned by someone or men who are free to do what they want to do, have all been baptized into the one body by the same Holy Spirit. We have all received the one Spirit. The body is not one part, but many parts.

1 Corinthians 12:12-14 NLV

At some level, every one of us has a need, a desire, to fit in. It is a powerful internal force, something I believe God has planted in each of us. It is this desire that prompts us to wonder *how* we fit in.

Is my life part of a bigger plan? How do my creative gifts, my talents, fit into that bigger plan? These are natural questions that stem from a godly seed.

He has made everything beautiful in its time. He also has planted eternity in men's hearts and minds [*a divinely implanted sense of a purpose working through the ages which nothing under the sun but God alone can satisfy*], yet so that men cannot find out what God has done from the beginning to the end.

Ecclesiastes 3:11 AMPC

As Christians, indeed we were all created with a purpose and a plan: God's plan. And we were equipped to fulfill that plan.

I am here to reassure you that God created you and gave you your gifts and talents to serve in His divinely orchestrated plan, for your life and for His people, the Church. Our gifts and talents are meant to be made manifest in the Christian Church.

Who and what is the Christian Church? Simply stated, the Christian Church is the body of believers who believe in the God of Abraham, Isaac and Jacob, who believe that Jesus is the Son of God and He died for our sins so that we would have eternal life in heaven. The Christian Church is the body of believers who believe and practice the principles of the Bible.

Contrary to the view of many, the Church of the Bible is not a building or meeting place where God's people gather. The Christian Church refers to who we are, not where we go.

In Romans, Paul the apostle explains how we are part of God's body and if we don't function as part of the body, and according to our designed purpose, we will fall victim to the practice of comparing ourselves with others.

> In this way we are like the various parts of a human body. Each part gets its meaning from the body as a whole, not the other way around. The body we're talking about is Christ's body of chosen people. Each of us finds our meaning and function as a part of his body. But as a chopped-off finger or cut-off toe we wouldn't amount to much, would we? So since we find ourselves fashioned into all these excellently formed and marvelously functioning parts in Christ's body, let's just go ahead and be what we were made to be, without enviously or pridefully comparing ourselves with each other, or trying to be something we aren't.
>
> Romans 12:4-6 MSG

Comparison is dangerous, since we were created uniquely and equipped uniquely to take our place in the body of Christ. When we compare ourselves to others, we risk losing our divine identity. When that happens, we cannot effectively fulfill our role in the plans and purposes of God. Comparison is especially common among creative people.

The body of believers has a specific intent and purpose. That purpose is to walk in the revelation of God's Word through the Holy Spirit, to be transformed into the image of Jesus Christ, and to share the Gospel with the world. This is the identity of the Church.

Comparison and social conformity have destroyed the identity of the Christian and the identity of the Church. Why? For the most part, many of God's people have not yet discovered their true identity, or they have abandoned it for a worldly identity. We were created uniquely to fit into the body of Christ and to play a role in the Church. Without this knowledge, the desire God has placed within us to "fit in" to the Church is misplaced in the world.

Think about it in terms of a puzzle. Imagine opening a puzzle box only to find all the pieces were shaped the same! Crazy, right? Every piece in a puzzle is unique, in the way it looks and the way it's shaped.

Every piece is important. Have you ever spent hours working on a puzzle, only to find at the end one piece is missing? At that moment, doesn't that missing piece become the most important piece in the puzzle? A puzzle is incomplete and worthless when there is a missing piece.

THE SNARE OF COMPARISON

Both Christians and non-Christians look to the world and to secular social circles in an attempt to figure out where they fit in the world. They compare themselves to others in the world as they construct their identity. Instead, we must construct a unique identity in Christ, and seek our place in the Church.

Why is the impact of such worldly comparison detrimental to the discovery of our Christian identity? It is contrary to God's principles of unity and order. It undermines the notion that we were created uniquely to work together in the body of Christ.

Worldly comparison is a snare set by the enemy. It is especially destructive for the creative person because creative gifts and talents are subject to public judgment and criticism in a highly competitive and critical world.

In worship, as part of the body of Christ, creative worship should be without judgment and criticism, since it is lifted up to God. In worship, God is the judge and critic. Since He created you, since He gave you these gifts and talents, how can He feel anything but love and adoration?

When your child dances for you, or delivers a carefully prepared drawing or painting, is your heart filled with judgment and criticism, or is it filled with love and adoration?

If you don't understand your unique identity in Christ, then your gifts and talents will not operate in the power for which they were intended. When we operate in our divine identity, our creative talents and gifts flow in freedom and confidence.

When we compare ourselves to others, we fall into a trap. For example, in the world, we often compare ourselves to people we admire, people who have achieved what we hope to achieve. We view these people as more accomplished.

This is where we get ensnared in the trap. Captive, the mind falls prey to attack: "I'm not as talented." "I could never be that good." "I can never achieve that." These are self-defeating thoughts.

We also fall prey to what others say about us: "You're too young." "You don't have enough experience." "You're not important." "You're not strong enough." "You're not pretty enough."

These are the dangers of a worldly identity, where comparison and conformity render us powerless. They obstruct our path. They exclude us, and others, from participating in God's plan and purpose. They set obstacles our in path and delay our journey.

The following examples show how comparison can become a destructive force in our lives and in the Church.

Comparison Leads to Doubt & Fear

> For you did not receive the spirit of slavery to fall back into fear, but you have received the Spirit of adoption as sons, by whom we cry, "Abba! Father!" The Spirit himself bears witness with our spirit that we are children of God, and if children, then heirs—heirs of God and fellow heirs with Christ, provided we suffer with him in order that we may also be glorified with him.
>
> Romans 8:15-17 ESV

Did you know the word "fear" is mentioned over 500 times in the King James Version of the Bible? That speaks to how fear is something every person will wrestle or deal with in their lifetime. Some struggle with fear more than others, but fear is a reality that we need to overcome.

Did you ever consider that the area of fear in your life is the very area God wants to empower you in?

When we engage in comparison, we take the power out of our creative worship! We become less, not more, like God. It's a tactic the enemy uses to keep us operating in the realm of doubt and fear (James 1:6-8), diminishing our true identity and our ability to live in our unique purpose and destiny.

Comparison Leads to Isolation

When we engage in comparison we put up walls or barriers in our own lives. Doubt and fear are the building blocks in the walls we construct between others and ourselves. They're building blocks in the wall we construct between God and ourselves.

Instead of humility, comparison leads to false pride. It erodes unity. It isolates us. All of these things prevent us from growing spiritually, finding peace and finding our place in the Church.

For He Himself is our peace and our bond of unity. He who made both groups–[*Jews and Gentiles*]–into one body and broke down the barrier, the dividing wall [*of spiritual antagonism between us*], by abolishing in His [*own crucified*] flesh the hostility caused by the Law with its commandments contained in ordinances [*which He satisfied*]; so that in Himself He might make the two into one new man, thereby establishing peace.

Ephesians 2:14-15 AMP

Comparison Leads to Discouragement & Defensiveness

When we engage in comparison, we become defensive. Fear and doubt change our perspective. We see others as threats and take a defensive posture to protect ourselves from anticipated attacks and the resulting wounds. Instead of being an encouragement, we become discouraged, and we discourage others. Instead of the freedom to run the race with endurance and persistence, (Hebrew 12:1), we become entangled in sin, keeping us from God's plan and purpose.

Some people have gotten out of the habit of meeting for worship, but we must not do that. We should keep on encouraging each other, especially since you know that the day of the Lord's coming is getting closer.

Hebrews 10:25 CEV

Comparison Leads to Jealousy, Division & Destruction

When we engage in comparison, we further isolate ourselves and invite jealousy to take root in our heart. Jealousy begins to corrupt our heart and mind. Jealousy leads to bitterness, which brings division and rejection. Division and rejection wounds God's people, one of the things that often leads to the destruction of churches.

Wherever you find jealousy and fighting, there will be trouble and every other kind of wrong-doing. But the wisdom that comes from heaven is first of all pure. Then it gives peace. It is gentle and willing to obey. It is full of loving-kindness and of doing good. It has no doubts and does not pretend to be something it is not. Those who plant seeds of peace will gather what is right and good.

James 3:16-18 NLV

Comparison Hinders Worship

Comparison promotes doubt and fear. It leads to isolation, discouragement, defensiveness, jealousy, division and destruction. All of these things hinder the move and flow of the Holy Spirit during worship. They hinder the flow of power in worship. They hinder our ability to commune with God during worship.

> If you are guided by the Spirit, you won't obey your selfish desires. The Spirit and your desires are enemies of each other. They are always fighting each other and keeping you from doing what you feel you should.
>
> Galatians 5:16-17 CEV

When we allow comparison to enter our mind, we allow sin to enter our hearts. We prevent ourselves from worshiping in the Spirit. The whole purpose of worship is to enter the spirit-realm, the supernatural realm, to stand before the throne of God and give glory and honor to God alone.

Since God created each of us uniquely, and equipped us with gifts and talents to accomplish His plan and purpose for our lives, then comparison is unnecessary! We are unlike anyone else.

We should look inward to discover those gifts and talents. We should pray that God would reveal them to us. We should seek God's face to get the revelation of who we are and what He has planned for us!

How do we do that? Worship! Face-to-face worship is one of the most powerful ways to engage with God. When we enter the spirit-realm, when we enter into Spirit-led worship, we become pure vessels for the Spirit of God to flow and manifest through.

To worship in spirit and truth, to operate in peace and power, we must walk in our true identity. We must not compare ourselves to others, or give power to what others say about us. Otherwise, we surrender our true identity and begin to assume a false identity.

Embracing your true identity empowers you to fulfill the plans and purpose God has for your life. It allows you to fit into the body of believers and do God's work.

Still, the world will continue to try to reclaim you. It will try to tell you who you are and what you should do. It will try to return you to a false identity.

When you feel the pull of the world, turn directly to God. Remind yourself that your identity is in Christ Jesus. Reaffirm with God that you are who He says you are, and you were made for such a time as this to fulfill His plan and purpose for your life.

Embrace God's plan and purpose for you, and know He's made a place for you in the Church, among the body of believers. When you find yourself engaging in comparison, *take these simple steps*:

- Recognize and appreciate the gifts and talents that God has given others.

- Pray for and encourage whomever it is you are comparing yourself to.
- Thank God for the gifts and talents that He has given you and that He made you unlike anyone.
- Pray that God would increase you and elevate your gifts to serve Him in the plans He has for you.

This approach allows us to put God first and to pour God's heart into one another. It allows us to give of ourselves and to build one another up in the Lord.

> Do to others as you would like them to do to you.
>
> Luke 6:31 NLT

These steps give us a godly way to deal with and overcome comparison.

Comparison is one of Satan's tactics, designed to choke the life out of our God-purpose and God-destiny. Satan will tell you to conform and be like others. But God says I created you uniquely to be extraordinary and to do extraordinary things. **Believe God!**

Additionally, when we turn to God and pour into others, taking these steps shifts our perspective. It takes our focus off ourselves and puts it onto the heart of God. We may have faced a rough day, but sacrificially following these simple steps, allows us to take our minds off our own feelings of failure, or what we see as our short-comings, and shifts our focus on God and what He says and thinks about us.

Building a supportive culture, or community in the church among creative people is important. As a body of believers, we are a godly culture and community. The Church should provide a safe environment for us to pray and encourage one another. It should provide a community in which we can be vulnerable with one another and with God. It should help us to grow and mature in a trusting and loving environment, built on God's Word.

A healthy church environment promotes a healthy accountability, built on a godly humility. A healthy church launches and supports us into our God-designed plan, purpose and destiny. By giving of ourselves, by praying and encouraging other believers, we not only make a connection with people on a relational level, but we allow for the connection between God and ourselves to grow, strengthen and produce fruit.

IDENTITY CRISIS

In much the same way that many Christians have lost their individual identity in Christ, the Christian Church, at least in westernized societies, has also lost her identity in Christ. Just as our own identity is established in Jesus, so should the Church's identity be established in Jesus.

The Westernized Church has lost her power and her impact, in part because she has bought into a worldly identity, marked by a worldly culture and a community that has lost sight of the most fundamental objective, to seek the face of God and His truth, and to be transformed by it.

Believers in the Christian Church have relied on their own efforts, their own ideas and their own power to impact the lives of others inside and outside of the body. Instead of asking God, seeking His face, we ask people, we seek the wisdom of man for the answers.

Let us look at the next two scriptures, and consider the explanation of Steve Thompson, a biblical teacher and speaker, author, prophetic minister and business owner. I believe it speaks to my point here about why seeking God's face and God's truth should be the fundamental part of our supernatural lifestyle. God is speaking to Moses.

> But He said, "You cannot see My face. For no man can see Me and live!"
>
> Exodus 33:20 NLV

This suggests we would die if we saw God's face. But, how effective would our worship be if we believed that when God showed up, face-to-face, we'd die? Then, Steve observed in verse 11 the Bible seemed to contradict itself, because clearly Moses didn't die.

> The Lord spoke to Moses face to face, as a man speaks to his friend. When Moses returned to the other tents, his servant Joshua, the son of Nun, a young man, would not leave the meeting tent.
>
> Exodus 33:11 NLV

The Bible, under no circumstance, contradicts itself. So, when we find scripture that appears to be contradictory, Steve points out, we can be certain a revelation awaits us.

Upon reading these scriptures, Steve Thompson asked God for the revelation to this apparent contradiction. And after much prayer and study, God gave him the answer. It began in his reading of Deuteronomy 34 in verse 5. Moses died only because God told him to. He didn't die because he saw the face of God.

Later in verse 7 it tells us that Moses' body did not show any signs of aging or disease, confirming the Lord told Moses to die and that aging and disease did the cause the death of Moses.

> So Moses, the servant of the Lord, died there in the land of Moab, just as the Lord had said. Moses was 120 years old when he died, yet his eyesight was clear, and he was as strong as ever.
>
> Deuteronomy 34:5 & 7 NLT

As Steve studied further, he reviewed Exodus 33:20, studying the part of the verse that says, "For no man can see Me and live." He looked up the Hebrew meaning for the word "live" and discovered in this context it means: "to keep your life the way it was" or "to preserve your life."

So, if we put that in the verse below, Steve's revelation unfolds as follows:

> But He said, "You cannot see My face. For no man can see Me and preserve the way your life was before!"

We cannot see the face of God without being changed! Sharing and emphasizing this one simple truth is the most fundamental goal of this book.

I want each of you to seek God's face. I want each of you to enter into that place, the supernatural realm, where you can stand face-to-face with God. Through worship, I want you to learn how to enter into the throne room of God and have a face-to-face encounter with Him, and to be transformed whenever you want to. I want this for you, because God wants it!

CONCLUSION

The Christian Church of today must be completely transformed by the power of God. In order for that to happen, we must create an environment through which we can pursue a face-to-face encounter with God. Instead of an anesthetized Church, it must be revived and transformed to rise strong again. It must become healthy again.

This is so important, because a healthy Church is a unified Church. A healthy Church is a Church that operates in power. In order for each of us to fit in, to take our place in God's larger plan and purpose, to achieve the will of God in our communities, our nations and the world, the Church must operate in wisdom and power. All of this is available to us in the throne room of God, face-to-face with Him.

There, we will experience this glorious transformation in our bodies, minds and spirits. It will change us, like it changed Moses.

Imagine the Christian Church, victorious in everything She does. Imagine miraculous healings in every church. Imagine a body of believers that walk in divine health, prosperity and fullness. Imagine a Church where God's people lay hands on the dead and they are resurrected.

This is the power of God in action, through the body of Christ. This is what God expects from the Church. Healthy believers, united as a healthy Church, will operate in this kind of power.

"Most assuredly, I say to you, he who believes in Me, the works that I do he will do also; and greater works than these he will do, because I go to My Father. And whatever you ask in My name, that I will do, that the Father may be glorified in the Son. If you ask anything in My name, I will do it.

John 14:12-14 NKJV

God, our Father who loves you, created you uniquely. Before you were even born He knew and adored you. He knew the plans and purposes He had for you, and He gave you gifts and talents to accomplish all these things. He also created a place for you, a place in which you fit among other believers, a place within the Church.

My identity: I belong to Christ
My responsibility: to know Christ
My debt: to make Christ known

- author unknown

In unity and in power with other believers, we can fulfill the plans and purposes of God, at every level.

6

A GOD SETUP

When God Does Something Unexpected

Commit your works to the Lord, and your thoughts will be established. A man's heart plans his way, but the Lord directs his steps.

Proverbs 16:3 & 9 NKJV

God has a plan for you and me. It's up to us to ask God to reveal it to us. Faithful, He will reveal it in His good and perfect time. The key phrase: in His good and perfect time.

For the vision is yet for the appointed [*future*] time. It hurries toward the goal [*of fulfillment*]; it will not fail. Even though it delays, wait [*patiently*] for it, because it will certainly come; it will not delay.

Habakkuk 2:3 AMPC

There was a long season in my life when I yearned to know God's plan for my life. There came a point in my life, in my early twenties, I was faced with a decision.

On one hand, I could continue with my weekly routine of going to church, singing a few praise and worship songs, listening to a three-point sermon and saying a prayer, waiting for God to do something.

On the other hand, I could seek God's plan for my life. I could ask Him to reveal my God-given purpose and how I was to be a part of His big plan.

I chose the latter and have not looked back since. It was this decision that opened the door to God's plan and purpose for my life.

I'd been living in the U.S. for about eight years and there was a lot of uncertainty about my future, whether I would be able to stay in the States or have to go back to South Africa, or possibly move to another country.

But God was working behind the scenes in my life, even though I didn't realize it yet. His plan led me on an amazing adventure that started with a trip to Iloilo, Philippines in January of 2006.

I was invited to join a young ministry team from Australia and to dance at the Firestorm Youth Conference. It was at this conference that God initially launched me into my original plan and purpose as a creative worshiper.

I talk about this experience in greater detail later in the book. But for now I want to jump ahead and focus on the following trip in May of 2006, five months after my trip to the Philippines. It was on this trip that God showed me my roots and identity as a worshiper. God chose what I would call the most unexpected and obscure place to do it. He sent me on an adventure to Carrefour, Haiti.

Pastors Terry and Cary Nelson have been pastoring Light Ministries Inc. in Carrefour, Haiti since 1980. In April of 2006 they hosted a worship conference at their church.

God's setup began when a team from a church in Alexandria, Louisiana, scheduled to teach and preach at the Haiti worship conference, canceled at the last minute. I was going to travel with this team to assist in the workshops and I would dance during worship services. But when I got word the team had canceled, it was too late for me to back out because I had already booked and paid for my flights.

Pastor Terry asked if I would preach and teach in place of the team. Only I had never done anything like this before. I had never preached before. Even more troubling, it was a weeklong conference and I didn't have a program or plan of action. Remember, I was originally just going to offer a helping hand as needed and to dance during services.

When Pastor Terry made this offer, I almost fell on my back. It felt like the wind was knocked right out of me. I sat on the other side of the phone call having all kinds of thoughts rush through my mind. Those thoughts were thoughts of pure inadequacy, unpreparedness, fear, lack of experience. I felt like a deer-in-the-headlights and filled with a sense of inability.

It seemed like 5 minutes before I responded, but in reality it was just a couple seconds. When I finally managed to compose myself, still filled with mixed emotions, the Holy Spirit gently nudged me with a very familiar scripture.

> "Whom should I send? Who will go for Us?" Then I said, "Here am I. Send me!"
>
> Isaiah 6:8 NLV

At that moment, this scripture spoke loud and clear, "say yes and don't look back!" Oddly, amid these mixed emotions I felt an excitement that I couldn't quite explain. So, with trembling in my voice, I answered with a shaky "yes." I immediately asked if I could invite a friend to join me to help. I felt like I needed back up.

I don't know if you've ever felt this way, but when I feel overwhelmed I like to pull my husband, mom or dad close as a support or backup. In this case, it would be a dear friend.

Initially, I found it surprising that Pastor Terry would offer me this opportunity because he knew my background. He knew very well I lacked experience in this area.

God really works in mysterious ways and thankfully God knows me well. I might add that God has a sense of humor, especially regarding the things He asks me to do.

Today, when God throws me into these situations, when He throws me into the deep end, I'm not surprised. I just know now that if I just doggie paddle at first, I will end up swimming along gracefully, at least I think so…. wink-wink.

After the call with Pastor Terry, I immediately called my friend, Mattie Livesey, from Cape Town South Africa and asked her if she was available to fly out to Haiti right away! She said yes and hopped on the next available flight. That alone was a miracle. She was one of the worship pastors and the Dean of the Bible School at the church she was working for at the time. This usually kept her bound to a rigid schedule. But God had other plans.

I wanted Mattie to join me because I knew how she operates and flows in the prophetic. Additionally, she is a worshiper, musician, and a great biblical teacher. I felt like that was pretty good backup!

When Mattie and I arrived in Haiti, we both agreed in prayer that we were to be empty vessels for God to pour into, and out through us, into the lives of the Haitian people.

We had no clue how this was going to happen, but we chose to remain sensitive to the Holy Spirit and submit to the authority of Pastors Terry and Cary, who trusted us with their leaders and church members.

That week in Haiti proved to be one of the most profound experiences either Mattie or I had experienced to that point in our lives. We went with the purpose of teaching worship but ended up receiving way more than we bargained for.

Simply stated, we found our roots and identity as worshipers. To top it off, God orchestrated it in a foreign land, not the land of our birth or citizenship.

So much happened in that week that profoundly impacted me. The experience revealed the creative expression of my worship. It revealed that through worship, I am a warrior. And on this trip we battled for souls that were bound and held captive through witchcraft.

I'd say that was the deep end! Wouldn't you?

THE HAITIAN CURSE

I believe that God sent me to Haiti not only to discover my own identity in Him as a creative worshiper, but also to recognize that so many of the Haitian people have been bound up and held captive by the curse over Haiti.

The one thing that profoundly stood out to me was how the Haitian people are desperate to know their true identity. Instead of the truth, their identity in Christ, they obsess over their African roots, a worldly identity. This obsession has subjected them to the lies of the devil, through which they have been bound in a curse fashioned in fear and insecurity. This is all designed to turn their worship from God to the devil.

You see, it was a 200-year curse in which the Haitians had dedicated Haiti to the devil, hoping that this dedication would free them from the slavery of the French.

Once a very fruitful country, providing Europe with 40% of all its sugar and 60% of their coffee, Haiti was known as the Pearl of the Antilles. It was one of the richest colonies in the 18th century French empire.

Primarily Catholic, France populated Haiti with African slaves from twelve different tribes. Afraid of rebellion, the French believed it was less likely the different tribes would unite and overthrow the French, since the various tribes did not get along. The French also believed the Africans didn't have souls, so they excluded them from their Catholic masses and activities.

The French view and treatment of the African people in Haiti upset the Haitian slaves. As you and I know, these beliefs are false; every human, regardless of race, creed or culture has a soul and was created by God with equal value. The slaves endured brutal methods of punishment at the hands of their French masters. Desperate for help, they united and turned to a well-known native Jamaican voodoo priest named Boukman.

In August of 1791, two months before Boukman's death, they performed a voodoo ceremony called the "Freedom Covenant" at Bois Caïman. Under a very large tree, they offered the blood of a black pig to Satan. In this ceremony they made a covenant with the devil for freedom.

They signed this demonic contract with the blood of the black pig believing they would be freed from the brutal slavery of the French. This sparked the beginning of the Haitian Revolution. The African slaves believed their covenant with the devil worked, because in 1804 Haiti became an independent nation free from the French and slavery. Yet, they were still bound by the Freedom Covenant, committing them to the devil.

For 200 years, the covenant robbed the Haitian people of their identity, having sold their souls out to the devil. Everything God had put in their hearts and created them to be, the devil took and twisted; he distorted and perverted it all for his glory.

One example of this is in the way the Haitian people worship. They routinely have local ceremonial gatherings called Rah-Rahs. Voodoo priests dress in full ceremonial headdresses and skirts. Participants carry banners and flags that are accompanied by drummers and trumpets.

The rhythm of the worship music is unique with a strange sort of offbeat, which is also accompanied by the sounds of a cracking whip. The people fill the streets dancing in a procession and chanting. A young man waving a voodoo flag usually leads the procession. At times, you will see them carry a disembodied arm, head, or limb as they walk.

Western missionaries tried for many years to reach the Haitian people and teach them about westernized Christianity and how to worship God the western way. They taught them how to clap as part of praise, raise their hands as part of worship, and follow the western rhythms and beats.

Although their hearts were genuine in their missionary work, they were not finding success because culturally the western worship mold didn't fit into the Haitian culture. The western worship didn't allow for the Haitian people to enter into worship in spirit and in truth, which you and I know brings a glorious transformation.

A group of Christian missionaries that knew about the curse over Haiti remained prayerful and waited patiently for the curse to come to an end. As the end drew near, this group of Christians traveled to Haiti, with the intent of going to the very place in Bois Caïman where the yearly sacrificial ceremonies were held under the large tree.

Previously, no one was ever able to access this spot without permission from the voodoo priests. But God had other plans. The prayers of Christians from all over the world prepared the way for these Christian missionaries to not only access this site, but on August 14th of 1997 they were able to march around the tree seven times and declare the curse broken over Haiti.

The very next day the very large tree was dead. That alone was a miraculous sign, since the tree had stood alive for well over 200 years. The curse was broken, and it marked the beginning of a new start for Haiti. Hallelujah!

Nearly ten years later, the history and affects of the Haitian curse and voodoo practice still plague Haiti. But Mattie and I were about to engage in some serious spiritual warfare to help the Haitian members of this one church take back from the devil what was intended for God.

A New Sound

After the curse was broken, western missionaries flooded Haiti with evangelism. Unfortunately, these missionaries lacked an understanding and knowledge of Haitian culture. As a result, there was no breakthrough in certain areas, including worship.

So long entrenched in the voodoo worship culture, the Haitian people couldn't disassociate Christian worship from their past voodoo practices. After worshipping the devil for so long, teaching Christian Haitian's to worship for the glorification of God failed.

The instruments, the voices of the Rah-Rahs and sounds of Haitian music stirred up fears in the Haitians, reminding them of the voodoo spirits their music once conjured up. Many feared that their instruments and the music that came from them were cursed.

As we geared up for this trip and made our ways to Haiti, God had been dealing strongly with my friend Mattie on what message we were to bring to the Haitian people. So, as Mattie submitted to the Holy Spirit, He put it on her heart that we were to release a new sound of worship.

Of course, we didn't know what that meant, or even how we were going to do that, but we trusted the Holy Spirit would lead us through it all. So, God put it on our hearts to offensively take back what the devil had distorted and perverted, and release a new sound that would reverse the curse.

As His vessels, we allowed the Holy Spirit fire to pour through us and into the Haitian people to burn away the past and witchcraft, and then to release a new sound, a sound that would bring glory to God and only God!

Over the course of the conference we spent a lot of time preparing and teaching the Haitian people. I danced in all the evening worship services following the Holy Spirit's lead with every move and step I took. Before we began the last meeting of the 5-day worship conference we finally got a Word from the Lord and approached Pastors Terry & Cary with what God had laid on Mattie's heart and confirmed in mine.

We shared what we believed the Holy Spirit wanted to accomplish in the last meeting of the conference. As they attentively listened, we could see by their faces that they agreed, even before they verbalized it.

This was a very important step to Mattie and me. We wanted to be sure we were in agreement and under the rightful submission to their leadership.

We asked a few of the leaders to gather together as many instruments as they could, specifically the ones used in the Haitian voodoo ceremonies and Rah-rahs. They brought them into the church and laid them on the platform.

There were trumpets, drums, maracas, percussion, bells and drums. All these instruments, per se, are harmless. But as the members of the church entered the church, as soon as they spotted the instruments we saw how fear overcame them.

Fear is always birthed out of a place where there is a lack of knowledge or understanding. So, the key was to show the Haitians that a demon will not live in an instrument, because there are much more effective ways a demon can carry out the work of the devil than to live in an innate object.

Mattie began sharing a powerful message on sound, its purpose, effect, characteristics and power, how it affects us in the natural as well as in the supernatural. She taught on the sound of revival as well as familiar spirits. It was a powerful message.

Slowly we began to see their faces and bodies relax as they began understanding Mattie's teaching. By the end of the message we encouraged people to take an instrument and ready themselves to release a new sound, the sound of revival for Haiti.

Before we began, we led everyone in prayer. Everyone stood in prayer before God to present themselves as clean and righteous vessels.

As creative worshipers, this is a very important step for us to take. Before releasing a sound or any creative expression of flags, dance, singing, poetry, etc. we need to empty ourselves of self-serving thoughts and motives. We must allow the Spirit of God to fill us so that we can be found pleasing to God. That is how our worship taps into the very power of God's presence and this will send the enemy to flight.

Following this teaching, as the Haitians began to worship, as the instruments began to sound, they began to worship God in spirit and in truth.

Mattie and I were amazed as the sounds that came out of those instruments sounded so different than before. It didn't sound like the Rah-Rah sounds. It didn't sound like western worship or even European, or Eastern worship. It was a new sound, a sound divinely designed, a sound of true God-worship that God had been yearning to hear from the Haitian people. It was a sound that was true to their true identity.

This sound began to stir up a powerful anointing and the building began to fill with God's glory. A transformation began to take place. People on the streets heard the instruments and were drawn into the building. Some of them that were demon possessed came too. As the power of God overtook these people they were set free and delivered!

Haiti had never and will never escape God's notice. Not for a moment. God had a powerful plan to bring the Haitian people out of the bondage of the devil by destroying the curse.

Now the Haitian people are free from the chains of the curse and can find their true identity in Christ. I am humbled to have witnessed just a small part of this glorious experience, to see their lives changed before my very eyes. It was also the experience through which I found *my* identity as a warring worshiper.

A Warrior Worshiper is Born

This Haitian experience caused me to realize that each nation, culture and person has a unique, geographic sound. Being a white South African, I never thought that I would be considered African in my worship. I was very naïve to think that my skin color in a predominantly African nation affected and shaped how I was to worship God.

I may have grown up in a country where there was segregation, but as a child growing up in a Christian home, I never found myself treating other races differently. Because we bleed the same color blood, skin color was never an issue for me.

I just never realized that being Caucasian I would have found my identity in what is typically considered to be that of an African. The rhythms and beats of the drums brought to life the warrior in me. I just thought it was because I grew up in that culture and that it was a part of me.

Now living in the States, I rarely hear those familiar sounds and when I do it stirs up that warrior. My experience in Haiti made it very clear that I was truly an African warrior in my worship. The sounds that I heard at that worship conference caused the Spirit of God to rise up within me and led me to boldly go deeper in worship and enter into dimensions I'd not yet experienced.

A freedom came over me as I danced, holding nothing back! The moves that my body made felt perfectly *right*, as though I was born to move this way, and I literally allowed myself to get totally *lost* in worshiping Him. I felt as though He and I were the only persons in the building and I was giving ALL of my adoration and ALL of my worship to Him alone.

What a powerful and transcending experience; one that transformed my worship and completely changed my understanding of the power of sound, movement, creative expression. It set me up to discover my identity as a true God-worshiper.

Ignorance Isn't Bliss

Following my trip to Haiti I spent a few weeks pondering all that had happened there. I realized there are so many people in this world today seeking to experience freedom in worship. They want to understand and engage in true God-worship. But they have no idea how to get there. I want others to experience this freedom, whenever they want it.

One of the key lessons I learned is that without knowledge and understanding we cannot obtain freedom. As I observe creative worship around the world, I see so many creative worshipers, struggling to enter into true God-worship, to attain this freedom.

True God-worship begins when there is a shift in our focus. It's a shift from living our worldly life here on earth, to living a life that is eternally focused. We must recognize that our time here on earth is a momentary stop on our way to our eternal life. Our life is not meant for just the here-and-now, but this life on earth is a period of preparation for eternity with our Lord and Savior, Jesus Christ.

> For physical training is of some value, but godliness (spiritual training) is of value in everything and in every way, since it holds promise for the present life and for the life to come.
>
> 1 Timothy 4:8 AMP

Listen carefully. This life, our life that we are living today on this earth, is just a moment, a blink of an eye in our eternity. Our moment may be 65, 75, 85 years or more, but it is just a moment in terms of eternity.

We must start to think bigger and broader. Even that may not be big enough, because our mind will never comprehend the greatness and glory of our eternity with God. That is why it is so important to get back to the basics, the fundamental truth of God's Word. It always points to eternity; our eternal God, and our eternal place beside Him.

Digging into the Word of God, with the help of the Holy Spirit, will bring revelation. It will reveal our gifts and talents. It will instruct us how to use them to worship God, to serve God. The One who created everything, the One who created you and me, is the author and the finisher of our faith. (Hebrews 12:2) So, it makes sense that we would want to get to know Him as He is our beginning and our end.

When we make it a priority to get into God's Word, we start discovering who we truly are in Christ, how we are rooted in Him, what He thinks of us and what He wants for us. Not just in words, but also by the power of the Holy Spirit, we see and feel how He loves us and that He has a purpose and destiny carefully and strategically crafted just for you and me.

Through these revelations we begin to see a bigger picture of our eternity. We begin to see how awesome and ever-present is our God. We begin to see that it is impossible to escape the notice of God, whether we want to or not.

The Haitians turned to the devil for salvation and sold their souls to him. But God never stopped paying attention to the people of Haiti, because He has a plan for each one of them.

Each of us are important to God, and He has made us an important part of His *big* plan. That is why it is imperative we know who we are, our true identity, and our role in God's *big* plan.

Expanding knowledge, the God kind, is essential for growth in our life on all levels: mentally, physically and emotionally. Maturity is developed and a greater understanding of our purpose is revealed through knowledge. The popular quote "knowledge is power" is exactly that - power.

Without knowledge, our way of life would not be as advanced as it is today. Back in the *old* days we either walked or rode horses to get around and we were dependent on daylight for light.

Today we have cars, electricity, and technology grows at such a rapid rate that 2-year-old computer is considered out of date. Knowledge doesn't just allow us to go through life with more ease; it empowers us to be more efficient.

With so much knowledge available today, have you ever wondered why the world is in such a state of chaos? It's because of ignorance. The Webster dictionary describes ignorance as: lack of knowledge, education, or awareness.

With so much knowledge available today, I'd take it one step further to say ignorance is a rejection of knowledge.

Contrary to the adage, ignorance is *not* bliss. We pay a high price when we buy into ignorance. Ignorance leaves us powerless, weak and vulnerable. The worst kind of ignorance a person can have is ignorance of God's laws. It is sin.

We must also recognize that knowledge is not enough. **When we have**

knowledge, we have power, but when we have wisdom, we are powerful. Wisdom allows us to use knowledge to accomplish things. It allows us to apply knowledge to solve problems. It prevents us from making mistakes, or making the same mistake twice.

We read in Romans that even though we are no longer under the law of the Old Testament, we are still required to obey the laws.

> Well then, if we emphasize faith, does this mean that we can forget about the law? Of course not! In fact, only when we have faith do we truly fulfill the law.
>
> Romans 3:31 NLT

Sin is sin in the eyes of God. Through knowledge or ignorance, sin is sin, just as a crime is a crime, whether you knew the law or not. Obeying the law is using wisdom with knowledge! It is our responsibility to ensure we are always informed and have the wisdom to use knowledge wisely. When you recognize and understand biblical truths, and then apply them to your life, you are using wisdom.

Reflecting on the plight of the Haitian slaves, it was clear they didn't have knowledge or wisdom. This lack of knowledge led to a 200-year curse, one of death and destruction. It led to the corruption of their true God-created identity.

The reason I bring this up is that understanding your identity in Christ, and walking out the plans and purposes God has for your life, requires wisdom. Knowledge alone will not get the job done! The same applies as you learn to enter into true God-worship. Wisdom is essential.

People who ignore the truth, who walk through life blindly, not only fail to use wisdom, but subject themselves to the wiles of the enemy, who comes to kill, steal and destroy.

Just look at the world today. Truth is not recognized or respected. It's loudly rejected. Lies are not only welcomed as truth, but they're celebrated. This is dangerous, and we're seeing the consequences; anarchy played out in the streets across our nation.

> Woe to those who call evil good, and good evil; Who substitute darkness for light and light for darkness; Who substitute bitter for sweet and sweet for bitter! Woe to those who are wise in their own eyes and clever in their own sight!"
>
> Isaiah 5:20-21 NASB

Stop Thinking. Start Praying.

Sometimes knowledge and wisdom seem illusive, like the answers we seek are just not coming. In my experience, prayer is often the missing ingredient. Fighting the mind and wrestling with worldly knowledge is something we don't need to do alone.

Sometimes we just need to stop thinking and start praying. Prayer is a way to deepen our relationship with God and draw upon godly wisdom.

Have you ever been in the company of someone who deems himself to be an expert on God and what the Bible says, but they have no real relationship with God? They come across as arrogant and their mind and spirit seem to be disconnected from each other. They often sound like they come from a place of judgment rather than grace.

They can quote the Bible, seemingly from cover to cover. Yet, their life doesn't reflect what proceeds from their mouth. Their minds are not renewed and washed in the truth of God's Word, revealed through the Holy Spirit.

Dealing with someone who has the knowledge, but is without godly wisdom, can cause division and bring confusion for those seeking the one true God, the God of mercy and grace.

About a year ago, my husband Mike began to attend a bible study hosted by one of his friends. The teacher impressed Mike with his knowledge of the Bible. He was very astute. He studied Hebrew and the Hebrew and Aramaic traditions of Jesus' day. However, a few of his teachings seemed contrary to fundamental Christian principles. Mike told me that these teachings were very unsettling. He said they made his stomach turn, and for several weeks he wrestled with these new teachings.

Mike studied these new teachings, looking for scripture to support them, but they seemed contrary to scripture and the truths he'd learned over the years. They contradicted the basic truths and fundamental beliefs that had been confirmed in prayer and through the Holy Spirit.

Yet, when Mike presented his case and supporting scripture to the teacher, the teacher used other scripture to reinforce his own arguments and to disprove Mike's beliefs.

A battle between Mike's mind and his spirit raged on for several weeks as he went back and forth between scriptural truths and the teachings and arguments of the Bible study teacher.

In prayer, through reading and studying the Word, and with the revelation of the Holy Spirit, Mike quickly rejected these false teachings and refused to return to the Bible study. Immediately he told me this twisted burden in his gut was released and clarity returned.

Mike says this was a great experience for him because he experienced the move of the Holy Spirit within him as he engaged in a supernatural battle of the mind. He says this was the closest thing to a real, physical world battle. It affected him physically, mentally and spiritually.

Praise God for His grace and power. Prayer, the Word of God and the Holy Spirit brought godly wisdom, giving him victory in this battle. Mike came through this experience with a stronger and more confident faith and a closer relationship with God.

Many Christians, when they face these kinds of battles are wounded. Some are turned away from God. And for others, it leads their lives into destruction.

Without prayer, the Holy Spirit and the Word of God, godly wisdom is absent and ignorance reins. Without godly wisdom, the ability to balance our lives and make wise choices is lost.

Ignorance has diminished the creative arts as a form of worship to the point that there is no middle ground or logical understanding anymore. Creative worship is either fully embraced or it is rejected. It's either included blindly or completely excluded from worship services.

This is because there is little teaching on worship, especially creative worship. I hope this book will fill the gap, offering a balanced approach to creative worship.

There are many Christians gifted in the creative arts. Unless they are singers and musicians on the worship team, they will tell you they find it almost impossible to find a place in a church setting through which they can offer their gifts as creative expression, especially in worship. They are grossly misunderstood and often persecuted.

As a creative individual myself, I understand how this misunderstanding and persecution can injure people. Creative people are typically more expressive with their emotions. While emotion is important in your relationship with God, we should not to be led by our emotions. You are to be led by the Spirit of God. Still, new or maturing, and even mature Christians often learn this the hard way.

So, how do we seek and find a place for our creative gifts and talents in worship? **Wisdom!** Remember, embracing wisdom in every area of your life whether health, finances, relationships, emotions and reasoning will always bring balance. The moment we slack on using wisdom it throws our life into lack and chaos.

If you are not sure where to start, how to embrace wisdom, then start with reading the whole book of Proverbs.

> Wisdom *is* the principal thing; *Therefore* get wisdom. And in all your getting, get understanding.
>
> Proverbs 4:7 NKJV

When wisdom and knowledge are not applied to the creative arts in a church setting we will see either one of two scenarios. For example, the church does not accept dance at all in any shape or form, or it goes over the top and instead of worship, dance becomes a big show, nothing more than entertainment.

In both cases, what's lacking is the leading of the Holy Spirit, who can bring revelation and knowledge regarding the purpose of dance as creative expression in worship. Sadly, in many of our churches the Holy Spirit has been rejected, sidelined or forgotten as the Person who is the very One needed to lead us as we worship.

When we engage in true God-worship, whether it is in dance, flags, painting or any kind of creative worship, our spirit man is connecting and communing with the Holy Spirit who is God's spirit.

Godly wisdom leads to balance and true-God worship for the creative worshiper. This is essential to finding our place. But let's not forget that worship is not limited to any place, and worship can take many forms. You can worship in any way, anywhere and anytime.

Before I conclude, let's talk about taking our worship into the throne room of God! We are made in the image of God, which means man is also triune; three in one, with a body, soul and spirit. (Genesis 1:26)

Let's explore further this notion of the triune makeup of man. The body is our temporary earth suit that houses our flesh, nerves, cells, tissues, etc. The body functions through our 5 senses. The soul is our personality which functions through our emotions, thoughts, will and reasoning. The spirit man is the inner part of a person that primarily connects and communes with the Holy Spirit through faith, love and worship. Considering this triune makeup, let's look at what scripture says in the book of Corinthians.

> Don't you realize that your body is the temple of the Holy Spirit, who lives in you and was given to you by God? You do not belong to yourself, for God bought you with a high price. So you must honor God with your body.
>
> 1 Corinthians 6:19-20 NLT

Before salvation, before we are filled with the Holy Spirit, our body seemed as something we had to satisfy, through exercise, food or other pleasures. It was also often something we neglected through substance abuse, poor diet or sexual sin.

Once we chose to accept Christ, we voluntarily surrendered our will and life to God. Our bodies become the temple of the Holy Spirit. The price for our bodies and souls was paid in full when Jesus Christ was crucified.

So, while we live in our bodies on this earth we are to honor God with our bodies by taking care of them and sacrificing our fleshly desires, daily presenting ourselves holy and acceptable before God.

The Haitians spent almost 200 years sacrificing their bodies, their lives, to the devil. And it brought nothing but death and destruction. But when we sacrificially honor God with our bodies, it will bring life, and life eternal. (Romans 12:1)

The moment you said "yes" to Jesus Christ, your spirit man became alive. Being spiritually alive, your worship connects your spirit man with the Holy Spirit in communion, and a beautiful trusting relationship is built.

Worship is not whole or complete unless it is done in spirit and in truth. When we surrender our will over to God and seek His face, this is the place in worship God will begin to reveal His plan for our life.

I believe the discovery of my true identity as a creative worshiper was a God-setup that began in the Philippines 5 months prior and was made manifest in Haiti.

He did not put the weight of that assignment on my abilities. Instead, it was my yielding to the Holy Spirit and my trust in Him that opened this door. **He didn't consider my physical abilities. He considered my heart.**

As we yield our own agendas, abilities and ideas over to the Holy Spirit we will begin to see God's handiwork play out in our lives. The more we get to know Him, the more our desires will begin to become like His. His voice will no longer seem silent, but it will become louder and clearer with each day we spend with Him.

It is like a marriage. In a healthy marriage, the more time you spend with your spouse, honoring and celebrating each other, the more you two will become in sync. I know with my husband, we often find ourselves thinking the same thing at the same time. It's more than just a coincidence. It is a result of us spending time together, building our relationship and trusting each other.

Worshiping in spirit and in truth is like a marriage. We cannot divide the two because they are one. A marriage consists of two parts, a man and a woman, but in the eyes of God they are one. A marriage is not a marriage if there is just one part. Therefore, worship is not true God-worship when there is just spirit or just truth. We must have both.

CONCLUSION

In conclusion, God's plan for your life is a plan to prosper you, to give you a purpose and destiny. Once you recognize and embrace your identity in Christ, receiving God's plan should be the next step.

Anyone who's ever planned a trip knows the plan gives you direction, from point A to Z, a sense of how long the trip will take, timing, and some expectation of what you will do when you get there; your purpose.

However, we also know that sometimes along that route we might take a few detours depending on the circumstances. There might be road closures, heavy traffic, or we might decide to take a scenic route.

Regardless of the detours, point A and point Z remain, a beginning and an end. The beginning is where you are now. The end is eternity in heaven, in the arms of our redeemer, Jesus.

God has a plan for each one of us. In order to obtain this plan we need to go to the One who is the Architect of that plan, God. Communing with God through worship is how we can go directly to the source of that plan.

As we begin to receive this plan, the Holy Spirit will be our guide and we must yield to Him and let Him lead us. The moment we ignore the Holy Spirit and decide to go our own way, do it our own way, we will either get lost or end up in a wreck.

Personally, I prefer to yield my life to the Holy Spirit, as the journey is thrilling and adventurous with lots of great surprises lying in wait for me. My trip to Haiti was, what I affectionately like to call, a God-setup. It was one of those scenic trips that God planned for my life that brought a whole new level and perspective of creative worship in my life.

I understood the basic plan for my life. But by being yielded over to the Holy Spirit I got to enjoy a thrilling and adventurous experience in Haiti, just one of the amazing adventures I will be sharing with you.

As we turn the page to the next chapter, my story focuses on how, over the years, creative worship has become a touchy subject among many believers. We will explore the biblical backing of dance as part of worship and the power that lies in the knowledge and wisdom gained of arts and dance as part of true God-worship.

It's important to note, however: Knowledge and wisdom alone will not restore the arts and dance back to its intended purpose within the body of Christ. The key to making a powerful impact in both the natural and supernatural realm of true God-worship is the **motive of one's heart**.

Knowledge and godly wisdom engage the motive of a person's heart, which results in balanced and stable believers. **Balance and stability provide for a daily supernatural lifestyle, one that is sustainable through the end of our worldly chapter and into eternity.**

7

GOING THROUGH THE MOTIONS

But I will hope continually and will praise you yet more and more. O God, from my youth you have taught me, and I still proclaim your wondrous deeds.

Psalm 71:14,17 ESV

There is a fair argument that dance and the creative arts in worship can be a distraction. When this argument is made, how do creative worshipers biblically defend the creative forms of worship?

Creative worship is biblical. I'll present basic definitions and insights into the purpose of dance and the arts and show how it is supported biblically.

Also, we will focus on one of the most essential aspects of worship in any form: the importance of our motive. The motive of our heart is the key to nullifying the argument that dance and other forms of creative worship are not biblical and nothing more than a distraction.

God is the creator of everything. Recall the majesty and wonder of the world and creatures He made. He created us in His likeness therefore we are creative too. When we enter the posture of God-worship, our creativity will flow naturally as an expression and adoration of our heart as worship.

WHAT IS THE POSTURE OF GOD-WORSHIP

The posture of God worship is when we fix our focus onto Jesus as we behold Him, engaging Him with extreme submission and extravagant reverence. In this posture, God pours His individual plan and purpose into our hearts, which affirms our inward desire to serve Him.

As we realize our divine plan and purpose, this revelation compels us into action to willingly fulfill God's commission. This posture of God-worship unlocks and opens the door for God's perfect will to manifest in and through our lives.

When Creative Worship Becomes a Creative Distraction

How can dance and the creative arts become a distraction? We cannot ignore that in some cases creative worship does distract and draw our attention away from God.

When the Holy Spirit is side-lined and when we choose to let our own agenda or motive lead us in our creative expression of worship, we will no longer reflect the truth of God.

While it may be beautiful and perfectly displayed, this kind of worship will distract others. It draws their attention away from God. The result? Worship becomes merely lifeless motion, unpleasing to God, and without spiritual benefit for us or for those in worship with us.

This quote is a great example of why there are churches and leaders that would rather not embrace dance and other creative arts in worship:

> "If your Holy Ghost just makes you run and dance but doesn't help you live holy, then it is not the Holy Ghost. It is ADHD." -- unknown.

Worship should empower us and equip us, as we commune intimately with God. But, sadly, I have seen this type of self-serving, distracting worship void of the Holy Spirit. The results always lead to a powerless life.

There was a time I knew and admired people like this, but they now live away from God. To those around them they seemed to have their life right. But, the reality was they lived for the moment and their worship was self-serving. They missed the opportunity to have a life-changing transformation.

Worship in spirit and truth should produce fruit in our lives. When we engage in creative worship, our worship should produce fruit in those around us. It is how we cultivate a powerful relationship with God through the Holy Spirit.

When we sideline the Holy Spirit, and let our creative expression of worship become self-serving, seeking the approval of man, we are setting ourselves up for a powerless life, and we become a distraction to those around us.

Human nature would prefer the approval of man because it feels good and strokes our ego. The problem with human nature is that since the time of Adam and Eve, it has failed us every time. A momentary pleasure does not last a lifetime.

Our purpose as worshipers is to enter the throne room of God and to worship Him face to face.

In creative worship, our performance is for God, and our gifts and talents must point to Him. As we worship creatively, we commune with God. Sometimes He has something to say. And He uses our performance to do it!

The Holy Spirit is the key to effectively fulfilling this purpose. The Holy Spirit is our guide *to* the Father. He is also the messenger from the Father. In creative worship, our expression of worship is often the expression or message of God, as the Holy Spirit flows through us and leads our demonstration of it.

The affect can be a change in the atmosphere, as His glory and anointing will fill a place. Or, just as prophecy can come through the words of God's people, prophecy can also be expressed in creative worship expressions. Let us use dance, for example.

Remember, the Holy Spirit is the key! A dancer is like a shoe. A shoe without a foot in it is just a shoe. A dancer without the Holy Spirit in him is just a dancer. The only time the dancer can communicate an effective message from God is when that dancer allows the Holy Spirit to fill him or her.

When our spirit man connects with the Holy Spirit our creative expression of worship comes alive. Not only do we experience a radical transformation for His glory, but we can also effectively deliver God's message and impact the lives of others.

Dance is Dance, Even in Worship

To dance is to simply move your feet or your body rhythmically, particularly to music. To skip, leap, twirl; move in a quick and lively way as from excitement or emotion. Dance is often a normal part of many familiar occasions including social events, celebrations, political, and many others. It's even considered therapeutic.

Dance is absent of words, but not absent of communication. Dance can open a door for restoration. It can transform turmoil into peace. Where there is captivity it can bring freedom. Dance has the power to restore joy and happiness to the body of believers.

> I will rebuild you, my virgin Israel. You will again be happy and dance merrily with your tambourines.
>
> Jeremiah 31:4 NLT

Dance in the Old & New Testaments

Affirmations of dance in the Old Testament are plentiful. Dance and celebration were a central part of the culture. The Israelites used dance in the way it was meant to be used, as a creative expression or response to victories in battle, wedding celebrations, and as worship.

Throughout the New Testament there are references to dance. Aramaic was spoken during this period. The Aramaic word for dance can be interchanged with rejoice, be merry, and celebrate.

> "Rejoice in that day and leap for joy, for your reward is great in Heaven, for so were their fathers doing to The Prophets."
>
> Luke 6:23 Aramaic Bible

The prodigal son is great example of a reference to dance in the New Testament and the powerful portrayal of God's heart for the lost and toward dance. In this story, we see that even in our lost condition, apart from God, God is willing to forgive and celebrate us when we choose to repent and return to Him. The simple act of turning back to God and repenting will instantly bring you into the presence of God and He will celebrate you on your return.

The rejoicing (dancing) in the prodigal father's house was due to the salvation (return) of his child. What this means is that you must rejoice (dance, be merry and celebrate) in the God of your salvation. The message in the story of the prodigal son boils down to salvation. Salvation is the principal reason for dancing. (Luke 15:32)

We also read that miracles caused people to dance and praise God. This is clear in the case where Peter prayed for the crippled beggar in the book of Acts.

> And he jumped, stood and walked and entered with them into The Temple as he was walking and jumping and praising God.
>
> Acts 3:8 Aramaic Bible

In the Apostle Paul's letter to the Philippians, chapter 4 verse 4, he emphasizes the importance of rejoicing (dancing) and encourages the Church to participate in a full expression of praise and joy, similar to the way Old Testament psalmists instructed God's people. (Psalm 37:4)

As you can see dance is acceptable in the New Testament and God is pleased with dance. In the early church dance was something that Christians were accustomed to doing by celebrating in dance at worship gatherings and festivals. It was an essential part of the Hebrew tradition.

So, what happened to dance?

The Dance Controversy

So why is dance so controversial in today's Church? Let us start at the point where the fall of dance in the Church happened and consider the cause. I don't like pointing fingers, but history suggests, it was the Romans' fault.

In the 4th century, the Romans changed dance and ignited the controversy over dance that has lived on and continued into today's churches. The Roman culture seeped into the Church and transformed dance in the Church to mirror their traditional dances. The problem was the nature of Roman dance. It lost its reverence due to the worldly influence.

Fond of the theatre, the Romans introduced dance into theatrical performances, commercializing it to draw crowds. This simple act of commercializing dance for entertainment polluted what was once pure and holy in nature. It was meant for God's glory.

This transformation seared their spirits, and quenched God's Spirit. Dancers pursued fame and grandeur as they sought recognition and self-glory. The more they performed, the colder and more stony people's hearts grew. What was once meant to bring glory and honor to God in celebration and worship, had been corrupted for worldly entertainment.

By nature, Roman religious behavior was orgiastic, which made their dance sensual and immoral. This destroyed the purity of dance as worship in a similar way Voodoo rituals had destroyed the purity of Haitian Christian worship using traditional Haitian instruments.

Once pride, fame and self-glorification began to snowball, this corruption trickled into every form of creative arts. The motive behind their creative expression became tainted and impure. It becomes worldly.

This is what birthed the fall of dance as an expression of true God-worship. It was the fallen, sinful nature of man that turned the focus away from God. No longer did their motive and intent mirror God's heart.

By the 6th century dance in church worship services had become relegated to processional dances only. After Rome fell in the Early Middle Ages the use of dance was restricted and monitored, and the focus shifted from dance being a spontaneous celebration and act of praising God, to ritualistic processions.

This resulted in the church's grip growing tighter, exerting control over dance, allowing the clergy to determine when and how these dances could occur. As a result, dance was set aside for special occasions, like Christmas and Easter.

There is good news though. God is in the process of restoring dance and arts back to the Church body where it belongs. But He wants to do it with you and me.

How can we be part of this great restoration of worship in all its fullness in the Church body again? The key is to reset our focus, our motive, our intent and fix our gaze on Jesus. We must become sensitive to the Holy Spirit and let our heartbeat fall into sync with Father God.

Restoration of Dance & the Arts Back to the Church

In the previous chapter I answered a similar question, but I believe it is necessary to answer this question from a different perspective; addressing the motive and intent behind dance and the arts and how it will support or diminish this restoration process.

The motive and intent of the heart in worship should be centered on humility in our supplication before God and in our corporate worship alongside other believers. This kind of humility is one that earnestly works toward preserving unity.

When we walk alongside other believers who have different gifts and talents, we should accept and embrace them because there is a place for everyone in the body of believers. Humility will allow us to show gentleness, kindness, patience and love to one another. (Ephesians 4:1-16)

The character of humility is peace and gentleness at the core of one's heart, and displays inward strength and beauty, which is very special to God. Humility is beautiful.

> Don't be concerned about the outward beauty of fancy hairstyles, expensive jewelry, or beautiful clothes. You should clothe yourselves instead with the beauty that comes from within, the unfading beauty of a gentle and quiet spirit, which is so precious to God.
>
> 1 Peter 3:3-4 NLT

If all believers, not just creative people, have a motive and intent in their heart that is rooted in humility we will see dance and the arts restored back to the Church once again.

In the body, there must be order and unity to fulfill the will of God. (Ephesians 4:13-16) In creative worship, we must operate under authority, or there can be no order. However, we must also be careful not to let titles and positions manifest as pride and control.

The worship team submits to the pastor, and the worship team leads everyone in worship. The creative types submit to the worship leader. And yet, our worship must be fully submitted to God, led by the power of the Holy Spirit. This is a godly order that transcends the natural world.

To enter into the throne room of God, for our worship to be pleasing to Him, we must humble ourselves before God, and worship in unity as a body. Unity is crucial in the restoration of dance in the Church. It must be a natural part of worship that brings the creatives and non-creatives together, rather than a distraction that separates us.

If our motive is one that desires a title or a position of recognition, it will alienate us from God. This is how division and disunity starts, in both the natural and supernatural.

Titles are a natural part of organizing our churches and establishing order. But it is dangerous when leaders use titles and recognition to establish status, or to elevate themselves to a higher position.

Leadership, title or no title, must remain humble, especially in worship. As creatives we must operate with a pure motive, otherwise titles and recognition will get in the way of our relationship with God. Titles and positions of distinction will divide us rather than unite us.

Titles and recognition are good only when God has exalted us. When our motive remains pure by placing our title and position of recognition on the spiritual altar of sacrifice we allow a unified heart to develop within the Church.

It is important we never exalt ourselves, as it will open the door and welcome pride into our hearts. Unity is crucial and it is one of the most powerful ways we can restore the arts back to the Church. Unity and order are critical in maintaining humility, and it serves as a shield against other forms of attacks designed to bring division and disunity in worship.

It's not uncommon that people are sent on assignment from the devil to create distractions, to cast spells or hexes on the people or leaders of the church. I've seen this before, and through worship have sensed it.

It presents itself as a roadblock, a stronghold, seemingly preventing worship from going to the next level. It affects others in worship. Especially if they are tired or distracted, they become less engaged. Or, a simple miscommunication between the pastor and worship leader, or between the worship leader and the worship team can occur and cause confusion.

When dealing with attacks, whether they come from within (pride), or whether they are spiritual attacks from the outside, it is important that our response is to pull together in unity.

How do we pull together in unity and defeat the attack of the enemy? Submitted under leadership, as a dancer and flagger, I begin to intercede using my creative expression of worship. I open my spirit man and connect with the Holy Spirit so that I can begin to receive clear instruction on how I should proceed.

As I am interceding in worship and allowing my motions with my flags and dance to flow according to the Holy Spirit's lead, the people who were once distracted or tired are now drawn in. The more I empty my spirit and my heart of my own agenda and motives, the more God's Spirit can fill me with His will, which will overflow and impact others around me.

When the distracted and tired recognize that the creative expression is one that is drawing them in and then directing them to shift their focus and gaze upon Jesus, it will spark something. It will spark a desire in them and that will prompt them to engage in worship. This spark and change is often described as a change or shift in the atmosphere of worship.

My husband Mike often has a different response. When he senses strongholds, he begins to intercede in spiritual warfare, praying against these demonic strongholds. Worship leaders, sensitive to the Holy Spirit, will also respond accordingly. When they sense strongholds, they follow the leading of the Holy Spirit and direct worship into breakthrough.

Pastors sensitive to the Holy Spirit will join the worship leader in unity, to lead and direct the church into breakthrough.

Each of us has a role and function in worship, led by the Holy Spirit. Taking our place and doing our part, is operating in unity! In my role as dancer and flagger it is my responsibility to follow the Holy Spirit and ensure that my worship reflects God's heart. At no point should my worship draw attention to myself, or be done in a way that exalts myself with titles or recognition.

As we explore the different types of dance, keep in mind that if your creative gift or talent is not dance, apply the same principals and dynamics shared below to your creative wheelhouse.

Types of Dance in the Body of Christ

There are various types of dance as worship and they all have one purpose; to bring glory and honor to God (not man).

Worship Dance

Worship Dance or Sacred Dance is when our actions or movement are used for the specific purpose of worshiping God. Worship dance and sacred dance are devotional in nature. Either type of dance leads a person into a place of intimacy and devotion to God through movement.

> Oh come, let us worship and bow down; Let us kneel before the Lord our Maker.
>
> Psalm 95:6 NKJV

Both types of dance create a response of intimacy and the movements are usually in an upward motion. It reflects an attitude where the dancer is drawing near to God in the posture of God-worship.

> You have turned for me my mourning into dancing;
> You have put off my sackcloth and clothed me with gladness,
> To the end that my glory may sing praise to You and not be silent.
> O Lord my God, I will give thanks to You forever.
>
> Psalm 30:11 NKJV

Liturgical Dance

Liturgical Dance is dance that relates to formal public worship or corporate worship. Liturgical dance is described as movement that is incorporated into liturgies or worship services.

The dancer will respond with an appropriate dance that flows to the music and enhances the prayer or worship experience. It can be either spontaneous or choreographed. When choreographed it generally compliments the song lyrics or religious message.

Miriam, a prophet and the sister or Aaron was the first person to lead a celebration with liturgical dance and song. It stood to glorify God in victory after

He delivered them out of captivity in Egypt and destroyed Pharaoh's army in the Red Sea.

> Then Miriam the prophetess, the sister of Aaron, took the timbrel in her hand; and all the women went out after her with timbrels and with dances.
>
> Exodus 15:20 NKJV

Personally, I love the celebratory manner in which this type of dance flows. When I flow in this type of dance I respond to the beats, rhythms and cadence of the music. It is free flowing.

In my travels, I have experienced different forms of liturgical dance in different nations. My experience during a trip to Northern India is a great example of this.

When I danced in India, I flowed in what looked like traditional Indian folk style dance with symbolic gestures of my body, hands, fingers and feet. I had never danced in this manner before. I'd only seen it. But the music and sound that would come from the traditional Indian instruments stirred up a style of dance that caused my expression of dance to respond in this manner.

Intercessory Dance

Intercessory Dance is when a dancer allows their movement to be a form of communication on behalf of another, standing in the gap. The dictionary defines intercession as an interposing or pleading on behalf of another person; a prayer to God on behalf of another.

As an intercessor, we should allow our worship to bear the burden for another through our movement and for the purpose of another's breakthrough, healing or victory. Through intercession, we stand in the gap for others. It is an honor to be used in such a manner. Just as Moses stood in the gap for the nation of Israel, we can intercede on the behalf of others through intercessory dance. (Psalms 106:23)

How does this type of dance look to an onlooker? In many cases what appears is the response to the power and glory of God's presence. As the dancer bears his or her body before the Lord, their intercession connects their spirit man with heaven through the Holy Spirit. Their physical body will begin to tremble, shake, quiver and vibrate with deep groaning. This happens because our physical bodies are not designed to withstand the full power of God's glory.

Intercessory dance is a spiritual battle fought on behalf of another through prayerful worship. But spiritual warfare is a battle fought against the powers of darkness. So often, intercessory dance is doing both at the same time; prayer and warfare.

For the sake of explanation, and clarity, I address the two separately.

Warfare Dance

Warfare Dance is when intercessory dance graduates into a dance of spiritual warfare. As in a worldly battle, taking ground is key to victory, whether we are taking it back or taking new territories.

In spiritual warfare, there is ground that we are to take to advance God's Kingdom (Genesis 1:28), to achieve His plans and purposes. Warfare dance is a powerful weapon we can use to defeat the devil, to take or retake territories and regions for God's glory.

Using warfare dance we are to battle for the souls of people too. Many times, we've seen people who've come to church defiant, receive salvation. Through worship, even if they don't participate, through spiritual warfare their hearts are changed and they give their life to Jesus. (Ephesians 6:12)

How does this type of dance look to the onlooker? As the spirit of God flows through the dancer they will begin to make moves that represent offensive actions. There will be no passivity. Their motions are militant and warrior-like; repetitive actions of stomping one's feet, strong hand and arms motions, movement that emulates the battle and defeat of the enemy. Simply stomping one's foot represents authority as suggested in Luke 10.

> Behold, I give you the authority to trample on serpents and scorpions, and over all the power of the enemy, and nothing shall by any means hurt you.
>
> Luke 10:19 NKJV

This scripture establishes the believer's authority and victory over the power of the enemy. It offers a visualization of the battle, with a victorious end.

Personally, in times of worship when there is spiritual darkness or bondage that is holding people back, or quenching the free flow of the Holy Spirit, I will enter intercession. Through my dance, I will intercede for the worship team, the pastor and the congregation.

In almost every case my intercession graduates to warfare. I allow the Holy Spirit to lead my actions and I use my arms and hands to cut through spiritual darkness, breaking chains.

At times, I have pounded the ground with my hands or fists and I cry out with a call to war. The sounds that come forth as a warrior in worship sounds like a heavenly roar.

Apart from worship I have not been able to imitate this roar. It's a roar that sends the enemy to flight freeing those who are bound. It calls them into unity as we worship together. It is glorious!

Prophetic Dance

Prophetic Dance or "Interpretive Dance" is a dance in which the dancer allows the Holy Spirit to reveal a timely message through a demonstration of actions or movement. (Revelation 19:10)

Jesus is calling upon prophetic people who will hear Him, speak His words and demonstrate His purposes through movement.

Prophetic dance is movement that comes from the Lord's heart, from His throne, birthed in the spiritual realm and released through the dancer into the natural realm to accomplish His purpose. People who dance prophetically are typically very uninhibited and totally inspired by the Holy Spirit. They are a lot like contemporary dancers in my opinion.

I read a story of a lady, Sandi Ramsey, who is a worship dancer. It described her worship movements as spinning and twirling. The writer said it appeared as if she was unraveling or untwisting the bindings of the enemy on our lives. It made sense to me.

There is a Hebrew word *chuwl* (pro. khool), a verb that means to twist or twirl in a circular or spiral manner (Strong's #2342).

From my research of the word, *chuwl* as a verb in the Blue Letter Bible's Greek/Hebrew texts. *Chuwl* was not done purely out of giddiness or joy through the manifestation of dance and whirling, but also as a response of pain, travail, grief, anguish, and trembling.

Here is a scriptural example of *chuwl*, referenced in dance and whirling as an expression of joy:

> When the victorious Israelite army was returning home after David had killed the Philistine, women from all the towns of Israel came out to meet King Saul. They sang and danced for joy with tambourines and cymbals.
>
> 1 Samuel 8:16 NLT

Now here is an example of *chuwl* used as an expression of pain:

> Just as a pregnant woman writhes and cries out in pain as she gives birth, so were we in Your presence, LORD.
>
> Isaiah 26:17 NLT

Just this simple truth of the word *chuwl* started me on a journey to seek out the reason and purpose behind some of the ways I am led to move in my worship, my dance.

Guided by the Holy Spirit, the concordance became a great guide, giving me revelation regarding these things, regarding prophetic dance. It gave me great confidence knowing it was supported in Biblical truths.

As I looked for these truths, God's Word jumped off the page as the voice of the Holy Spirit began to speak clearer and louder. My personal worship began to grow into levels and depths I never knew existed.

Prophetic Dance in Haiti

On my second trip to Carrefour, Haiti I had a powerful experience I want to share that shows how prophetic or interpretive dance can be used as a powerful means of intercession and deliverance.

There was a Haitian lady who was a descendant in a long line of witches before her. As was customary, she was next in line to become a witch. One day she came to Pastors Terry and Cary for help in getting free from this generational family curse.

On that day, as the worship was progressing, she was brought up onto the platform for prayer. I was asked to join Pastors Terry and Cary to pray for her deliverance. As I walked over I felt a strong leading from the Holy Spirit to run around her. Pastor Cary confirmed it when she asked me to dance in a manner that would set the woman free.

As I began to run around her I saw how this action began to un-twist the chains that were keeping her bound in fear and anguish. She writhed and trembled. The moment I stopped I walked straight up to her and I saw terror in her eyes. I knew demons were looking at me through her eyes.

She had been bound in this fear and curse since she was born. She was in a state of paralytic fear. The demons knew they could no longer stay. It was in this moment they knew they had to flee.

After I took her and led her in a dance, as a daddy would dance with his daughter, one by one the demons left her and she was set free.

While what I did, running around this lady and dancing with her, may have been very simple, I would have never thought to do this in my own thinking.

When we worship in dance, if we worship in spirit and truth, the Lord will place significance on our actions and movements as they come from a place of obedience. Allow Jesus, through the Holy Spirit, to be your choreographer. It is important that He remains in control, and He will work through you to achieve His plans and purposes.

Regardless of which form of dance we flow in, it is important to note that we are there to impact the will of God, not our own will or agenda. We do not dance for recognition from our pastor, the worship team, or the congregation. We are simply there to be an extension of God's will and purpose to advance His Kingdom for His glory. We are His servants, holy and set apart for His purpose alone. (Romans 6:22, Hebrews 12:2)

To Worship God in Dance is Biblical

Interestingly, the Bible tells us that God desires every aspect of our lives to be an act of worship to Him in giving Him glory. Not only is dance biblical, but so is any other form of creative expression a demonstration of worship to God: painting, poetry, singing, drama, instruments, banners and flags.

In the book of Psalms, we can see how worshiping God in the dance and with instruments is biblical.

> Let them praise His name with dancing. Let them sing praises to Him with timbrels and a harp.
>
> Psalm 149:3 NLV

> Praise Him with timbrels and dancing. Praise Him with strings and horns.
>
> Psalm 150:4 NLV

Creative Worship is Biblical

Creativity is a gift from God and it can be expressed in many different ways. Since God is the source of our creativity, there should be a place for creativity and every gift and talent in the body of Christ, the Church. In Exodus 35:31-35 we see many other creative gifts in action:

> and He has filled him with the Spirit of God, in wisdom and understanding, in knowledge and all manner of workmanship, to design artistic works, to work in gold and silver and bronze, in cutting jewels for setting, in carving wood, and to work in all manner of artistic workmanship. "And He has put in his heart the ability to teach, in him and Aholiab the son of Ahisamach, of the tribe of Dan. He has filled them with skill to do all manner of work of the engraver and the designer and the tapestry maker, in blue, purple, and scarlet thread, and fine linen, and of the weaver— those who do every work and those who design artistic works.
>
> Exodus 35:31-35 NKJV

Expressing ourselves creatively, as worship, is not limited to having an ability to sing or to play and instrument. Worship is not limited to a pretty song with a catchy tune that stirs our emotions. True God-worship is about a person offering God everything with extravagant love and extreme submission. It's showering the Lord of lords and King of kings with every affection as we worship. This is not the end, but the beginning of an awesome eternity with Jesus, worshiping God!

As noted previously, we must not restrict our creative worship to the confines of a building or worship service at our church. The artists tasked to construct the tabernacle laid their gifts and talents before God in praise and worship **as they worked**.

Dance is Healthy

Did you know that dance and movement have health benefits for people as well? God not only wants us to live healthy spiritual lives, but He desires us to live healthy physical and emotional lives too.

> The young women will dance for joy, and the men—old and young—will join in the celebration. I will turn their mourning into joy. I will comfort them and exchange their sorrow for rejoicing.
>
> Jeremiah 31:13 NLT

Many emotions like anger, depression, sadness, bitterness, hurt, and unforgiveness have a devastating effect on our health. These emotions are ungodly, like a cancer to our soul, even to our physical body. Dance and movement is God's way for us to have an outlet for emotional stress, like a heavenly medicine.

Personally, I have left a worship service with such joy and peace after I put all my worries and issues under my feet and I danced a victorious dance all over them.

There are many articles and research on how dance is beneficial and a vehicle in which a person can deal with or release stress. Stress is just a broad term for all kinds of issues ranging from anxiety, depression, trauma, PTSD, tension and the list goes on. There are even occupations that specialize in dance and movement therapies.

I am so glad we serve a God who doesn't require us to first "clean up our act" before He will pay us any attention. We see a great example in John 12:3, an account of a sinful woman, Mary of Bethany, who washed the feet of Jesus with her tears and a bottle of very expensive perfume. She didn't let her sin or her shame stop her from boldly going to Jesus.

She wiped the feet of Jesus dry with her hair. She didn't ask for a towel, instead she used her hair, which spiritually represents a woman's glory. Her glory meant nothing to her when she was in the presence of Jesus. Others may have labeled her a sinner, but Jesus saw her heart and her sacrifice.

Mary's account in the Bible stands as a reminder to us all that Jesus wants to meet us right now, right where we are today. Mary's sacrificial act of love for Jesus, even though her life wasn't right, even though her life was a mess according to man, she came to Jesus, and because of it she will live on with Him for eternity.

Personally, on a few occasions during worship, the Holy Spirit has prompted me to stop for a moment, to put my flags down and just adore Him, offering Him every part of me. I find myself laid bare in complete vulnerability as I pour my most costly perfume of tears out on His feet, giving Him all the glory that is due to His name.

It's amazing how all fear, worry, stress and the concerns of my day are melted away. When I get up from that place I feel like a whole new person who is revived, loved and secure. These times of dance in worship have prepared my spirit to receive healing and stabilizing emotional wellbeing. This is powerful spiritual medicine that has many spiritual benefits.

On the flipside of the coin, dance releases endorphins that have a physical benefit for our emotional health. These endorphins benefit our physical body by bringing pain relief. It's been studied and found that endorphins are anywhere from 18 to 500 times more powerful than painkillers made in a lab.

Dancing as opposed to exercise has also been found to be more beneficial for emotional happiness. Imagine adding God's Spirit in the mix of that equation. It can only make for a glorious healthy experience on all levels. I believe the more people express themselves through dance the shorter the healing prayer line will become.

We are faced with all kinds of emotional stresses in our day to day. Whenever you feel the stress of the day weighing you down, here is a great way to give it to God. Get some anointing oil and anoint yourself. Then, write down all your fears, worries, hurts and emotions. Put that paper on the ground and dance a dance of joy on it with all your might!

When we do this sacrificial act during trials or hard times, giving God all praise, we will be liberated and set free from the burdens of stress. We can see in the Beatitudes how these burdens build and weigh upon believers. If you read Luke 6:20-22 Jesus describes these burdens. But in the next verse He says to "rejoice" and "leap for joy" when these things happen:

> Rejoice in that day and leap for joy, because your reward in heaven is great!
>
> Luke 6:23 ISV

Indeed, the burden will be lifted and the yoke will be broken as His Holy anointing falls on us. (Isaiah 10:27) Our praise and worship as a sacrificial offering releases a sweet aroma that attracts God and compels Him to *smell* our worship and take pleasure in the fragrance of our sacrifice. (Psalm 141:2)

God will meet us right where we are and rain His fresh healing presence on us to revive and heal our physical and emotional stress.

As you worship, I want to encourage you to let the Holy Spirit direct your steps and movement. Don't just simply rely on your ability. As you worship, do as Mary of Bethany did when she knelt before Jesus and poured her most costly gift upon His feet.

You might not feel like it emotionally at the time, but your sacrificial demonstration of worship, your sacrificial dance and vulnerability brought to Him with boldness will bring you into the presence of Jesus where He will defend you when others condemn you.

What Does <u>Going Through the Motions</u> Mean?

Simply going through the motions comprised of steps and movement with no heart behind it, with no real intent, is dead. It is equivalent to that of what a robot would do. It's not exciting, there's no life, emotion or presence.

I am so passionate about this because I see this happening in churches more than I should. There are so many in our church bodies that just simply go through the motions *lacking life*. Not only is it boring and dull, but also God says that it is not pleasing or delightful to Him.

> Going through the motions doesn't please you, a flawless performance is nothing to you.
>
> Psalm 51:16 MSG

Going through the motions without revelation and power speaks of a lack of understanding of the posture of God-worship. Somewhere, there lies a disconnect between our motive or agenda and God's design. I believe there are two causes of this disconnect; having a heart of complacency, or having a hidden motive for self-gain or gratification.

This is a very dangerous place to be. It opens us up to the wiles and influence of the enemy. It gives the devil influence over our minds and steals our focus from God. He shifts our focus to where he wants it: on man, and then ultimately on him. The moment we take our focus off God we are no longer pursuing Him.

Our Treasure. Our Focus.

God should always be our treasure and our focus. (Matthew 6:21) When we stop our pursuit of God we taint the purity of our heart and our motive. Our flesh will seek gratification. The fallen nature of man will always seek self-gratification. When we don't allow God to fill that need, the world will.

When we worship with our creative gifts and our heart is not pure, our motive or intent will seek gratification drawing attention to our ability. Our creative expression of worship will become self-serving and sinful. It becomes a show or performance.

There is another dynamic that results when we seek self-gratification or recognition in our worship. It leads to inappropriate motions or actions in our expression. The Bible warns against sensual, lewd behavior, lustful and inappropriate dancing, which will lead you and others into sin.

In the book of Exodus, we see what happened while Moses was up on the mountain, interceding for Israel. The Israelites chose to forsake their purity and satisfy their need to worship by building a golden calf.

> The people got up early the next morning to sacrifice burnt offerings and peace offerings. After this, they celebrated with feasting and drinking, and they indulged in pagan revelry.
>
> Exodus 32:6 NLT

A little bit further in this chapter we read how this type of worship led them to lose control. Below, two versions of the same scripture are compared. Note, in the

King James version it says they were naked.

> Moses saw that Aaron had let the people get completely out of control, much to the amusement of their enemies.
>
> Exodus 32:25 NLT

> And when Moses saw that the people were naked; (for Aaron had made them naked unto their shame among their enemies:)
>
> Exodus 32:25 KJV

The Israelites' lost their focus on worshiping God. They built an altar to satisfying their worldly need to worship. They were simply going through the motions of worship. It led to sin and allowed evil to enter their hearts. Ultimately, the sin and evil manifested in their worship, and it nearly led to their destruction. (Exodus 32:11)

Appropriate vs. Inappropriate

In today's popular culture, rock stars, pop idols, television, movies and social media have painted a very different picture as to what is appropriate and inappropriate behavior, compared to past generations.

If we took a group of churched and un-churched millennials, played popular music and asked them to let the music move their body, without exception, we would see how music directly influences movement.

Music is a powerful means of communication and it can have a powerful effect on the way a person moves in dance. It can affect our mood, attitude and even daily behavior. In most cases, when we play different styles of music, like classical, rock, pop, rap, hip hop, heavy metal, etc. a particular type of body movement will match the style of music.

Classical music will produce graceful motions. On the other hand, heavy metal music will produce harsh motions and erratic movement; even to the point of self-injury. What do you think would happen if this same group of churched and un-churched millennials was asked to respond to worship music? We would probably see confusion, and maybe even disgust on the faces of the unchurched. As for the churched, they would likely begin to imitate what they have seen in their church with hand clapping or raising of their hands.

The world has become the devil's playground. He has influenced so many to draw their ideas of dance from movies, TV, and social media, and desensitize people to accept sin as *cool*.

Thankfully, if we look to Romans, we have this promise from God regarding His grace.

But where sin abounded, grace abounded much more.

Romans 5:20 NKJV

As a worshiper who loves music, I have made a conscious decision to ensure the music I listen to brings glory and honor to God. Music has a powerful impact on me as a person and I choose to let music build me up and not feed my spirit man with deception, illicit behavior and hate.

In doing this, I choose God and His will for my life. We must recognize, music has the power to either bind a person up in the bondage of sin, or the power to liberate and free a person from the bondage of sin.

How to Prepare Our Heart With a Pure Motive

First and foremost, if we are to prepare our hearts with pure motives, we must acknowledge the only way this will work is if we are willing. We need to be willing to put aside our own agenda and willingly open our heart and spirit man to God so He can fill us with His Spirit.

Our own ability, training and talent are no longer required. In fact, training, talent and ability can, in most cases, get in the way because our mind tends to override our spirit man.

In true God-worship, we must be careful not to allow our mind to take control, because pride is looking for any opportunity to take root in our lives. **Trying to worship in the supernatural, relying on the natural, is giving pride an open door.**

If we follow these 3 steps we can close the door to pride:

1. Ready Yourself – We must first lay our *self*, our agenda and ideas on the spiritual altar of sacrifice.
2. Light the Fire - Embrace the Holy Spirit. Let Him light the fire and burn away any pride, fear, and rebellion.
3. Drink of the Spirit – Let the Holy Spirit fill you up to overflowing. Let Him flow through you as a creative expression of your worship through your gifts and talents.

These steps bring us into a deeper dimension of worship and in closer relationship with God. Our creative expression of worship will produce good fruit and we'll start to see pride, selfishness, arrogance, self-consciousness and our worldly self-image fade into the distance.

As worshipers, we are to imitate Christ. (1 Corinthians 11:1) The motive behind our creative expression of worship should promote God. Our purpose is to be available, sensitive and ready to be used by God.

I heard a story many years ago about the obedience of a lady who was prompted by the Holy Spirit to do cartwheels during a worship service. Those cartwheels resulted in the salvation of a man and his entire family. If God asks me to step out and do a cartwheel because He has a purpose in it, I want to do it.

A place of availability, combined with a pure motive creates the perfect environment for God to perform miracles and set people free.

If you are well trained, have amazing abilities with dance, flags or banners, paint gorgeous art pieces or write award winning poetry, please hear my heart when I say that training, talent and ability can potentially become hindrances in your creative expression of worship.

When our heart and motive is pure and connected to the Holy Spirit, we can express our gifts and talents in worship in a way that connects with God. It's when our training, talent and ability are under submission to the Holy Spirit in purity, that our creative expression of worship will attract God's heart and our worship will produce an aroma pleasing to God.

When this happens, God will swoop into the place with His glory and radically transform the hearts and lives of the people present.

Dance in the Church Today is Fulfillment of Prophecy

In the book of Jeremiah, it talks about the virgin rejoicing in the dance in the last days. The word for virgin in scripture is typically used to describe the bride of Christ. We are preparing ourselves to be His bride.

> Then shall the virgin rejoice in the dance, and the young men and the old, together
>
> Jeremiah 31:13a NKJV

In the book of Revelation, it goes on to say:

> Let us be glad and rejoice and give Him glory, for the marriage of the Lamb has come, and His wife has made herself ready.
>
> Revelations 19:7 NKJV

In these two scriptures, we see that there is significant importance on being prepared and ready for the return of Jesus. Not only will our preparation be fulfillment of biblical prophecy, but also our true God-worship will bring all glory to God.

In heaven, we will worship God for eternity. If worship and glorification to God is to be our eternal emphasis, then it makes sense that we would learn how to do it well now, here on earth.

How Our Gifts & Talents Prepare Us to Be His Bride

As we prepare and ready ourselves for God, as we prepare ourselves to use our gifts and talents to help restore the arts back to God, there are several steps we need to consider.

1. First, we need to identify our gifts and talents? In my case, it is dance and flags.

2. Second, we need to establish the motive of our heart when we use our gift or talent as worship. Our motive will be either one of self-gratification and promotion, or one of humility and servant-hood. I recommend the latter!

3. Finally, we should recognize how the first and second steps will affect others. It will either distract them by drawing their focus to you and your ability, or it will point them to God, shifting their focus off man and onto God Himself.

Once we can confidently say we understand the importance of getting these three steps right, and applying them effectively to our life, we are ready to be used by God to advance His Kingdom. At this stage, our creative expression of worship will have an eternal and everlasting impact.

God-worship leads to living a life of fullness, filled with the promises of God. The only way to come to this understanding is to embrace the Holy Spirit and dig into God's Word allowing Him to reveal Himself to us. We must be determined to keep our focus on the One True God, and honor Him with extravagant worship with extreme submission.

Expressive Actions as Worship

Dance in worship should occur naturally, although some will argue that it's unnatural and hard to do. Many struggle to worship because there is a fear of what others might think. They worry about how others might judge them or even laugh at them.

When we celebrate our favorite sports team winning the world championship, or when we jump for joy after winning a trip to an exotic destination, or when our favorite band comes to town, we will experience some level of excitement that will most likely manifest actions like jumping up and down, waiving our hands excitedly, squealing, spinning around, or running around the house, right?

These actions are an expression toward, and a response to, the good news. In the moment, we don't care about what others may think, because we won't care. Our actions clearly establish that we are very happy.

When we enter into worship and receive a revelation, a glimpse of how awesome God is, a glimpse of the things He has done for us; when we realize how much He loves us or what awaits us in eternity with Him; we should receive this as very good news, right?

If we are in the posture of true God-worship, then our response will naturally manifest in ways that we will not be able control. We will begin to express our excitement with movement, leaping, spinning or dancing. These are motions of worship.

God does not need our worship, but He delights in our worship. He is worthy of it and our worship acknowledges this, and it demonstrates that we know who He is. Our worship tells God how grateful we are to be His. It tells Him we are thankful for what He has done for us through Jesus' sacrifice on the cross.

> Oh come, let us sing to the Lord!
> Let us shout joyfully to the Rock of our salvation.
> Let us come before His presence with thanksgiving;
> Let us shout joyfully to Him with psalms.
> For the Lord is the great God,
> And the great King above all gods.
>
> Psalm 95:1-3 NKJV

Even though dance and the creative arts in worship are viewed as controversial and often frowned upon, the Bible is filled with evidence that God finds it normal and welcomes it. God created each of us with gifts and talents expressly to bring glory to Him, especially in creative worship.

One reason we see a resistance or rejection of dance and the creative arts as a form of worship in our churches today is because there is a lack of knowledge and proper teaching on it. The very good news is we can solve this with knowledge and proper teaching!

The Importance of Our Motive

Another reason dance and the creative arts are not accepted in worship today can be related to the motive and the condition of the heart in worship.

> Every man's way is right in his own eyes, But the Lord weighs and examines the hearts [of people and their motives].
>
> Proverbs 21:2 AMP

According to the Webster dictionary our motive is the reason for doing something (hidden or not obvious); something (as a need or desire) that causes a person to act.

There are many people whose motives will become clear when we see them use their gifts and talents as a platform to seek promotion, self-gain, fame and recognition. This is the wrong motive. Our motive should be pure, one of love, adoration and passion for God.

As humans, we live in a body made of flesh. Our flesh seeks gratification. The flesh will always try to override the spirit and suppress the voice of the Holy Spirit. Bringing the flesh into subjection requires discipline and commitment. It is not just a one-time deal; it requires vigilant attention and sacrifice.

Don't let anyone tell you that once you are saved and become a Christian that life is going to be easy and a bed of roses. The truth is that as believers we live in a body made of flesh in a fallen world where the devil "prowls around like a roaring lion, seeking someone to devour." (1 Peter 5:8)

As long as we live in this world we will need to live in an offensive stance to advance God's Kingdom and fight off the attacks of the devil. We are not of this world, but we are living in this world and that will require us to keep bringing our flesh into subjection and set our heart and mind on Christ. (1 Corinthians 9:27)

When going through the motions our motive should be pure and exalt God. The Holy Spirit is here on earth to empower us as we worship the Lord our God through our gifts and talents. Anything that focuses on self-promotion in worship is dead and distracts others causing them to lose focus and to stumble.

It is normal for others to watch us because that is one way people learn. Because people are at different levels in their relationship with God it is important that our motive is pure. Some are new in Christ while others are at different levels of maturity. As believers, it is our responsibility to become aware of the impact our lifestyle, our worship, has on others.

Premature Judgment

We all know quite well the story of King David when he danced with great enthusiasm as the Ark of the Lord was brought to the City of David. The Ark of the Lord was where God's presence dwelt in the Old Testament. King David was overjoyed at the fact that the presence of God was going to reside in the tabernacle, the very place King David had built and prepared for Him.

> Then, as the ark of the Lord came into the City of David, Michal, Saul's daughter [*David's wife*], looked down from the window above and saw King David leaping and dancing before the Lord; and she felt contempt for him in her heart [*because she thought him undignified*]...Michal the daughter of Saul had no child to the day of her death.
>
> 2 Samuel 6:16,23 AMP

Saul's daughter, Michal failed to understand the significance of this event unfolding beneath her window as she looked at King David with contempt and judgment. Michal's heart was filled with judgment and condescension because she didn't understand why David danced as he did. She thought he was being undignified and she allowed it to offend her. Her failure to understand David's heart and his motive, caused her to be barren the rest of her life.

Michal opened a door to lack in her life through her judgment. She considered David's response, his worship, to be indecent and undignified. This is a great example of how careful we must be when we see others doing something we don't quite understand, or haven't seen before.

How we judge others can either produce life or bring lack, or bareness in the case of Michal. There is only one way we can judge, and that is to judge someone by their fruit. (Matthew 7:20)

CONCLUSION

When we worship God in spirit and truth, with total abandon in His presence, giving Him glory with a pure heart and motive, we'll experience freedom. This freedom will bring us the revelation we need to grow in faith. In this way, we allow God to use us to reach the "Michal's" of the world by manifesting God's truth, not our own motives or agendas. The truth will set us free!

The story I talked about earlier, where the lady did cartwheels that resulted in someone else receiving salvation, would serve as a great example as to how we can reach the Michal's of today.

During worship this lady felt led by the Holy Spirit to do cartwheels in the front of the church. She wrestled with God about it because she thought that it would be seen as undignified or unacceptable.

The unction grew stronger and stronger in her until she decided to step out and obey. After doing her cartwheels she headed back to her seat and felt a release in her spirit and the burden that impressed her to do it had lifted.

Nothing significant appeared to happen until later, when a man who was present during the service shared his story with one of the salvation counselors afterwards. He told the counselor that he was a very tried and hard man with a stone-cold heart who came to church as a last hope, and with an ultimatum.

He said that he made a deal with God that if God was real and loved him like he'd been told, he would accept Christ only if someone did cartwheels in the church. Lo and behold, if it weren't for the sensitivity to the Holy Spirit and obedience of that lady, this man would not have accepted Christ.

When our motive is pure and spirit-led, all focus automatically shifts to God and off man. I love what John the Baptist says here, one of my favorite scriptures:

> He must increase [*in prominence*], but I must decrease.
>
> John 3:30 AMP

The more we seek Him and His presence in our life, our flesh and sinful nature cannot remain and must submit to His glorious presence and decrease. I won't say that it is easy to live a life where our spirit man must rise above our soul man. But I can say that when we renew our mind daily with God's Word, washing our spirit with the rain of His presence in worship, it makes it easier to command our flesh to submit.

I encourage and challenge you to evaluate your motive, to inquire of God what

He wants, and to submit to the Holy Spirit in truth. Choose to worship God in a manner that brings glory and honor to Him. Choose whom you wish to celebrate, God or yourself. You cannot have both.

Let your creative movement prompt others to shift their focus to God. When going through the motions of worship, let it reflect God's heart and be pleasing to Him. When you worship in this way you will experience what true God-worship is and your motions will begin to paint a beautiful canvas of movement that edifies the body of Christ.

8

A FLAWLESS PERFORMANCE
Lessons Learned Along the Way

So then, let us [*who minister*] be regarded as servants of Christ and stewards (trustees, administrators) of the mysteries of God [*that He chooses to reveal*].

1 Corinthians 4:1 AMP

We serve a wonderful God of mysteries. He reveals these mysteries to us in many ways. Often, He chooses us, you and me to reveal the mysteries of His heart.

God also uses the creative arts and creative people to reveal these mysteries. This is what makes being a believer such an exciting journey. I like to think of it as a treasure hunt. The Bible is our map, the Holy Spirit is our revelator and guide, and our treasure is Jesus.

As believers, we are not here to hide away these mysteries for ourselves, but rather we are to reveal them for the benefit of others. These mysteries are revealed through the Holy Spirit as we dig into God's Word and grow in our relationship with Jesus. They provide us with reliable and accurate knowledge that strengthens our foundation in Christ and empowers us with boldness.

Casting judgment and ranking ourselves according to popular opinion is pointless because with God there is not one of us more important than the other.

For God shows no partiality [*no arbitrary favoritism; with Him one person is not more important than another*].

Romans 2:11 AMP

Seeking to outdo and outperform one another leads us down a road that welcomes comparison. We established in Chapter 5 that comparison is dangerous and puts us at risk of losing our divine identity in Christ Jesus. The only opinion that should matter to us is that of Jesus. Jesus is the only one who we are to please. (Galatians 1:10)

In the previous chapter, we explored the importance of the motive of our heart in our creative expression of worship. In this chapter, we uncover why a flawless performance is not the key to pleasing God.

Recognition and praise, and being ranked according to the popular opinion of man, is momentary and short lived. Receiving God's stamp of approval is all that we should seek and live for.

How do we receive this approval? We simply surrender our heart and love to Jesus. Before we loved Him, He loved us. (1 John 4:19) This is a powerful truth and when we grab hold of it with all our heart, we realize that no matter what we do, how good, talented, or flawless we are, it will not change how much He loves us. All Jesus wants is our whole heart, a broken and contrite heart.

In the following chapter, we will dig deeper into the importance of a broken and contrite heart and how it is necessary for our spiritual growth and development in preparation of eternity in God's Kingdom. For now, I want to focus on the heart of a worshiper in the context of performance.

PERFORMANCE & THE HEART OF A WORSHIPER

There is nothing wrong with a performance if it is intended for entertainment purposes. However, a performance in the context of a worship service should be avoided.

Merriam Webster defines the word performance as "the act of doing a job, an activity: the execution of an action; an activity (such as singing a song or acting in a play) that a person or group does to entertain an audience."

Let's also look at the definition of the word flawless. Dictonary.com describes it as "having no defects or faults, especially none that diminish the value of something."

We'll bring these two together in a moment, but first let's dissect the performance.

A performance is comprised of two parts, the performer and the audience. To the performer, the word performance triggers the need to execute with excellence to please the audience and achieve the desired praise and recognition. To the audience, the word performance prompts one to sit back, watch, judge and be entertained.

The typical goal of a performer is to entertain with the hopes of pleasing the audience, often striving for recognition and fame. The performer measures success by how the audience reacts and responds to their performance. This mindset of the performer, seeking man's approval, is worldly and man-driven rather than Spirit-led.

When this mindset enters into the context of a worship service we are presented with a worldly, man-driven worship, rather than a Spirit-led worship experience. The worship team becomes merely performers, and the congregation becomes the audience, expecting to be entertained.

This kind of worship is powerless and void of the promises of God. Too often this is how worship is conducted. Instead, the goal should be a Spirit-led worship.

Why would we want Spirit-led worship? Simply because the Holy Spirit will lead us into complete truth, a truth that will set us free, bring healing and restoration, reveal God's heart and mysteries, and give us a hope of a future in Jesus Christ.

> But when He, the Spirit of Truth, comes, He will guide you into all the truth [*full and complete truth*]. For He will not speak on His own initiative, but He will speak whatever He hears [*from the Father—the message regarding the Son*], and He will disclose to you what is to come [*in the future*].
>
> John 16:13 AMP

The flaw in a performance-based worship is the congregation sees themselves as passive participants, rather than active participants. Entertainment should play no part in worship. Worship requires participation of all who are present, the worship team and congregation members alike. And the goal should be a Spirit-led worship.

The way I like to envision it is that the Holy Spirit takes each person by the hand and leads them through their worship, into the loving arms of Jesus. When the worship team brings a performance mindset and sees themselves as entertainers, they will do the congregation a huge disservice by leading them astray in their worship. Worship ends up being self-serving and self-soothing.

A performance will always have two parts, the entertainers and those who are entertained. Whereas, with God-worship there is only one part: man seeking the face of God. When performance enters into worship, there is a shift from the heavenly realm to the worldly realm. In the worldly realm the doors of division are flung wide open. The posture of true God-worship is diminished.

Instead, we must shut up and lock away the worldly nature of performance. We must stow away our own agendas and welcome God's Spirit. We must allow the desires of God's heart to manifest. Following the Holy Spirit, the worship team and those in the congregation will come together in unity.

When the congregation sits in a posture of entertainment, this passive role opens the door to complacency and judgment. Spectators judge. They judge whether the show or the entertainers were flawless or not.

Can you think of anyone who is flawless? I can think of only one person who fits this criterion, and that is Jesus Christ. Being flawless and without sin, **Jesus wasn't sent to this earth for our entertainment**. His life, the miracles He performed, the stories He shared, the fellowship He had with His disciples and followers, and ultimately the crucifixion, were not performances to attract crowds but were representations and reflections of God's heart for a broken people in need of a Savior. Jesus is the only flawless person that walked this earth.

In the book of Psalms, we can see that God does not desire materialistic sacrifices, like our gifts and talents. It is not enough.

> You do not desire a sacrifice, or I would offer one.
> You do not want a burnt offering.
>
> Psalms 51:16 NLT

> Going through the motions doesn't please you, a flawless performance is nothing to you.
>
> Psalm 51:16 MSG

What God desires is for our spirit and heart to be broken and repentant before Him. (Psalms 51:17)

We cannot find true repentance without having faith in Him and accepting His forgiveness. We often understand repentance to mean we need to clean up our act, do good, pray and read the Bible in the hopes that God will overlook what's in our heart. God desires a heart that is vulnerable and malleable.

Offering up a performance to God with a heart and spirit that is not yet broken or contrite before Him will end up being nothing to Him. It will not please Him.

Mankind views vulnerability and brokenness as weakness, an undesirable trait. Thankfully we serve a God who does not despise weakness, those who are vulnerable and broken.

If God chose to despise the brokenness of mankind's heart, then we would not have salvation through the sacrifice of Jesus on the cross. Jesus was the ultimate representation of brokenness and we can see the heart of God towards Jesus during the biggest trial He faced on this earth.

God used Jesus' brokenness to overcome death. He used it to take all sickness and disease to the grave. He did this so that we may have victory over death and have eternal life through Jesus, including the power over sickness and to walk in divine health. Just imagine what God can do with you and me in our place of brokenness and true repentance.

God is always concerned with the condition and motive of our heart. (1 Samuel 16:7) **No manner of religiosity or personal accomplishment can ever replace the internal motivation of a person's heart.** Without true repentance, there cannot be reconciliation with Him. No amount of excuses, reasons, or arguments can ever justify the internal motivation of our heart and spirit.

One of my husband Mike's favorite scriptures demonstrates this in a very simple way. In Luke, Jesus is crucified and talking to two thieves crucified beside Him. One is broken and repentant, while the other is defiant and rebellious.

Regarding their sins, they are no different. They are both guilty. Regarding their hearts, however, they are very different. Look at how Jesus responds to the broken and repentant man.

> We are *suffering* justly, because we are getting what we deserve for what we have done; but this Man has done nothing wrong." And he was saying, "Jesus, [*please*] remember me when You come into Your kingdom!" Jesus said to him, "I assure you *and* most solemnly say to you, today you will be with Me in Paradise."
>
> Luke 23:41-43 AMP

The devil is no fool and he knows the power of repentance. To keep us from repentance, the devil will feed us lies, so that as we examine our sin, we rationalize and try to justify it. He shifts our focus away from our offense and onto our self. Then he will point us to others, so that we begin to compare our sin to that of others, and then to give it a measure.

The flaw in this thinking is that God sees sin as sin. In His sight, there is no measure. A little white lie is a sin. Theft is a sin. Commit either and we have sinned.

Personally, I often rationalized and reasoned with God about some of the things I was doing. I didn't see anything wrong with going to nightclubs. It was purely to have an outlet to dance. God gifted me with dance and I didn't have an avenue to use that gift for God in a church setting.

Even though I didn't drink, smoke or do drugs, I was still allowing the music to influence my mind and body, and I would move in ways that was not pure in the eyes of God. Being in that environment desensitized me to God's purity and it caused my heart to draw away from God and to focus on satisfying my fleshly need to dance.

God sees sin as sin and there is no rank or measurement for sin in His eyes. The good news is that repentance leads to forgiveness, whether you told a white lie or robbed a bank. True repentance rejects the lies of the enemy and launches you into a newfound freedom in Him.

THE POWERFUL VOCABULARY OF DANCE

To illustrate how dance has a vocabulary, I want to share some personal experiences from ministry trips I've taken to foreign countries. Prior to my arrival in each, I was not familiar with their cultures or ways of life. It was in these experiences that I learned a lot about the difference between a performance and Spirit-led worship. **It was not the perfection of the performance, but rather my heart in the execution of it that made the difference.**

In creative worship there is one very important key that opens the door for God's transforming power and glory to set people free. It is the motivation of your heart toward God, not having a flawless performance.

Every language is distinguished by its own vocabulary and it is delivered primarily through speech. When learning a new language, part of the process is learning the vocabulary, or translating if from the language we know to the one we're learning. To become fluent in a language we must also speak it.

Dance can also be viewed as a language, a language translated by one's body. So, it is safe to assume dance has its own vocabulary.

With dance, the vocabulary of the language is primarily made up of movement. You can also say that the language of dance also has different dialects, styles of body language. Each can speak specifically to a certain group or culture of people: classical, contemporary, break dance, tap, rock, hip-hop, etc.

As with any language, the more extensive our vocabulary the better we are able to communicate a message. The same is true of dance. Just like worship is taught and not caught, so should be our creative expression.

For example, a successful ballet dancer doesn't just wake up one morning with a dance vocabulary and the ability to walk into any professional dance academy and take the lead role. There must be a level of teaching and training that takes place.

As a worshiper, we don't just wake up with the knowledge and vocabulary of worship, we need to be taught. Browse the web and you'll quickly find 100 dance studios within driving distance. However, when it comes to worship, even in our churches, worship is rarely taught. So, this begs the question: Where do we find a worship teacher?

When Jesus ascended to heaven He promised us He was going to leave us with a Helper. The world will not know or see Him, but because He lives inside of us as believers, we have the privilege and benefit of having the best Helper and Teacher in all of creation. (John 14:16-17, 26)

When our heart and spirit are connected with the Holy Spirit we will encounter supernatural revelation and know what actions or moves are needed to communicate God's message with accuracy.

So, the Holy Spirit leads our worship, and He will teach us as we dance and move in worship. In the natural, our movement is led by the music. But as we dance in worship, the Holy Spirit leads us in worship, and the music is nothing more than an accompaniment.

However, there is also the physical aspect of our dance. You don't have to know how to dance well to worship. But, I believe it is reasonable to encourage you to learn and broaden your vocabulary of movement. Learn to dance, and practice a lot! This not only helps build confidence but it provides you with greater communicative reach.

My daughters love to worship. They also love to dance. And we often dance together and worship with flags. We crank up worship music in our little sunroom and dance for hours, practicing new moves and choreographing dances.

In 2016, my daughters and I were invited to demonstrate creative worship as part of their school's preschool chapel service. We spent time practicing and preparing a short worship dance with flags. As the music began to play, we entered into worship and let the Holy Spirit lead us. It was an amazing 4 minutes of worship! The Holy Spirit filled the auditorium, and many were in tears as they worshiped with us.

My daughters didn't hesitate. Their boldness and confidence came in great part from God through the Holy Spirit. But it was also bolstered by their many hours of experimental play and practice.

In the foreign countries to which I have traveled, there are strong traditional styles of dance, rooted deeply in their cultures. I could have allowed this knowledge to be very intimidating, but instead I opened my spirit to the Holy Spirit and trusted in His lead.

My availability and submission to the Holy Spirit allowed a vocabulary of dance to flow through me that spoke God's heart loud and clear, and my dance spoke in the dance vocabulary of the locals. I had never before danced the way I danced, nor had I been trained in their traditional cultural styles or steps. But my worship dance was familiar to them!

I would never have thought, not in a million years, that the Holy Spirit would take me on such an amazing journey. What happened in my dance, in each of these countries, not only blew my mind, but also felt so exhilarating.

My background in dance includes 12 years of classical ballet training. It gives me a pretty good foundation and understanding of movement. However, as I began to engage in worship through dance, I learned very quickly that I should not depend on my training and my own ability. **I should allow my training to be the platform on which the Holy Spirit can build upon**.

Honestly, in many cases I have found that my training was more of a hindrance than a benefit. As I worshiped, my mind would wrestle with my spirit, telling me to move my body in ways that were familiar to me, instead of trusting the unfamiliar moves that the Holy Spirit was showing me.

When I finally overcame this mental battle and submitted to the Holy Spirit, He added styles and steps to my dance vocabulary that made for an awesome and liberating experience. Personally, I like to think of it as on-the-job training from the

Holy Spirit.

As we echo God's heart in worship through our spirit-led moves we become successful messengers for Jesus. God desires us to have life and peace. He wants us to forget about obsessing over our own thoughts and simply trust in Him. Our way leads to dead-end ways. God's way leads into open and clear communications that communicates His heart and not ours. (Romans 8:5-6)

The people of many nations speak many different languages, many languages I don't speak. We serve a God who can use us in dance to communicate His message to people anywhere. The language of dance crosses borders, barriers, cultures and continents without having to utter one spoken word. How awesome it is to be used by God to deliver His message to His people through dance and the creative arts?

PORT AU PRINCE, HAITI

Of all the countries I've visited, Haiti is my favorite. It is where I tapped into a dance style that revealed the warrior in me. I affectionately call it *warship*; warring in worship.

The Haitian people's origins are in the tribes of Africa. They were brought over from Africa by the French to work as slaves. After the French left Haiti, the Africans remained. Born in South Africa, I have a basic understanding of traditional African dance and rhythms. But I never really understood it's true nature and purpose. In Haiti God showed me the significance of the drum beat and drum rhythm and their purpose, especially in the context of warfare.

Between these revelations and how God was leading me in dance, my new dance vocabulary consisted of warlike moves; stomping feet, a low crouched posture, war-like arm actions as if I was wielding a sword and shield. The moves were repetitive, but very simple, which made it easy for others to join in and follow suit. It appeared as if an army marching into war.

Being classically ballet trained, these moves felt very different from the smooth, controlled, and graceful actions I was accustomed to. As the Holy Spirit pulled these moves out from deep within me, I realized they had been there all along. I found my purpose as a worshiper, right there in Haiti. I am a warrior for Christ, dancing to break down and destroy demonic curses and strongholds.

As I danced I felt a warrior rise up within my spirit. A deep-bellied roar welled up within and when it escaped my lips, it was a battle cry calling all fellow worship warriors to unify and take ground to advance God's Kingdom.

I read an interesting article about drumming and its effect on people. Oxford psychologists found that the endorphin-filled act of drumming increases positive emotions and leads people to work together in a more cooperative fashion.

Wow! Isn't that awesome? Even scientific research backs what I experienced during *warship* in Haiti. If the sound of drums has such a powerful impact on us in the natural, imagine the impact it has in the supernatural.

In warfare, unity and simple clear communication are key in achieving victory. The drum beat and rhythm brings people together in unity. It unifies them with one voice and one body. That is why I love it so much. It's a call to all warriors to come together and enforce our victory over the devil and his demons.

I want to add that as I was learning new Holy Spirit-led dance vocabularies over the course of a few years I was able to war in worship using moves that were perfectly orchestrated for a specific culture and group of people.

Not all warring moves look the same. In fact, I learned **it is not simply the moves that make a person a worship warrior, but it's what's in your spirit.** When you connect your spirit with the Holy Spirit, your heart follows suit. As the Holy Spirit pours into your spirit, leading you in all your moves, your role is to translate the moves as an outward expression for the purpose of revealing God's heart for others. His heart is to heal, deliver and set the captives free.

Personally in *warship*, I had to deal with some personal battles against my own mind, battling with negative thoughts that would flood my mind: I look foolish. What do others think of me? I feel silly moving this way. Am I really hearing the Holy Spirit?

Once I overcome these personal battles I began to war for others. Usually, I don't know exactly what I am warring for, or who I am warring for. But I am assured by the Holy Spirit that my obedience to follow His lead, and to fulfill His purpose, are all that He needs.

ILOILO, PHILIPPINES

In January 2006, I took my first ministry trip to Iloilo, an island in the Philippines. I was invited by a friend, Sheryll Weyers. I had met her 3 months earlier at the Breakthrough Conference hosted by Rey des Reyes in Buenos Aires, Argentina.

Sheryll wanted me to join her and her Australian youth ministry team, Firestorm, as a freestyle worship dancer. At this point neither Sheryll nor I had any idea what "freestyle worship dancer" meant. But God did.

Several months prior to this trip, during worship at the Breakthrough Conference in Argentina, God gave me an open vision of the angel He's assigned to me. You see, at this point I had a burning desire in my heart to take God's revival fire to the nations. But I had no idea how or when it would happen.

God allowed me to see my assigned angel because He wanted me to know that I didn't have to worry or be afraid of traveling alone. He wanted to assure me I would be safe and protected.

I was in awe of just how big and brilliant this angel is. God showed me He is three-stories tall. His wings are of the most brilliant white I'd ever seen and they span the width of a 747 Boeing airplane.

With an excitement in my spirit, and an assurance that I would be safe and protected, I decided to accept Sheryll's invitation.

This trip to the Philippines was the birth of the ministry God called me to. It was the scariest and most awesome experience I had had up to that point in my life.

At this 5-day youth conference, during worship the Holy Spirit took me on an interesting and exciting journey. Many times, I felt anxious and wanted to bow out. But, I remembered someone in my past once told me: **When God is in it and you are scared, just do it scared.**

As I yielded my body and mind to the Holy Spirit, I realized that God used Sheryll as an instrument to reveal my passion for dance, one I had had since a little girl. He showed me that my passion for dance was God-given, meant for worship and for God's glory.

Unlike the warrior-like moves I learned in Haiti, my dance vocabulary in the Philippines was energetic and light-footed. I would liken it to what people would do at raves with lots of hand and arm actions while keeping steady repetitive running rhythm with one's feet.

The age group of the youth present was predominantly 13-16 year olds and these movements impacted their youthful, active nature. These movements drew them into worship.

Very impressionable, it was important we engaged the youth in worship. The world is aggressively seeking this age group because they are easily influenced. It is during these years they face big decisions that affect the direction of their lives.

Impacting them with God's Spirit, showing them that surrendering to God is not only exciting, but also instrumental in impacting every aspect of their lives, even their career decisions.

Equipped with these new Holy Spirit-led dance movements, God used them to draw the hearts of the youth together and to unify the group. Together this group made a declaration that God had set them free from fear, low self-esteem, poor self-image, pride and rebellion. It was powerful!

I also tapped into a whole new level of worship dance at the conference when Sheryll was instructed by the Holy Spirit to have me dance right after she had finished preaching. God used this time, as I surrendered my dance as worship to Him, to shift and prepare the atmosphere before people came forward for prayer.

Prior to this conference, I had no idea how powerful dance could be to impact people's lives for God's glory. Words alone could never prompt this level of participation and activation. Many young people gave their lives to Christ that week.

Finally, something else amazing happened in the Philippines. A group of young street dancers heard about the conference and came out of curiosity.

They were Baptist and didn't believe in baptism of the Holy Spirit. By the time they left the conference, they were baptized with the Holy Spirit, filled to overflowing. They never expected to be changed in this way. They walked out of the conference with a newfound passion to use their street dancing skills for the glory of God. No longer would their dance be for the world.

NORTHERN INDIA

While in the Philippines I used flags only on two occasions. The first was in the opening dance for the Firestorm Conference to a song called 'Burn' by Planet Shakers. Although I talk more about flags later, its important to note that it was my experience here in India through which I learned the profound impact of flags in worship. This trip completely changed the way I worshiped, particularly how I used flags in worship as warfare. Especially compelling in this story is how the men of India reshaped my entire worship.

My trip to Northern India took place at the end of 2006. I traveled with a group of ministry school students. We arrived in New Delhi and traveled on to Jaipur, Jodhpur, and Agra.

India is a very interesting country in terms of culture, language dialects and religions, and this brought a whole new dynamic to my worship dance and flagging. There are strict cultural laws establishing how women are to dress, particularly in Northern India. I was sure to respect these laws. **It makes no sense to rebel against a culture and expect to reach them.**

My attire consisted of long palazzo pants with a knee length skirt on top. I wore long sleeve shirts and made sure that when I raised my arms my shirts were long enough to keep my abdomen covered. Finally, I covered my head with a scarf. The headscarf was a bit of a challenge, only because it wouldn't stay on my head as I danced.

Among other cultural traditions of interest, men and women sit separately, so the conference services were segregated accordingly.

During worship the Holy Spirit taught me very traditional, waltz-like moves. With my hands raised I would flick my wrists, I would do high and low turns and my body was very poised and precise.

Following each church service in which our team ministered, women approached our team saying that for the first time they felt a joy and freedom awaken within their spirit as they worshiped.

I noticed during worship how one by one the women began to smile and relax. Just this simple gesture by the Indian women allowed the atmosphere to shift and the heaviness of fear and bondage lifted. I sensed a confidence and reassurance rise within these women.

I went to India with a personal prayer. I prayed that as I walked in godly confidence, wherever I set my feet to worship in dance, idols would bow and break and the chains of oppression would fall off the people.

Having this confidence in my heart and through the outward expression of my worship I saw the manifestation of it. Everywhere we went we had favor with the locals and saw people's lives set free and delivered.

The men surprised me the most. They didn't hesitate at all during worship. They picked up some of the dance flags that I had brought, and before I knew it, they were joyfully dancing with my flags. Their movements were very powerful and masculine, proclaiming God's victory over their region.

This emotionally moved me as I saw how the men recognized the power of flag worship. I was also moved by how readily the men accepted dance as part of worship, especially since it was introduced by me, a woman.

The Philippines, Haiti and India are just a few examples of how having a basic dance vocabulary can be translated into a much broader vocabulary when we are open and yielded vessels of the Holy Spirit. With a teacher like the Holy Spirit, we will impact people without having to utter one word, even in foreign speaking nations.

When we can grasp this concept of speaking without using words, using our bodies to communicate, we have opened a whole new world of communication that God will happily use to advance His Kingdom on the earth.

These three experiences made it clear to me that there is more than one way, more than one style of dance that God chooses to communicate through. Had I let my own ideas about dance limit my dance vocabulary, the people we ministered to would have walked away unchanged. I would have walked away unchanged.

I was blessed to be a part of these experiences, to serve God and witness countless lives changed for His glory. My life was also radically changed in the process!

It is amazing how God can use every situation and opportunity to benefit all involved. Through it all, I had learned and developed a new sensitivity to the Holy Spirit, one that is rooted in trust.

THE UNIQUE ROLES OF MEN & WOMEN IN WORSHIP

God created men and women differently. This doesn't mean He made one gender superior to the other. We simply have unique roles that God created us to fill. (1 Corinthians 11:11-12)

God created men and women with different strengths and abilities, each unique to their genders. Our outlooks on life vary in terms of our relationships, work and marriage. Men and women were created to complement each other and they function best when operating according to their individual strengths and abilities.

When men and women operate outside of their God-designed strengths and abilities, they can undermine and interfere with the plans and purposes of God. Instead of unity, there is conflict.

While God has created us to fill certain roles in the relationships between a man and a woman, there are many misconceptions or fallacies regarding gender roles.

For example, there is a preconceived notion that dance in worship is a role that only women are to fill. I believe this notion entered the Church because of two factors.

Firstly, modern society has emasculated men by assailing their role as protectors and providers. Secondly, most men don't consider dance to be a masculine activity. Both of these notions have shaped the attitudes and behavior of men in the body of believers. They don't believe they have a role in creative or expressive worship.

Because of this, there is a lack in the power and authority that a man brings to our corporate worship sessions.

Men in Worship

In today's culture, we are faced with a feminist agenda that has emasculated men and put them in the corner. God did not create man to be superior to women. But God did create man with certain superior abilities for the benefit of mankind.

Science and biology proves a man is generally physically larger and than women. God also designed men with strong leadership traits and aggressive physical characteristics designed to protect and provide for his family and community. I believe that men carry a completely different level of anointing when they step out with expressive movement as worship. The anointing a man carries is strong, authoritative, bold and confident.

Men are an essential part of warfare in worship, or *warship*. God created a man to take the role of a protector. The man will fight to protect those he loves. The man is a leader, provider and protector and is physically built and wired for battle.

In my years of experiencing dance at different conferences, churches and outreaches, I have observed that women typically fill the role of worship in dance. I believe this is mostly because women are more comfortable with dance.

As young girls, moms are more prone to expose their daughters to some type of dance training, or cheerleading, whereas this is not common with little boys. Having this exposure as a child typically makes dance more comfortable for women than for men. I have seen very few men step out and begin to worship with expressive movement and total abandonment.

I have spoken with men who have attended my creative worship workshops, and the consensus among the men is that even though they want to dance, they feel it's not the place for a man to do so. On the few occasions I have seen men step out and dance, their movement brought a whole new level of authority in worship. It shifted the atmosphere to a whole new level, where any dark forces had to bow or flee. It brings this scripture to mind.

> For we do not wrestle against flesh and blood, but against the rulers, against the authorities, against the cosmic powers over this present darkness, against the spiritual forces of evil in the heavenly places.
>
> Ephesians 6:12 ESV

As these men danced in worship, a righteous authority entered the atmosphere through their strong and bold moves. It awakened a confidence and security in the women, who would then operate on a whole new level of anointing.

The authority a man adds to the dynamic of creative worship brings a confidence, boldness and security to women as they worship. There is nothing more powerful and life changing than when men and women led by the Holy Spirit worship together operating in their superior individual abilities.

After witnessing the men in India worshiping with the flags, and seeing how it shifted the atmosphere to a whole new level, a desire was birthed in me to start teaching creative worship workshops. I wanted to provide an environment where men could freely express themselves devoid of ridicule and judgment. I realized there is a role in worship that only a man can fill.

When men come together in worship it's like a unified army of warriors that has taken its position on the battlefield. This is a position of strength and advantage. It is the position from which the Church, the body of believers, must stand, attack and destroy the powers of darkness, the principalities and the strongholds that hold our families, cities, regions and nations captive.

An opportunity presented itself when a couple in our church, Jody and Jackie made their barn building, called Green Acres, available to me to begin teaching creative worship workshops.

Jody, the husband, had always struggled with a desire he had to dance as part of worship. Before he became a Christian and chose to give up the pleasures of the world, he used to spend his leisure time at dance halls. Now, as a Christian, Jody did not know what to do with the love he had for dance. He just figured that he had to quench that love and desire, hoping he would eventually forget about it.

No matter how hard he tried, every time he would worship he would see himself dancing, wild and free. He related to King David who danced in total freedom and abandon. Yet, guilt would set in because in his own way of thinking he thought it was unacceptable for a modern day Christian man to dance like that in a church worship session. His heart would tell him it was fine, but his mind wrestled against it and kept him bound in fear.

At the first workshop I taught at their place, I focused on biblical teaching that supported dance as part of worship. Jody took a hold of the teaching and when we went into the practical part of the workshop, he broke out with such freedom that it not only shocked him, but his wife and daughter too.

His dance made such an impact and shift in the atmosphere of worship that all preconceived ideas and notions were kicked to the curb. It was not a flawless execution of dance, but every move and step he made broke down any walls that were built up over the years.

Walls came crumbling down as God's glory filled the barn building. We worshiped in dance, with flags, banners and billows. One by one our worship entered into deep intercession and we began to war for the region and the state of Louisiana.

Many spiritual battles ensued as we met monthly. Each time we warred with creative worship until each battle was won. **The battles, being spiritual in nature, required us to take the fight to the supernatural realm using spiritual weapons**.

Our weapons were strategic prayer, scripture and true God-worship. Flowing in our gifts and talents, wholly and completely surrendered to God, we worshiped until we witnessed and experienced personal breakthroughs and victories.

As time passed, more and more men started to join these workshops with their wives, and at times there were more men than women. The men and women came together, and with a cohesive and unified heart they brought their superior individual abilities into the fold. This kind of worship brought victory upon victory. Hallelujah!

Women in Worship

God created woman with her own superior abilities. In relationship with a man, He fashioned a woman to be a helpmate to the man. A woman is not there to compete with a man, but rather complete a man.

Too often today, people see this as subservience or subordination. However, according to scripture God sees a husband and wife as one. (Genesis 2:22-24) So it is also true that a woman completes a man.

It is amazing how God preordained us to complement one another for advancing His Kingdom's purposes, whether in marriage or in the Church. **I believe that the woman is there to compliment the role and anointing of a man, and cannot replace it**.

For example, during worship the role and anointing of a woman centers on her ability to understand grace. She can stand confidently knowing how to approach the King with reverence, purity and tenderness, and yet she can stand strong and courageous when needed. Queen Ester demonstrates this in the book of Ester.

> So it was, when the king saw Queen Esther standing in the court, that she found favor in his sight, and the king held out to Esther the golden scepter that was in his hand.
>
> Esther 5:2 NKJV

Both men and women fill a unique role and purpose in worship. When the two come together and fill their rightful places it brings order and unity into the body of Christ and order on a personal level.

Actively and aggressively, the devil has been attacking the identity of men and women, not just on a personal level, but across society. The devil has planted the lie that your gender is a matter of how you feel, not a matter of biological fact.

Satan wants us to find flaws in our identity, to misinterpret God's original intent in creating us. God created us for a specific reason and purpose to complete His plan. As in the puzzle analogy, we are all part of God's puzzle of life. If there is one piece missing, it will be incomplete and it won't function properly.

Not only did God decide when we would be born, and how long we will live here on earth, He also planned the days of our life. Our sex, race and nationality are no accident. God has left no detail to chance. We were created male and female by His design.

> You saw me before I was born. Every day of my life was recorded in your book. Every moment was laid out before a single day had passed.
>
> Psalm 139:16 NLT

Another lie the devil wants us to believe is that God has favorites and that He only provides gifts and talents to some, and not all. The truth is that our earthly status is not important to God. In His eyes we are all His. He created us out of His pure love and to have a relationship with Him. He doesn't pick and choose to whom He gives more or less love. His love for a successful doctor is no more than His love for a beggar on the street.

> He doesn't care how great a person may be, and he pays no more attention to the rich than to the poor. He made them all.
>
> Job 34:19 NLT

> For God does not show favoritism.
>
> Romans 2:11 NLT

> And Peter opened his mouth and said: Most certainly *and* thoroughly I now perceive *and* understand that God shows no partiality *and* is no respecter of persons,
>
> Acts 10:34 AMPC

These scriptures show that these are lies from the pit of hell. They are a direct attack on our identity. We must be confident in who we are and in what God thinks of us. When we walk in this knowledge and revelation, we walk according to our identity in Christ, and the devil will never have power over us.

Because God assigned different roles to a man and woman, it doesn't mean he made one superior to the other, or one more important than the other. In God's eyes both men and women are equal.

When we don't fulfill our own gender role, when we try to fill the role of the other, it brings confusion. It weakens us and nullifies the impact we were supposed to have on others and in our churches. It creates disunity. It creates conflict. Ultimately, it will lead to our destruction.

A heart is no more important than a pair of kidneys. If the heart decided today it would start doing the job of the kidney, it will surely be the death of the body. The heart is not equipped to do the job of the kidneys. Just like a woman is not equipped to fill the role of a man, and vice versa.

AN APPROPRIATE TIME TO DANCE

There is something the Lord taught me over the years, not just in worship and dance but in life also. God is a God of order. (1 Corinthians 14:33)

Timing is an important aspect of God's order. We must trust in the Holy Spirit and allow Him to lead us. If we're paying attention, if we're sensitive to His leading, the Holy Spirit will prompt us when it's appropriate to dance.

It's when we get caught up in striving to create a flawless performance in our creative worship, we become deaf to the voice of the Holy Spirit. When we have our hearts set on executing it flawlessly, instead of following the Holy Spirit, we fail in fulfilling God's plan and purpose for that specific moment.

Instead of furthering God's agenda, we become a stumbling block. Obedience to God's voice, His commandments and His principals position us perfectly to allow God's blessings to fall upon us and to overtake us.

> And all these blessings shall come upon you and overtake you, because you obey the voice of the Lord your God:
>
> Deuteronomy 28:2 KNJV

Personally, at times during worship, when a battle ensues in my mind, or an urge or impression prompts me to dance, and I wrestle with whether it is the Holy Spirit or my own will, I must calm my mind and surrender my thoughts to God.

Because I have a strong desire to be Spirit-led and not self-led, I feel these mental battles emerge more often than usual. My desire is to have as little of myself in the execution of my creative expression of worship as possible.

The reason this is so important for me is so God's heart will be seen in the expressive moves of my dance, and it will cause the attention of onlookers to shift onto the One I am worshiping, Jesus.

We live in a fallen world. Battles will need to be fought, and challenges overcome. I don't believe I am the only one who faces these kinds of mental battles during worship. Whether in creative worship, or other types of worship, we all face these battles.

The questions that run through my mind are: Am I really hearing God's voice? Is He truly prompting me to step out? Is it my mind telling me it is the right time? What if I step out and dance and it's the wrong time?

These are typical questions that I believe floods most creative worshipers minds during worship when the Holy Spirit prompts them. When this happens, the Lord has taught me to first calm my mind, and then to ask myself one simple question: If I do not obey, will I regret it later? This little tactic has made it much easier for me to distinguish which voice I am hearing, God's voice or my own voice.

THE BATTLE AGAINST THE FLAWLESS PERFORMANCE

The following is a typical example of the kind of battle I have experienced on many occasions during worship. This usually happens when I am lacking confidence or when I feel I am not quite "in the groove."

Part of the insecurity on these occasions appears when my mind tells me I will be a spectacle if I don't execute flawlessly. Having a heart to reflect God's heart as my own through my worship, I have to overcome these thoughts of a flawless performance and knock down these roadblocks in my spirit.

Here's an example of how the battle often goes:

When I feel an urge or impression to dance or flag, the reasoning game ensues in my mind. I immediately make a conscious decision to arrest my mind. I close my eyes and focus on Jesus. When I don't do this, my humanness seeks affirmation from either the worship leader or the pastor, hoping to receive an affirmative nod that it's my time to come out and dance or flag. I've just hit the first roadblock.

If I don't find the affirmation from my leaders, I then shift my focus onto the congregation and gauge the spiritual temperature by how many people are engaging in worship. Another roadblock pops up.

When a large part of the congregation is not engaged in worship, the environment is intimidating and insecurities arise. My confidence wanes.

Not every believer has the revelation and knowledge of the purpose of creative worship, so by nature they will judge what they don't understand, especially if they have had no teaching on it. In my humanness, these thoughts wear on my confidence.

So, as these mental battles rage and these thoughts begin to flood my mind there is one word that makes its way to the surface; **feelings**. If I depend on my feelings I will miss the God-moment completely, and later I will regret it, kicking myself for not being obedient.

In the Bible, David sings a heart's cry to God which echoes my heart when I feel overwhelmed amid worship due to insecurity and a lack of confidence.

> From the end of the earth I will cry to You, when my heart is overwhelmed; Lead me to the rock that is higher than I.
>
> Psalm 61:2 NKJV

I know that in my humanness I am fallible. I don't want to make a mistake and miss God. The simple question I ask myself in these situations has many times helped me differentiate between my own agenda and God's plan: If I do not obey, will I regret it later?

Your question may differ from mine. But whatever your question is, if it eliminates the battle in your mind, then you have tapped into a newfound freedom in your expression of true God-worship.

The more you exercise this new freedom, the less and less power insecurity, inadequacy and imperfection will have over you. You can trust that **God will never lead us into failure or embarrassment**.

When we focus on God, and the need to execute a flawless performance for man fades, we will tap into two very important truths in our lives as true God-worshipers:

1) We find favor in God's eyes and we can be used to accomplish the plans and purposes He has set forth for us. (Genesis 18:3)
2) We reflect God's heart, not our own, and we leave a remnant of His Spirit everywhere we set foot in our worship. (2 Corinthians 3:18)

The deep cry of my heart is that all believers, especially creative worshipers, will desire to be found favorable in God's eyes and be available whenever and wherever God wants to use them; the workplace, our homes or our churches.

Our life is not our own. Daily, we should give it back to God as an act of true God-worship. You and I are on this earth for such a time as this to fulfill the purpose and destiny God created us for.

In the book of Acts, we read a very powerful portrayal of what our heart should be like in worship. As believers, we will all be presented with assignments to advance God's Kingdom. When our life is empty of self and full of His Spirit, fulfilling these assignments will be easy as we find our confidence in God's ability rather than our own.

> But I am not worried about this. I do not think of my life as worth much, but I do want to finish the work the Lord Jesus gave me to do. My work is to preach the Good News of God's loving-favor.
>
> Acts 20:24 NLV

CONCLUSION

In conclusion, if you want to be used by God in creative worship, you don't need all kinds of professional training. All you need is a willing heart and a desire to follow the lead of the Holy Spirit. It doesn't hurt to have training and experience, but it is not a requirement. You are a child of God, and this is what qualifies you.

There have been many people who attended my creative worship workshops who have had no dance experience, no experience with flags, banners, or billows, and yet they have glorious encounters and transformations that have led to supernatural breakthroughs, both personally and corporately.

When your heart, motive and spirit are ready, when they are in the right place, your motions will unlock the transforming power of Jesus and open the door for God's glory cloud to fall in the building.

You might experience a spiritual rain of His presence that washes over you like waves of glory. Other times His glory will rest upon you like a weighted blanket, to where you are unable to move. And then there may be moments in time where you just lay flat on your face, prostrate before Him, on the floor weeping at the beauty and glory of the Lord.

These manifestations bring breakthrough and freedom, breakthrough and freedom from fear, insecurity, hurt and depression, simply because the environment we created being wholly surrendered to God, welcomed God's manifest presence to transform our lives.

As a result, we walk away from these encounters filled with passion and purpose as we fall more in love with Jesus. I have personally experienced these things many times over, and the powerful testimonies from my workshops participants, children and adults alike, confirm it also.

A flawless performance, void of the Holy Spirit will hinder, distract, and even disrupt a worship service. It is imperative that we empty ourselves before God and submit to the Holy Spirit so that none of our self will be translated in the delivery of His message or assignment as we engage in creative worship.

As worshipers, our gifts and talents are not just for us to express ourselves and to commune with God, but it is also for the impact and transformation of the lives of others.

My husband Mike is not typical by any measure, but like many men he see's himself as a tough guy, so the following revelation is a little surprising. He's told me that often during worship services, he is moved nearly to tears when he witnesses someone pouring out their heart to God in worship, someone engaged in true-God worship.

He says he doesn't understand it, but it is a powerful joyful emotional state that overtakes him. He says that what he feels in the natural can be translated to: Look at how much she loves our God! In the supernatural, He believes it is the Holy Spirit inside of him responding to the love, adoration and true surrender to God.

God deserves all the glory, honor and praise in every move we make. We must surrender wholly to Him. We must let Him transform our performance into a beautiful display of our hearts surrendered to Him. We must let Him turn what is flawed into a reflection of His own heart toward us, His beloved.

Through the Holy Spirit our performance is made flawless, and it becomes holy and sacred in the eyes of God. We are His canvas, a living canvas on which He continues the good work He began before we were even in the womb. (Jeremiah 1:5)

9

MY PRIDE WAS SHATTERED

How God Worked a Miracle in My Life

The sacrifices of God are a broken spirit. -- Psalm 51:17a NKJV

There are many believers who are brokenhearted, discouraged and confused, because of sin. Through sin, we leave ourselves vulnerable to attacks by the enemy. These attacks lead to strongholds in our lives, though which the enemy will try to destroy us.

Pride is one sin that many of us face. In today's world pride has grown deep roots and is so common that often we don't even realize it's a problem until we're faced with uprooting this enemy stronghold in our life.

I want to begin this chapter by sharing a very troubling time in my life, when my pride was shattered. When this happened, it was a profound awakening in which I discovered how powerful worship could be. God delivered me from pride and a powerful enemy stronghold. I learned that God's healing could be delivered through worship!

MAN'S APPROVAL VS. GOD'S APPROVAL

The biggest obstacle in my life that hindered my worship and relationship with God was allowing man's approval to outweigh God's approval. Even though I loved God with all my heart, I still had pride and it had become an ugly thing in my life.

I allowed pride to bind me up with the chains of an eating disorder called

Bulimia. Pride convinced me that it was a good thing to control my body by controlling *what* I ate and *how much* I ate. I measured personal success by whether or not I obtained lead roles in ballet productions. So, I believed this *control* was necessary to stay skinny enough so my dance teachers would pick me for lead roles.

As a little girl, probably since I was about age 6, I had dreams of becoming a professional ballerina. I worked hard at it and practiced many hours weekly, including private training.

I spent countless nights bending my feet with bands, and soaking them in methylated spirits to toughen my skin so that my toes could handle the abuse of point shoes. I was committed, dedicated and ready to face this tough life choice. Nothing was going to stop me from achieving it, not even food. In my mind, I found power in taking control of my body. After all it was my body.

Years later I realized how wrong I had been. As a believer, my body is the temple of the Holy Spirit. When I became a Christian, it was no longer mine. This obsessive commitment and dedication to becoming a ballerina opened a door to pride in my life. I got to the point where I didn't want to listen to anyone except those that fed my pride.

MY PLAN VS. GOD'S PLAN

God had a plan for my life, but I was so blinded by pride that I couldn't see His plan. I knew God blessed me with an ability to dance and I loved dancing every moment I could. What I hadn't yet realized was how God would use dance for His good and for the good of others.

> God has given each of you a gift. Use it to help each other. This will show God's loving-favor.
>
> 1 Peter 4:10 NLV

This is a scripture I often think of now, understanding that dance was part of God's plan for me. At this time in my life however, it had not yet become a revelation to me. All I desired was to dance. That desire often led me to go to dance clubs with friends. We did not drink alcohol. We just danced. Ballet class was the other outlet for dance.

These were worldly venues that influenced my life. They were places where pride was free to take root in my heart. I began to learn what the world wanted and began to experience the pressures of attaining success.

In these worldly venues, Bulimia was accepted as a normal part of attaining success. Even though it was physically destructive to my body and health, I allowed pride to tell me that I was invincible.

I could explain away the destructive behaviors of Bulimia. I could remove the thoughts from my mind, ignoring them. And I made sure the words "I have Bulimia" never escaped my lips. That way, I didn't have to acknowledge I had a problem. I believed the lie that I had control over it. But in all truth, Bulimia controlled my whole life.

I battled with Bulimia for 5 years, until I decided to have a conversation with God. I made a deal with Him that I was going to let our big move to the USA be a brand new start for me. I would get plugged into a good church, make new friends, and get victory over Bulimia. A good church and new friends were the easy part. However, overcoming the power Bulimia had over my life was much more difficult than I ever could imagine.

I had no idea how strong its hold was on me. Relinquishing control over to God and learning self-control were the two biggest challenges. On top of it all, my pride kept getting in the way, keeping me from admitting that I was in way over my head. God knew I needed an intervention and in His perfect way He started me down the road to victory.

BREAKTHROUGH!

The family we were living with at the time invited us to join them at their church's home group meeting. I was 22 years old then, and we had been living in the States for 2 months.

At the meeting there was a lady who began to share her personal testimony of how she had struggled with food and obesity. She had an eating disorder also. In her case she couldn't control the amount of food she ate. With Bulimia, I would binge and purge.

The more she shared, the more self-conscious I became. I felt like every person knew my big dark secret. On the outside, I appeared calm and collected but on the inside I was screaming out, embarrassed and afraid.

The words, "I have Bulimia" had never escaped my lips before that night. That was how the stronghold of pride kept me bound. I remained in bondage, bound by my very own tongue.

The Holy Spirit was gently exposing the pride in my life through the testimony of the lady who was sharing her personal struggles. As the Holy Spirit was doing this, I began to recognize that I had blinders on my eyes all these years. I was blinded by the fact that I was never in control.

Even though there was a raging war going on inside of me that night, I knew I was going to have to decide whether I wanted the approval of man or God.

For years I focused on my appearance and abilities. I correlated success in ballet with my weight. I thought getting skinny led to getting lead roles. Strangely, I also equated success in my friendships, being accepted socially, with being skinny.

So, when I was faced with the decision to choose man's approval or God's, my mind tried everything to convince me that I was fine. I told myself that I had control over Bulimia and I wasn't physically sick.

Now, the bible study had ended and everyone was visiting, having tea and cake.

But I was still consumed by this lady's testimony from earlier. There was an overwhelming feeling and emotion that took over my body. My heart was racing. I was sweating, and there was a voice crying out from deep within my spirit. It felt like someone was pulling me by the hand, moving my feet one step at a time toward the lady who spoke earlier about her eating disorder.

Before I realized it, I was standing right in front of her. As soon as she greeted me the words "I have Bulimia" rolled right off my tongue. I was stunned and embarrassed because I had every intention of greeting her back. Instead, I just blurted it out.

This very night, my pride was shattered. The Holy Spirit walked me right up to this lady. It was Him who untied my tongue so I could admit I had Bulimia.

Admitting I had a problem was my first step. I was humbled, vulnerable and felt ready for what God had started to do in my life. I may have felt humiliated at first, because my pride tried to tell me I was a fool for walking over to that lady. But God turned that feeling of humiliation into humility. He turned what was evil to good. (Proverbs 29:23)

That night I learned first-hand the meaning of humility. Humility was the place where God began to restore my self-esteem. I was not ridiculed by anyone at the meeting. Instead I was accepted in my brokenness and humiliation. With my emotional wounds exposed for the first time for all to see, God swooped in and held me.

Until that night, not my parents or my brother were aware of my problem. It was their response I was most worried about. I expected them to reject me, to be upset and angry toward me. But instead I received nothing but love, support, compassion and acceptance from them.

We can see here in the book of Proverbs that God's Word says that true humility and godly fear ultimately lead to prosperity and long life.

> True humility and fear of the Lord lead to riches, honor, and long life.
>
> Proverbs 22:4 NLT

HEALING & RESTORATION

Still not completely set free and healed from Bulimia, I began to allow God's love, acceptance, compassion and healing to wash over me in my times of worship.

These were some of the most healing times in this journey. My times in God-worship, enveloped in His presence, became one of my favorite places to be. It was where I felt unconditional love and acceptance; I felt safe and secure.

Most of all, I received amazing nuggets of revelation from the Holy Spirit during my worship. These revelations gave me purpose and direction in my life. Over the course of a year my spirit began to grow stronger and stronger and my faith began to rise to a level it had never been to before. I knew that I was unable to break the control of Bulimia over my life alone, and that God was the only one who could heal me.

At times, I did stumble and fall, briefly relapsing. But I didn't let it stop me from humbly pursuing God and trusting in His healing power to set me free. I knew that only in His power, not my own, I would be set free.

Throughout this journey, I believe I was learning a valuable lesson. I learned how to maintain humility through true brokenness and repentance, with the acceptance of God's forgiveness.

FREEDOM

A little over a year after I admitted I had Bulimia an evangelist from South Africa came through our town and ministered at two services I attended. The first service was to our sister youth group in a neighboring town about 40 minutes away.

Our youth group would participate together with our sister youth group in many events and outreaches. So, a large group from our youth group took one of our church vans and drove to our sister church to hear the evangelist preach.

I was super-curious; partly because he was South African and it wasn't very often we had a visitor from my former home, let alone have one preach.

The message he shared that night was about God's miraculous healing power and how He desired for us to be healed and to walk in divine health. Listening to him sharing testimony after testimony, an intensity of God's presence began to fill the room as the level of faith began to grow in people, one by one.

My personal level of faith was up there too, but I was more interested in having a God-encounter and desired to experience the power of God for my life that night. The result of my increased faith awakened a level of hunger I had not had before. I just wanted more of God's presence in my life.

After he finished his message, the South African evangelist challenged each of us to walk through a "glory tunnel." A glory tunnel is made up of two rows of people standing shoulder to shoulder, one row facing the other, about five feet apart.

This formed a tunnel. The people in the two rows began to pray in the Spirit, interceding for the others who were about to walk through the tunnel. When the evangelist felt the Holy Spirit release him, he gestured for everyone else to form a line at the one front of the tunnel.

One by one we walked through the "glory tunnel." Suddenly a strong cloud of His glory came over me and I could not stand anymore. I just collapsed under His power. I was dragged off to the side. As I lay there, it felt like someone was holding me down on the floor, but no one was touching me. Physically it felt like I weighed a ton. All I could do was lie there and weep.

It was getting late, and since most of the youth that came with our group had curfews, we had to head home. Thanks to my brother and some friends, I was carried to the church van and driven home.

The best way I can describe the next couple of hours would be that it felt like I was undergoing spiritual surgery. My abdomen was filled with tangible heat and there was a supernatural holy churning; it was so tangible and holy that I was not able to touch my own belly. It felt like the power of God was pulling all the pride, self-hate, control and Bulimia out by the roots.

The very next morning when I woke up I knew that I was completely set free and delivered from the bondage of Bulimia. I knew that God had healed me and this was the beginning of the rest of my life serving God without the yoke of Bulimia hanging around my neck. I praise God to this day for my healing.

After this painful, but oh so glorious, experience the Holy Spirit began to reveal the purpose God had for me. My pride was the biggest obstacle that stood in the way. It caused me to become spiritually deaf, dumb and blind to the Holy Spirit.

I was not a bad person. I loved God, followed His principals in the Word and I attended church regularly. But there was one very important dynamic I neglected in my Christian walk and that was to embrace the Holy Spirit. My pride shut Him out.

Thankfully, God's ways are above our ways and when I felt like I had no way out, consumed with my food issues, I cried out to Him. That's all that God needed, my surrender, and He answered me immediately.

God will take any situation in our life that the devil intended to destroy us with and turn it around for our good and for His glory. When we surrender, when we open our hearts to the Holy Spirit, we give Him permission to empower us to overcome challenges and obstacles, just like He did with pride and Bulimia in my life. (Romans 8:28)

Bulimia may have intended to destroy me and to rob me of the passion I have for dance. Both physically and mentally, pride intended to keep me deaf, dumb and blind. But once I surrendered and allowed God to remove these obstacles, it became very clear that I was born to dance. The most important key in this miracle was that I knew I needed more of God.

A.W. Tozer, a well-known preacher in the early 1900's hit the nail on the head with this quote. He says in one sentence what took place in my life; the miraculous healing from Bulimia and pride.

> "Pulled out of the mud of your own ego, so that you have stopped thinking that you are somebody, at last you are delivered from yourself and are seeking God for Himself alone."

All I needed was to be willing to surrender and open my heart to Him and give Him full access. I had to turn control over to Him, give God the reins, and that was when He started the healing process.

Pride is something that will always knock on the door of our hearts in the dark of night. Never answer that door. Instead, turn on the porch light of humility. Humility is the antidote to pride. Continue to embrace the Holy Spirit and heed the conviction He brings.

"A conviction by the Holy Spirit may not feel good, but it will save your eternal life if you do not ignore it" - unknown

Through this whole experience, God turned Bulimia around for good. He healed me, delivered me and set me free. He gave me the opportunity to use this experience as a testimony for the sake of others.

The life we live is not for us only; we are here to serve Him and others. Our testimonies are very important. They testify to the greatness and goodness of our God. This experience demonstrates how God can work through worship. In this case, He healed me, encouraged me and gave me hope. He removed my pain and replaced confusion with peace and truth.

In great part, the power of worship in our relationship with God is the reason I've written this book. God has called me to draw creative people back into the Church. He's shown me there is a place in His Church for creative worship, for His creative people.

Unfortunately, creative people have a hard time finding a place in today's churches. Unless you're a musician or singer on the worship team, there isn't really a place for other creative types.

God is a creative God, and He created us in His image. So why wouldn't our worship be creative also?

Sadly, many people in today's Church have done more harm than good in terms of understanding and accepting God's creativity in worship. They tend to reject what they don't understand.

There are outliers. Churches like the well-known Bethel Church in Redding, CA and Morningstar Ministries in Fort Mills, SC have embraced create worship. But it is still not widely accepted.

Instead of the Church accepting people who are gifted and talented, they have often rejected them and even scoffed at them for thinking that God could use their creative gifts and talents as an expression of true God-worship.

The Church is comfortable with preachers, evangelists, missionaries, teachers and prophets, but they don't recognize creative worshipers. Unless you sing or play a musical instrument on the worship team, there aren't acceptable roles for creative people in the Church.

For creative people, this rejection often leads to hurt feelings, discouragement and confusion.

Even though this is the reality for creative types, our churches are not fully to blame for this problem. I believe that pride is at the root of this problem. Pride is the main reason the creative arts have been neglected or sidelined in a corporate worship setting.

This pride leads others to cast judgment on creative worshipers, simply because of a lack of knowledge. Churches bear the burden of this part of problem because they do not have the knowledge and understanding.

SHATTERING PRIDE IN CREATIVE WORSHIP

When it comes to creative worship, creative types should also take responsibility for the rejection of creative worship in our churches. We must recognize and address our own lack of knowledge and understanding, and we must avoid the pitfalls that have played a part in the rejection of creative worship.

One of the major pitfalls is pride. Pride will lead creative worshipers into performance rather than true God-worship. It leads one to seek attention rather than focus attention on God. This happens simply because of a lack of teaching and training. When others in the congregation witness prideful worship, they recognize it is not true God-worship, and it becomes a distraction.

The root of pride is selfishness, which puts focus on our ourselves, our ability and our own strength. Pride loves control. Pride fuels a motive of self-gain and promotion. Pride seeks titles that promote our status and fame.

When we are focused on our own gain and promotion we will never be satisfied. No matter what we achieve, apart from God, it will never satisfy the drive that pride fuels to obtain success.

Pride will operate in our worship, just as it was at work in my aspirations to become a ballerina. It eventually led me into my Bulimia, which nearly destroyed me.

Pride is a powerful tool Satan uses to divide us, and it causes people to do very foolish things.

I've made some foolish mistakes in my life over the years. I will be the first person to tell you that. I am no better than anyone else, and I've had to learn some hard lessons in my life. Its through these hard lessons I know that pride is a very powerful force that can bind us up in the chains of bondage and eventually lead us into destruction.

The Origin of Pride

The more we study the Bible, the more we understand that we are not battling other people. Our battles are in the supernatural against the powers of darkness.

> For we do not wrestle against flesh and blood, but against principalities, against powers, against the rulers of the darkness of this age, against spiritual hosts of wickedness in the heavenly places.
>
> Ephesians 6:12 NKJV

Pride is a supernatural problem. Pride opens the door to the spirit of Leviathan who is a strongman, or a very powerful spirit. The Strong's Concordance (3882, 3867) defines Leviathan as a wreathed animal or a serpent. (Isaiah 27:1)

The spirit of Leviathan bends and twists the truth in such a manner that it is hard to distinguish the truth from the lie.

In Job 21, we see a terrifying depiction of Leviathan. In these verses, we see how difficult pride is to penetrate, suggesting nothing, not even the truth can penetrate its scales.

> His rows of scales are his pride, shut up tightly as with a seal; One is so near another that no air can come between them; They are joined one to another, they stick together and cannot be parted.
>
> Job 41:15-17 NKJV

> He beholds every high thing; He is king over all the children of pride.
>
> Job 41:34 NKJV

The spirit of Leviathan has absolute power over its captives, a power that only God can overcome. (Job 41:10-11)

Pride is a big obstacle in our relationship with God, and it robs us of a humble and peaceful life. It prevents us from surrendering control over to God and entering His presence in worship. As a result, we block the Holy Spirit who facilitates a healthy spiritual growth in us.

God makes it clear in scripture that we should not boast about our abilities apart from God. The only boasting God finds acceptable is when we proclaim and give glory to God. (2 Corinthians 10:13)

Opening the door to pride closes the door on true humility. **Humility says that in the end, it's not what we say about ourselves, but what God says about us that matters**.

I heard John 4:24 paraphrased in a way that gave me a whole new perspective of this scripture: "those who worship Him must worship Him in spirit and in the truth of what God says about them."

God wants only the best for us. He sent His son Jesus to die for our sins and salvation, all because He loves us that much. So, when that truly sinks in, and we call out to God, pride will be overcome and we will be free to embrace humility.

Considering the power of pride, we must guard ourselves, and never give pride a foothold or place to operate in our lives.

The Shout of Pride vs. the Whisper of Humility

Pride tells us to feed our own ego while pointing out other people's sin. Pride brings condemnation. It finds pleasure in what the world offers. It delights in self-promotion, recognition and fame.

If this is what the voice of pride sounds like, then humility should sound the quite different.

Humility opposes pride. Humility compels us to welcome the Holy Spirit into our lives, allowing Him to bring conviction. Conviction opens the door to repentance and forgiveness, and makes way for the truth.

Humility finds satisfaction and contentment in God, and delights in service to others without seeking promotion, recognition or fame. Humility is gentle. Humility is a whisper.

God demonstrates very clearly how He feels about pride and humility in the following scripture:

> Likewise you younger people, submit yourselves to your elders. Yes, all of you be submissive to one another, and be clothed with humility, for "God resists the proud, but gives grace to the humble." Therefore humble yourselves under the mighty hand of God, that He may exalt you in due time.
>
> 1 Peter 5:5-6 NKJV

You have heard this throughout this book, and I believe it should be heard repeatedly throughout our lives: We must embrace the Holy Spirit and give Him complete access to all areas of our life, access to reach every recess of our heart.

One of the purposes of the Holy Spirit is to convict believers when they sin, or in some cases to convince believers they have sinned. Then, He leads the believer into repentance and to the truth through the Word of God.

> And when He has come, He will convict the world of sin, and of righteousness, and of judgment: However, when He, the Spirit of truth, has come, He will guide you into all truth; for He will not speak on His own authority, but whatever He hears He will speak; and He will tell you things to come.
>
> John 16:8, 13 NKJV

As we embrace the Holy Spirit and accept the conviction of any pride in our life we should be quick to repent, allowing our pride to be shattered so we can learn how to worship God in spirit and in truth.

LET GOD MAKE THE WAY

As a creative type, you might be walking through some tough circumstances but please know it does not make you a bad or weak person. The battles, storms, pain or seasons of waiting are not punishment from God.

As I've learned over the course of my life, God allowed these tough times in my life not to destroy me, but to show me that I am victorious. If God kept us from walking through any difficult season or situation we would never have the opportunities to work out our spiritual muscles of faith and authority.

Yes, at times we make wrong decisions and open the door to pain, failure, hurt and disappointment, but the key is in how we handle it. Do we try to do it on our own, or do we surrender to God, embrace the Holy Spirit and walk in the faith and knowledge that He will take care of us and our obstacles?

What obstacle or vice is holding you back from walking in the fullness of your gifts and talents? Pride was mine. The moment I surrendered my heart to Him, I not only allowed God to shatter my pride but I received healing in my body and my mind. The veil was torn from my eyes and I began to see what my purpose was in the body of Christ.

God knows us better than we can know ourselves. When we look through our natural eyes **we might see and experience failure, but God sees an opportunity for victory**. God sees in us what many of us cannot even see within ourselves. (Psalm 139:1)

God knows everything about you and me, right down to our secret heart's desires. Let us surrender to Him, give Him full access to our heart and see how glorious our walk with Him will be. We will no longer have a "victim mentality," but instead we will be overcomers.

It is very important that even though our local church or leadership does not understand the importance and purpose of creative worship, that we still allow God to prepare and make the way for us.

We can't let pride cause us to step out in worship with creative expression prematurely, inappropriately, or completely give up on creative worship.

We must trust that God will make a way. Otherwise, we will find ourselves stepping out from under His protective covering, exposed to the attacks of the enemy. Being exposed makes us vulnerable to judgment, hurt, confusion and discouragement.

Instead, let us be vigilant and protect what we know to be pleasing to God; our creative worship. Let us be on guard for when the enemy will try to destroy the gift that God has given His creative sons and daughters. Let us watch out for the death of creative worship in ourselves.

In my experience, there are three stages of death that can occur in our creative worship when we find ourselves stuck.

- We know that our heart is in the right place, and we have a desire to worship God with our gifts and talents, but the church has rejected us because of a lack of understanding.
- We are stuck in a place where we believe we hear the call to worship God with our gifts and talents, but because the church has rejected us, we have decided to satisfy the need to express ourselves creatively outside of the church.
- Our desire to worship creatively has been quenched, so much so that we don't know how to bring it back to life again.

Humility and patience are two key virtues that can help revive and restore life, no matter what stage you might be going through. We often must wait on God to make a way, and waiting is sometimes the hardest thing to do.

I've been through many seasons of waiting and I've learned a few keys that have helped me to remain humble and submitted to the leadership in my life. This helped me to understand the *when* and *how* God could use me in creative worship.

Four Keys to Apply While God Makes a Way

Remain Prayerful

Bring all your petitions to God. I found the more I talked to God, not others, about my concerns, feelings, questions, etc. the less I desired validation from my leaders, peers and their thoughts. (Philippians 4:6)

Remain Humble

We can handle all unfair treatment peacefully when we are humble. We will also find peace amid unfair judgment. (Philippians 2:3, Ephesians 4:2)

Surround Yourself With Wise Counsel

We must choose our counsel wisely; people who will speak the truth, people who challenge us to better ourselves, and people who have a genuine desire for us to succeed. (Proverbs 19:20)

Worship God in the Secret Place

We must set time aside to be quiet before the Lord, offer our gifts and talents to Him as an extravagant expression of love. Personally, I love to put on an anointed worship CD, turn up the volume and worship Him uninhibited. (Psalm 91:1)

The following scripture in the book of Peter is also a very good key on where we should keep our focus in our walk with God.

> You have never seen Him but you love Him. You cannot see Him now but you are putting your trust in Him. And you have joy so great that words cannot tell about it. You will get what your faith is looking for, which is to be saved from the punishment of sin.
>
> 1 Peter 1:8-9 NLV

Let us love Him, trust Him, and allow the joy of the Holy Spirit to fill our hearts. Let us allow our faith to increase in Him and protect us from the pride that knocks at our door. As we embrace Him, He will make a way and empower us to shed light on some serious issues that plague the Church today.

He will show us, through His Word, how we can be used, how to play an instrumental part in restoring the creative arts back to the Church where it originally belonged. He will also help us to shed light on the truth of the impact that the creative arts have on our personal growth as creative types and as creative worshipers.

There have been many theological and religious battles over this very topic. My focus in this book, and the purpose of it is to highlight the importance of the heart of the worshiper, whether they are creative or not. When we have given our heart to God, it doesn't confine us. It sets us free from ourselves and liberates us in our worship.

This brings us to the next question about worship and the creative arts.

WHY ARE THE CREATIVE ARTS MISUNDERSTOOD?

To answer this question, we return to the spirit of Leviathan. This twisted spirit has led the Church to believe that embracing the creative arts as part of worship is not meant for the Church.

Instead, this spirit wants us to believe the creative arts belong to the world. This spirit has defiled the creative arts, making it an idol that serves the world as entertainment and self-gratification.

The spirit of Leviathan knows that the Kingdom of God is unshakable and if he can get us to believe a lie, He can conceal the truth and keep us from God's will. We are unshakable when we focus on God, when we worship Him in spirit and truth with holy fear and reverence. Anything that comes against us will be devoured by God's holy fire. (Hebrews 12:28-29)

We live in a fallen world and there are battles that believers face every day, especially regarding the topic of creative worship. These battles are intended to shush creative types into a corner, stripping them of their confidence and self-esteem through suppression, mockery and control.

This is all because of the lie the spirit of Leviathan has woven into the hearts of those who have not yet embraced the Holy Spirit and the truth of God's Word regarding creative types.

In James 4:6-10 we are given clear instructions on how to resist the devil and overcome the enemy. Once again we see, Humility is the antidote to pride.

> But He gives more grace. Therefore He says: "GOD RESISTS THE PROUD, BUT GIVES GRACE TO THE HUMBLE." Therefore submit to God. Resist the devil and he will flee from you. Draw near to God and He will draw near to you. Cleanse your hands, you sinners; and purify your hearts, you double-minded. Lament and mourn and weep! Let your laughter be turned to mourning and your joy to gloom. Humble yourselves in the sight of the Lord, and He will lift you up.
>
> James 4:6-10 NKJV

Yes, it is hard to face battles, especially when it comes from people we expect to have understanding. Trust me, I've been there and it hurts. It is in our human nature to want to fight back and prove ourselves. It only makes matters worse when the person we are trying to convince doesn't have a renewed mind in the Holy Spirit towards the arts.

We read in the book of James that it is God who will oppose the proud. So, it is not our battle but God's. Then James tells us that those who choose to remain humble will be given grace. Grace is powerful. Grace grants favor and honor that usually comes from someone in leadership. So, God will vindicate us as long as we submit ourselves to Him in humility.

How can we obtain God's grace during trials and temptations? We simply ask for it. In my case I cried out for it when I didn't know where else to turn because of the bondage of Bulimia.

I reached a point where I didn't care what anyone else thought about me anymore. I was miserable. The pride in my life fought hard to keep me bound by the grips of Bulimia, but my surrender released the Holy Spirit to shatter the pride in my life. I knew I could not do it in my own power.

As we choose to understand and embrace humility and grace, we will be empowered to resist the world and its enticing devices. The pleasures of the world will lose its shininess and fade away. Do you want to walk in power? Grab a hold of God's grace. His grace is truly all we will need especially in our weakest moments. (2 Corinthians 12:9)

PEACE & HOLINESS

Peace is something the world cannot offer or provide. Dating back to biblical times there have been many battles and wars. Today, we face opposition and battles daily that threaten to steal our peace.

When a car suddenly pulls out in front of us, a simple errand to the grocery store can rob us of our peace. The many years I strived to succeed in my career as a ballet dancer never produced peace. I was in constant turmoil watching my diet, practicing many hours every week and competing as often as I could.

I was striving for recognition in all the wrong places. Only when I surrendered and embraced the Holy Spirit did I finally find the recognition I yearned for. It was only then that I found peace. The recognition I needed no longer came from man. It now comes from my Father, God.

It is interesting that God's Word tells us that we must pursue peace. Pursue means: *to chase after with the intent of apprehension.*

> Pursue peace with all *people*, and holiness, without which no one will see the Lord:
>
> Hebrews 12:14 NKJV

The pursuit of peace does not just mean we must desire peace. It means we must also do our part to apprehend it through action.

How do we do this? We surrender our lives and agenda to God. We worship Him in the posture of God-worship. This provides God with a bare canvas He can creatively work on, and through, with the purpose of impacting our lives and the lives of others.

God is the one who makes us holy. We advance His Kingdom through a willing obedience to the leading of His Holy Spirit. Our God-worship empowers us to confidently take back territory from the devil and his demons. The creative arts is territory we must reclaim and restore to the Church to glorify God.

I love how teacher, speaker and prophet, Steve Thompson puts it, "We are supernatural beings living in a natural world. Our purpose is to advance the Kingdom of heaven on this earth until we push the devil and his demons off." – paraphrased.

When my pride was shattered I found a peace that I hold dear, even to this day. When I find that my peace is being threatened I focus my energy on entering His presence through His Word, through prayer and through worship. It doesn't take long before the peace of God fills my heart again.

CONCLUSION

In conclusion, there is a place for creative types in the Church. We must re-establish it in faithfulness to God's Word. We must resist the devil's lies and traps in doing this. We must resist the temptations of this world.

Pride is a big one, and one of the most powerful spirits we will battle. But we can rest assured that nothing is too big for God to overcome, as long as we are willing. God cannot work through someone who is prideful. He must have our surrender, our humble heart.

I encourage you to surrender and embrace the Holy Spirit as you draw closer to God through worship. If there's not a place for creative worship at your church, then find a place, even if that means doing it in your living room or back yard.

We cannot effectively pursue what is in front of us when we keep turning back to our past and rehearsing it over and over again. **Let go of what is behind you so that you can reach for what is in front of you**.

When we pursue the heart of God, trust that He fights our battles for us, the spirit of Leviathan must release the grip it has on our lives. Use the natural antidote of humility to allow God to defeat the supernatural stronghold of pride.

Remain humble and turn your back on the ill feelings that come from being misunderstood or unfairly attacked by those who are not walking in the full knowledge of God's truth regarding the creative arts as part of worship.

Turning your back on these feelings is not ignoring them, but rather rejecting them. Instead of looking back, face forward and pursue God. When you do this, you give Him permission to take care of it for you.

This will make letting go of offenses easy. Revenge will find itself kicked to the curb, and the critical voices of pride will fall on deaf ears. As we forgive others who operate out of ignorance, we reveal the heart of God to them. Jesus is both the answer and our deliverer. Forgiveness is a strength. Forgiveness is not the admission of wrong or a sign of being weak.

In fact, it takes a strong person to forgive, even when the opposing party won't accept your forgiveness, or when they are unaware that they have hurt or offended you. (Matthew 6:14-15)

There is no condemnation in Christ. Pride is paralyzed by humility. Offense is disabled by love. Forgive and forget. Walk in peace and know that Jesus is seated at the right hand of Father God. He is still on the throne, and His Spirit fights our battles for us.

> He who overcomes [*the world through believing that Jesus is the Son of God*], I will grant to him [*the privilege*] to sit beside Me on My throne, as I also overcame and sat down beside My Father on His throne.
>
> Revelation 3:21 AMP

10

TOOLS OF CREATIVE WORSHIP

Flags, Banners, Billows, Color & Sound

And there are [*distinctive*] varieties of ministries and service, but it is the same Lord [*who is served*]. And there are [*distinctive*] ways of working [*to accomplish things*], but it is the same God who produces all things in all believers [*inspiring, energizing, and empowering them*].

1 Corinthians 12:5-6 AMP

It is well known that the creative arts have a powerful impact on people. It can attract and captivate one person or an entire audience. The performer has all the power to take us on an emotional journey wherever they choose. That is when the performance is directed toward people.

However, when God is our audience we have seen in scripture that going through the motions or having a flawless performance are nothing to Him. We can only please Him when we surrender our whole being over to Him, for His glory, in creative worship.

Creative people are generally passionate and artistic. These are gifts from God that we are naturally inclined, even driven, to use in our lives. When we engage in creative worship, we offer these gifts back to God, and that expression can take many forms.

As we express these gifts, we often use creative tools. In this chapter we explore the use of tools to express our creative worship, and the power they have to impact our worship, the people around us and the Church, God's people.

We'll see how these tools will glorify God and benefit others. We'll explore the purpose and function of flags, banners and billows. We'll look at how color and sound can speak without words.

As we explore the purpose and use of these tools I will share some of my personal experiences and how they have impacted my journey.

If you haven't been already, you should be wondering at this point: How powerful, captivating and impacting can a Holy Spirit led creative worship experience be?

Even though I have been a part of many amazing creative worship experiences, I still wonder about it. I still desire a greater and greater engagement with our God through worship.

When I was first exposed to the use of flags in worship, I couldn't quite wrap my mind around the idea. All I knew about flags was how they were used in color guards and dance routines. The use of flags by an individual flag dancer, or flagger seemed odd, and ineffective. Flags are meant to be used in groups, right?

I wasn't as naive when it came to the use of banners or sheets of fabric. As a trained dancer, I could envision how fabric, flowing beautifully during intimate moments of worship would not only look pretty but also add to the dynamic of a dance routine.

Billows on the other hand were not even on my radar. Until I saw billows in action at my friend's church in Cape Town, South Africa, I would never have thought that it would have any place in a worship setting.

Flags, banners, billows, sheets of fabric, instruments, voices, paintbrushes, etc. are just tools we can use as part of our worship. They each have a unique function in communicating a message, achieving an expression, action and unified response.

If you want to build a house it requires lots of tools to get the job done. It requires supplies like bricks, mortar, wood, nails, windows, doors, roof tiles, etc. These supplies cannot just sit on the job site and be called a house. It takes a coordinated team of construction workers, working together with one goal in mind and using the necessary tools to build a house.

I was introduced to dance as a form of worship when I was in my early twenties shortly after immigrating to the USA. When I visited a couple churches, I saw the flags and banners being used as part of worship. I was surprised by what I saw. I didn't see much technique in terms of what I had grown up seeing as part of my dance training. My formal ballet training technique was always a very important part of being successful as a performer.

As a little girl in South Africa, I attended a church that would do a yearly production. It would require auditions for vocals, dancers and musicians. My understanding of what was acceptable was framed by my earlier experiences where ability and excellence were the keys to being successful in the arts.

Given my background and training in the arts, when I was first exposed to creative worship I wasn't humble. I admit that I was critical. As I watched and observed dancers or flaggers participate in worship I struggled to understand their purpose because I was so focused on critiquing their performance and technique.

There was an internal conflict between what I was taught and what I saw. I didn't recognize how their creative expression of worship prepared the way for God's glory to fall, to transform lives.

I saw lots of motions and actions, but I didn't see the expression of real feeling or raw emotions in their eyes. It seemed like there was a disconnect between the actions and the heart. They didn't seem fully engaged with their whole being in the expression of worship.

It's hard to explain in mere words, but ultimately it seemed like there was no heart, no passion, just motions. I was taught in dance that these were essential elements.

This bothered me because just the motions without true and honest emotion lost its impact. The sincere emotion from one's heart is what moves or prompts others to focus on Jesus and engage in worship. In a way, the sincere emotion is like a street sign that gets your attention and then redirects your attention to where you should go.

Other things that became evident were a lack of understanding of the connection between motion and emotion, as well as a lack of emphasis on any kind of training beyond the basics. I was looking at this through the critical eyes of a dancer. I was looking at it through the critical lens of the world.

Because of my background and what I saw, I became less interested in dance as part of worship. I was more focused on what was lacking instead of considering what I could do to support creative art worship groups.

Then, the Lord responded. He began stoking a fire in my spirit that ultimately started me on the journey I am on today. I thought, if the world requires training, practice and the 'it' factor to be considered acceptable and pleasing, what would happen if Christians also committed to pursuing excellence as they offer their gifts and talents to God in worship? God wants our whole heart and being, but shouldn't we also be committed to giving Him our best?

I could see the Church has plenty of talent and ability. Many members of our churches are using those talents in worldly occupations and pursuits. But I recognized the 'it' factor isn't quite there yet. For the most part, the Church has yet to tap into the 'it' factor. This point strikes at the worshiper's heart and the emotional part of the creative arts.

In the world, the 'it' factor normally translates to when a dancer or performer has an inward substance and raw emotion that comes from deep within them, in addition to their talent and ability. It draws the audience in and takes them on an emotional journey.

This inward substance and raw emotion is usually birthed from experiences of hurt, pain or an impressionable experience that caused the person to tap into a deep and strong emotion.

I began to imagine the powerful impact the Church would have if we applied similar principals of training and practice with sincere emotional expression (the 'it' factor)? I began to imagine a Church that rises up as the example to the world of arts. Instead of the Church looking to the world, the world would glean inspiration from the Church. This vision and dream is one that looks absolutely glorious, powerful and transformational.

As God was planting these seeds in my heart, I envisioned a glorified Church that has a face-to-face encounter with God in true God-worship, a Church completely transformed by His glory. It is a Church set on fire with passion and purpose that impacts and transforms the lives of many; the hurt, rejected, the prodigals.

I can see a revival coming that will sweep across this world through a nameless and faceless people, who are empowered and transformed, and who reach people in all areas of society, cultures, and sectors.

As my journey continued from that point, it was clear God had put His plan for me in motion. He started me on a path to find people who shared a similar passion and vision of true God-worship. He connected me with people who understood that when adding our gifts and talents to the mix it would take our worship to a whole new level.

It became impossible to deny the strong call I felt deep inside my spirit to restore the arts back to God and the Church.

In the book of Ephesians, we can see a prayer that the apostle Paul prayed for understanding. It became my prayer:

> I pray that your hearts will be able to understand. I pray that you will know about the hope given by God's call. I pray that you will see how great the things are that He has promised to those who belong to Him.
>
> Ephesians 1:18 NLV

As I began to study the Word of God and what it said about dance and the creative arts, I started seeing truth after truth revealed, and it set me free from the discouragement I originally felt about my desire to restore the arts back to the Church.

All I wanted was to be used, to be a part of the restoration. But I had no idea where to start. So, I started to educate and familiarize myself with what tools a dancer and creative artist would use, and what their functions were in the realm of the supernatural.

A very dear friend of mine, Ms. Joy Tate, was one of the first people God used early in my journey to help shed light on the arts and how it could be used as true God-worship. As time progressed my core group of friends began to grow and we began to see some common issues that would pop up when the topic of worshiping with flags, banners and billows were mentioned. So, it just made sense to figure out how to answer these questions about the purpose and function of our worship tools and their benefits.

KNOW YOUR TOOL

It is very important that as a creative worshiper we know the ins and outs of the tools we use to express ourselves through our gifts and talents. Our tool is just a means through which our gift or talent can manifest.

In my case my, my tools happen to be my body through dance, as well as flags and fabric. Our tools each have a function and are merely a means through which we communicate God's heart to others, and boldly declare to whom we are worshiping.

For a drummer, a set of drums is his tool. Imagine, in the throes of worship, someone who has never played drums before jumps on the drum set and starts banging on the drums. Worship will certainly end up in a train wreck.

The same applies to someone who has never worked with a flag before. When they pick up a pair of flags and start flailing the flags about, they could potentially injure someone, and will most definitely draw attention to themselves for the wrong reason, despite having pure and genuine intentions. It will distract others and draw them out of worship.

Just as musicians and singers take the time to practice, there needs to be a time of practice for dancers, flaggers, etc. It is not the time and place to practice in a corporate worship setting.

We need to set aside time to train and practice. In the privacy of our own homes, during practice sessions with the worship team, in creative worship workshops, we must train and practice with the intent of becoming familiar and proficient with our tools of worship, and their functions.

Conferences and corporate worship settings are not the place to learn. In my experience, my favorite times of worship have been the private times where I am worshiping, trying new and different moves. It's during these private moments I experience a different level of freedom.

In private, a person tends to be freer, and a greater level of creativity pours out. Being in a conference or corporate worship setting has other factors that affect our freedom, so it's harder to just let go and flow in your moves unless you have a high level of proficiency.

In corporate settings, fighting our mind and the thoughts of what others are thinking is the greatest battle.

FLAGS & BANNERS

Basic Purpose and Function of Flags and Banners

In the Bible, flags are typically referred to as a standard, banner or emblem. Since the word flag is rarely used in the English translations of the Bible, if we look at the Hebrew word for standard it is **degel**. **Degel** means a chief flag or banner. So, flags and banners are used interchangeably.

> "...When the enemy comes in like a flood, the Spirit of the Lord will lift up a standard against him."
>
> Isaiah 59:19b NKJV

Just by reading the above scripture we can safely assert that a flag can serve as a weapon to stop enemy advances into our lives and circumstances by raising a standard against him.

In the Merriam Webster dictionary, the definition of a flag is: a conspicuous object formally carried at the top of a pole and used to mark a rallying point especially in battle or to serve as an emblem; an organization flag carried by a mounted or motorized military unit; a long narrow tapering flag that is personal to an individual or corporation and bears heraldic devices.

In the Bible, flags were used for multiple reasons and it's usually related to battle. In Biblical times flags were used to identify the tribes and families of Israel. (Numbers 2:2) They were used extensively by Israel as governmental or tribal markers and as signals during wars. If flags weren't flown during battle, it would make the identification of different groups or nations very difficult, and lead to confusion. (Isaiah 62:10)

In the book of Jeremiah 51:27 we see an historical account of how flag or banner bearers would go out before the army. Their purpose was to signal that their army was approaching to conquer an area. The banner would make a declaration. It would send a message without using words. The message was clear and singular and it was interpreted the same without confusion on either side.

During worship, when I raise a flag, I declare the authority and power of the Lord Jesus Christ over the region. It's a signal that I represent and give authority to God, and that I proclaim He is the head of the region. I establish that I intend to conquer the region for Jesus.

Flags and banners are great tools designed to attract attention. In worship, the attention is not drawn to ourselves but directed to whom we represent, to whom we serve, Jesus Christ. Because flags are attractive and catch the attention of others it has the power to bring others into unity.

For example, during worship the Holy Spirit would prompt my heart with an urge to pick up a pair of flags, to signal that we are opening our hearts and welcoming the presence of Jesus into our worship. These motions appear as if I am opening a gate, except I'm holding flags. I hold the flags out in front of me in an upright position with my arms outstretched, and then I open my arms in a scissor-like motion, like opening curtains. I repeat this until I sense, through the Holy Spirit, that people are in one accord.

The basic functions of flags and banners in worship are simple: to declare that God is on the throne, to take back enemy territory, to advance God's Kingdom and to foretell of our victory!

I affectionately call my flags, my weapons of warfare for *warship*. The sound that a flag makes in *warship*, as it cuts through the air sends demons fleeing.

As I flag, I normally feel a spiritual stirring as people begin to unify in their worship. The level of their faith increases, their hunger for the presence of Jesus intensifies, and a supernatural shift takes place in the atmosphere. This shift creates the perfect environment for strongholds and bondages to be broken and cast down.

When we wholly surrender to the Spirit of God, the motions of the flags communicate a clear and precise message. They speak louder than our very own spoken words. Action speaks louder than words, especially at times when we don't know what to say or what to declare. (Titus 1:16)

Flags and banners are not only used as spiritual weapons of warfare to send the demons fleeing, they are also used to express praise and to rejoice over our circumstances. (Psalm 20:5)

A little different from a flag, a banner is a large rectangular piece of fabric, about 3-5 yards in length and usually used without a stick. Personally, I am drawn to worship with a banner when my worship becomes more intimate.

In the book of Song of Solomon, we see a collection of love songs. In the scripture below we see how a banner symbolizes love.

> He brought me to the banqueting house, and his banner over me was love.
>
> Song of Solomon 2:4 NKJV

Song of Solomon is filled with descriptions of romantic love between a husband and wife. It is also a beautiful symbol of the love relationship between the Lord Jesus Christ and His bride, the Church.

When worshiping with a banner in this manner I have tapped into a level and depth of worship where I feel His acceptance and unconditional love as I pour my affection on Him and present myself as a living sacrifice.

Banners are used to symbolize the sovereignty of Jesus, His authority, and His power and promise to protect us. Jesus is our standard (flag) and His standard is powerful, pure and holy. As we pursue holiness in our lives, we are raising up a spiritual standard against the enemy, under which we are safe. (Isaiah 59:19)

Here is an important key to keep in mind. We must know the *what* and the *why* when we engage in worship with our creative expression. When there is a lack of understanding and we don't know why we are using flags or banners, they will certainly become a distraction.

Comedian Michael Jr. once said this at a speaking engagement. He said that without knowing the *why* your *what* will not fulfill the purpose it was intended for.

Let me elaborate. If your tool is a flag then that flag is your *what*. The motive of your heart is the *why*. When you properly add the *why* to the *what*, God's plan and purpose will be fulfilled. The pure motive of your heart will ignite a holy passion in your moves, and it will breathe life into every action that follows suit.

The *why* is like a supernatural infusion of the Holy Spirit into our gifts and talents that will result in a divinely inspired message that is delivered through the *what*.

> Blessed be the Lord, my Rock and my keen and firm Strength,
> Who teaches my hands to war and my fingers to fight—
>
> Psalm 144:1 AMPC

David talks about the importance of training, especially for battle. We need to become familiar with our tools or weapons of worship. Practice, practice, practice. If we are not familiar with its function and purpose we will not benefit from it. Our tool will lose its divine impact and we will be deemed defeated in spiritual battles.

Training and practice prepares us. It makes a clear statement to God that we are ready and willing to obey His lead (unction) and be victorious in spiritual battles. (1 John 2:20)

Benefits of Flags & Banners in Worship

Flags and banners communicate a message that we might otherwise have difficulty verbalizing.

Are you familiar with the maxim: a picture is worth a thousand words? Instead of using words to communicate a message, the simple movement of a flag in worship can proclaim a powerful message with a different level of impact. A flag might be simple in its design, but it has the potential to speak directly, clearly and powerfully.

Personally, I find that when using the flags, I declare Jesus as the Lord of lords and King of kings. My movements tend to get bigger and greater. It makes a greater statement than I can by simply using my arms.

It is important to me that as I worship with flags that it is not about the flag itself. I do not depend on a flag to enter into the attitude or posture of God-worship. True God-worship starts in my heart. The flags are only the outward expression of what I am experiencing inwardly.

I like to think of the flags as an amplifier. I am the cable plugged into the source, Jesus. The supernatural current that flows through me is the anointing of the Holy

Spirit. His message is amplified and delivered through me for all to see.

I like to describe the use of flags in worship in another way. My flags become an extension of my arms. They become one with my body. There is no separation between me, the stick and flag. There is no distinct spot where my hand ends and the flag begins. This allows the movement of the flags to be one with me. If I were to drop the flags, my movement and expression should be unaffected.

Flags facilitate unity.

Flags encourages others to join in with rejoicing and glorifying God. I have found, especially with young people, that flags have a great influence on breaking the ice and drawing them in to engage and participate.

In sports, this is very common. Flags, pom-poms and other tools are used by spirit teams, cheerleaders and dancers, to engage and unify their audience.

Flags represent a spiritual weapon.

When raising up a banner we are raising up a standard against the enemy. Banners declare and enforce our victory over spiritual forces and wicked principalities.

> When the enemy comes in like a flood, the Spirit of the Lord will lift up a standard against him.
>
> Isaiah 59:19 NKJV

Personally, I find that when I worship with my flags I most often enter into warfare worship, or *warship*. When the flags make a "crack" sound, demons flee. The sharp direct movements that cut through the air with "cracks" enforce God's truth, power and victory.

The flags represent a spiritual weapon of warfare that I submit to the Holy Spirit as I confidently yield them as swords on the spiritual battlefield enforcing our victory as believers.

In the book of Psalm 47:1 we find a scripture that talks about the clapping of our hands and a shout of victory that sends demons fleeing.

As I "crack" my flag, which sounds a lot like a loud clap, this scripture comes to mind. Also, as I *warship*, the presence of God becomes so intense and powerful on the inside of me that I feel a deep roar building. It grows louder and louder until it escapes my mouth with a loud shout. I envision that with every "crack" or clap, loud roar or shout, I send demons to flight.

There are times that evil spirits are sent on assignment to disrupt church services. In my experience, witches like to target worship services to interfere and block people from engaging in and entering into worship.

When people are unable to enter God-worship they are prevented from coming into unity, operating in power and experiencing freedom. To the natural eye, it will appear as if people are distracted, apathetic, tired and don't want to participate or engage in worship. It requires a much greater effort for them to join in with song, clapping or raised hands.

These evil spirits function within the supernatural realm. So, if we want to break the power of these evil spirits we must take the battle into the spiritual realm with our worship.

> For we do not wrestle against flesh and blood, but against principalities, against powers, against the rulers of the darkness of this age, against spiritual hosts of wickedness in the heavenly places.
>
> Ephesians 6:12 NKJV

It is amazing how effective the flags are as weapons of warfare to battle against spiritual darkness. Personally, I *warship* until I sense a noticeable shift or change in the atmosphere. I battle until I sense there is a breakthrough and a release from the chains of the enemy.

Once there is a breakthrough, we notice that people begin to focus, engage and join in with song, raise their hands and participate as they begin to go deeper in their personal worship.

We don't stop here. We continue to pursue God in worship, even after we have the breakthrough and have overcome the tactics and assignments of the devil. With a breakthrough in the spiritual realm, the atmosphere is free of hindrances and obstacles. This is the spiritual atmosphere in which miracles happen.

Spiritual Breakthroughs

There are various manifestations of spiritual breakthroughs. As people receive the transforming touch of God and are set free, they often break out in spontaneous and celebratory clapping.

Others may start jumping, become undone and run around the building. While others find themselves twirling and spinning without inhibition or restraint. Breakthrough in worship is total freedom, no matter what the cost and regardless of the obstacles.

God desires for us to be free of anything that would hold us back or block us from entering intimate God-worship. He desires freedom and liberty for His children. I cannot put it in better words than what God's Word says in Hebrews:

Therefore, since we are surrounded by so great a cloud of witnesses [*who by faith have testified to the truth of God's absolute faithfulness*], stripping off every unnecessary weight and the sin which so easily and cleverly entangles us, let us run with endurance and active persistence the race that is set before us, [*looking away from all that will distract us and*] focusing our eyes on Jesus, who is the Author and Perfecter of faith [*the first incentive for our belief and the One who brings our faith to maturity*], who for the joy [*of accomplishing the goal*] set before Him endured the cross, disregarding the shame, and sat down at the right hand of the throne of God [*revealing His deity, His authority, and the completion of His work*]. Just consider and meditate on Him who endured from sinners such bitter hostility against Himself [*consider it all in comparison with your trials*], so that you will not grow weary and lose heart.

Hebrews 12:1-3 AMP

Story of the Fire Flags

I have a pair of flags that I call my fire flags. They are satin and they look like flames of red, orange and black. They were the first pair of flags I made and owned and hold a special place in my heart, not because of how they look, move or feel, but because of how God used them to orchestrate and set His plan for my life and ministry into motion.

God's hand was in it from the minute I bought and made these flags to the moment I first worshiped with them in Iloilo, Philippines.

As much as God has done for me, He never ceases to amaze me. For nearly 10 years prior to the Philippines trip, it was prophesied over me that I would be a revival fire carrier to the nations.

Then in 2005 at the Breakthrough Conference in Buenos Aires, Argentina, God confirmed these prophesies in a vision. He showed me that I would travel the world as a revival fire carrier. At that time I was apprehensive about traveling internationally on my own. Knowing this, God showed me I wasn't alone. In Argentina He revealed to me my guardian angel and told me I had nothing to fear. This was the setup for the Fire Flag story!

I believe this story is so important to share because it not only fulfilled these prophecies, but it impacted my life, increased my faith and trust in God, and impacted the lives of others in deep and intimate ways.

These fire-flags, while at the center of the story, they are simply the tools that God used to work through me in strategic warfare, nothing else.

The story begins in 2006 when a dear friend, Sheryll Weyers Pedroja, invited me to join her on a ministry trip. She was taking a youth ministry team called Firestorm, from Australia, her home country, to the Philippines. I had met Sheryll about 3 months earlier in Argentina at the September 2005 Breakthrough Conference.

As a teenager God had birthed a passionate fire in my spirit, one I wanted to use in dance as an expression of worship, not just as a special church performance. This trip is where this growing passion and expression would find a place in God's plan for me.

It was on this trip to the Philippines that I also learned what it was to rely on the Holy Spirit alone, and not on my own ability for dance.

During the Firestorm conference in the Philippines, my passion was finally released and given purpose. I recognized that God didn't just gift me with talent to dance for mere pleasure but He wanted to use me as a trigger, a spark to ignite His fire within others.

I am His Firestarter. His holy fire not only burns away our old ways and old thinking, but it brings renewal in our minds and a glorious transformation of our whole body.

As I considered Sheryll's invitation, I struggled with whether or not to accept the invitation. I wanted to be sure this trip was part of God's will and plan for me. I felt like God was moving in my life, and I didn't want to make a mistake.

Being curious by nature, I hopped onto Google and searched images. As I clicked the search button, the first picture I laid my eyes on stunned me. I was literally speechless. Suddenly, two dreams that I had flashed before my eyes.

Five or six months before I met Sheryll, I had two God-given dreams, each about a month apart. Both dreams were similar in terms of the venue, setting and theme. The venue was at an airport, in a tropical setting. Lots of young people were everywhere, all excited about attending a conference or concert.

I was stunned because these pictures were snapshots taken right from my dreams! I remembered the young people's excitement. I have always been drawn to the youth. I know that if I can impact and influence just one young person, speak Christ's identity over them, and show them the power they have when they have a heart connected and knit together with Jesus, they will graduate into adulthood with ease. They will find that living a supernatural lifestyle with passion and fire is attainable and sustainable.

I believe there is something unique that can be said of young people. They have a fearless passion and drive, and they exhibit a vulnerability that hasn't been quenched due to hurt or disappointment.

As for adults, that is not quite the case. Biologically adults lose that youthfulness, and life's challenges tends to stifle that passion.

I was prepared to accept the invitation to join Sheryll and her team, but I had no clue what lay ahead. I didn't even know where in the world the Philippines was located. As I sat there, I told God that if this was part of His plan for me I would accept it by faith and trust that He had it all laid out.

That is when He responded by flooding my spirit with complete peace. Even though my mind was yelling at me, telling me that the Philippines is too far, especially traveling much of the trip alone, and that the flights and accommodation would be too expensive.

At that moment I had confidence God was completely behind this trip, so I accepted with great enthusiasm.

As I began planning and booking flights and accommodations, my mind was still doing its best to talk me out of it. But I was committed and I declared that if I had somehow missed God's instruction, then I would consider it a lesson and not a mistake.

I would commit to serve the team and the people with the same heart and passion as if it were His plan. I chose to submit my heart as a servant to Him for the advancement of His Kingdom, and not worry about whether I was right or wrong in deciding to take this trip.

As the preparations continued, God affirmed my decision at every turn. The recollection of my two dreams became clearer, and the prophesy of being a revival fire carrier began to materialize. I realized the name of the ministry team I would join was Firestorm, and the song Sheryll emailed me to dance to for the opening of the conference was "Burn" by Planet Shakers.

While God ordained this trip, I also learned that no one is exempt from spiritual opposition. By faith, I had to remain focused and push through enemy opposition. As I began working on choreography for the song, my mind and emotions were the target of attacks. I kept hitting a wall. Nothing would flow or come easily.

Staying focused by faith, I began to cut the fabric I purchased to start making a pair of flags. The satin fabric would fray after I cut it and moved it. This was not a good scenario for flag worship, since they would be vigorously moved about.

Not owning a sewing machine at this point, I grabbed our fireplace lighter. I figured since I was only using these flags for one song, they just needed to last that long. I took the lighter and carefully melted the edges, shaping them to stop the fabric from fraying.

Thinking back on this, God showed me the symbolism in this. This burning symbolized a burning away of the chaff, the worthless and trivial things that clutter & busy our lives. This burning welcomed the fire of His presence to purify and shape me as a person.

God revealed to me that when I use these flags, His passion and fire would flow from my surrendered heart through the fabric and out over the people, igniting them on fire.

At the international airport in Manila, I met up with the Firestorm youth team from Australia. The domestic airport was another 30-minute drive away so we took a taxicab to make our connecting flight to Iloilo, one of the islands.

Once we arrived at the domestic airport, as we waited on our last flight I sat down to relax. Looking around, I looked up, and once again, a vision from my dreams came rushing back from memory.

This airport was exactly like the venue in my dreams. It was also constructed of glass. I was overcome with emotion and humbled that God would speak to me this way. His love overwhelmed me as I sat there and experienced how much God cared about me, how He knew I needed reassurance, and how He had already taken care of all the little and finer details in advance.

I was finally able to choreograph my dance, and I danced for the opening song of the Firestorm Conference.

There were 9 more meetings remaining in the conference, and at the end of the first meeting, Sheryll asked me to dance for each of the remaining meetings. It was super scary because at this point I had relied on my talent and ability to dance according to my choreography.

When dancing before 13-20 year olds, there is a high level of expectation and a keen perception of whether I was dancing according to my own ability, or whether I was being led purely by the Holy Spirit.

But God had other plans. He wanted to stretch me. He set me up to rely on the leading of the Holy Spirit alone. He put me in a place where I had to trust in Him.

Sheryll was a blessing to me throughout this trip. God used her to broaden my idea of how dance can be used in worship. She would have me dance between her message and the altar call. The purpose was to prepare an atmosphere through which God's miracles would be available to anyone who might need them.

This simple but powerful gesture of giving my gifts and talents over to God and following the Holy Spirit in my dance allowed His manifest glory to fall upon the room like a blanket.

I remember vividly the moment Sheryll asked me to swirl the fire flags above her head as she kneeled. Later, she described the experience as physically unbearable, but spiritually charging and transforming. Sheryll described that experience as the moment God burned away the chaff in her own life.

I was truly humbled by this whole experience. I learned that I should never take anything for granted and that I should not ignore the small things. Had I ignored my dreams or dismissed the fire related symbols, I would've missed out on God's communication and reassurance.

The ministry team name, the song I danced to, and the burning of my fire flags were not merely coincidence. It was God leading me through His amazing creative Spirit.

BILLOWS

Just as a flag is a tool of worship, so is a billow. A billow is a long stretch of fabric about 5-6 yards in length and requires two people to handle it. Two people work together to create large wavelike motions.

The motions of the billows remind me of the way Native American Indians communicated through smoke signals, creating billows of smoke in the sky. They use a wet blanket and hold it over an open fire to contain the smoke. When they would lift the blanket, the smoke would escape, creating billows of smoke.

They would do this intermittently to create the smoke signals. They used this practice to quickly and visually communicate messages to one another over long distances, or across areas that were difficult to travel.

When I host a workshop, I like to start out with using billows. Not only does it break the ice, but it also shifts the atmosphere. When people are relaxed and at ease they tend to be more sensitive to the Holy Spirit. Using the billows begins to shift the atmosphere and brings everyone into unity.

As we worship together in unity, we create an environment for the presence of God and His glory to manifest in our presence. In corporate worship, the billows do the same, just on a different scale.

On one of my ministry trips to Haiti we used 6 billows during worship. They were arranged side by side, as if they were stacked horizontally. They were all billowing in unison. From the congregation's view, it looked like a river. As the billows moved with the rhythms and beats of the African drums it created a vibrant and energetic billow river. I danced up and down between the billows, and an atmosphere of joy and celebration filled the building.

People began dancing up and down the aisles while others just danced right in their seat. It shifted the atmosphere to a whole new level of glory, one that empowered everyone present with a joy and boldness.

Billows are a great means to communicate visual messages during worship. When I use billows, I like to use them in ways that move, or stir the atmosphere. A simple, but exaggerated wavelike motion of the billows creates a sense of majesty.

When 2 or more billows join together and cross over it looks like a canopy. As the canopy of billows stays up, people like to dance or simply walk under them. I've heard people testify that they received healings and deliverance during these worship sessions.

Billows can be used in more complex ways; crossing over and weaving to create different shapes or symbols, for example. Using 2 billows, strategically crossed over each other can create the shape of a cross. Moving the billows from side to side is a way of shifting and directing the atmosphere over the people.

As I am in the throes of worship and the Spirit of God is moving powerfully, I envision the billows catching the glory of God from heaven and pouring it out over the people, releasing transforming waves of His glory.

This reminds me of a profound experience I had at the 2010 Louisiana Outpouring meetings I attended in Pineville Louisiana.

My husband and I were part of the worship team. My husband worshiped through prophetic painting while I *warshipped* with the flags. The presence and power of God began to manifest with such intensity that at one point His glory cloud filled the sanctuary.

To the natural eye, it appeared as a thick hazy mist. A profound moment lingered as the worship team paused, but remained worshipful. You could sense something extraordinary was about to be released, something that had been building in the Spirit. It was a moment that hovered, waiting for the right moment to pour out over the congregation.

This moment, or pause, made me think of the transition phase a mother experiences just before she gives birth. Medically, the transition is typically described as the time where the mom enters a short quiet phase, just before the baby emerges.

Metaphorically, I believe this applies to our worship also. When we worship and reach a moment where it gets quiet, where there is a momentary stillness, it is at this point that we need to be sure not to lose focus. It is imperative that we are not distracted, ready for what God is about to birth through the Spirit.

As this moment of stillness hovered over the Louisiana Outpouring congregation, I looked over at the worship leader and he looked back at me. I knew by his expression he couldn't sing. I glanced over at my pastor. His eyes were closed as he basked in the moment.

I looked at the congregation and many were also basking like my pastor. Others were looking around the sanctuary as if they were trying to figure out was going to happen next. When I looked back at the worship leader, he was lying flat on his face on the platform in complete surrender.

The place fell beautifully silent. I quietly motioned to my dad to help pull out and stretch a red billow across the platform. We began to wave the billows. At first the motions were slow and deliberate, moving up and down. It transitioned into more forceful waves going out over the congregation. I saw visions of waves of God's fire and glory pour out over His people.

A low groan began to grow and stir in the hearts of the people. One by one a roar began to escape the mouths of the people. It was a sound of war, a victorious roar against the forces of darkness. The roar kept intensifying until almost everyone began to shout. It was so intense I thought the roof was going to blow right off the building.

This was the delivery of God's glorious impartation of fire, power and victory. An army of victorious worshipers arose at that moment on that day. It was a glorious and powerful moment that forever transformed the lives of hundreds of people in attendance that day. There was a true outpouring of His holy and empowering anointing.

After that service, while I was in the green room, I heard an account from a lady about what she had experienced during this transition, the quiet moment in worship.

This lady urgently needed a restroom break. So, she hurried down the aisle to the restrooms in the lobby area in the front of the church. At this point, she was unaware that the sanctuary had fallen silent. Standing in the restroom line, she was suddenly overwhelmed with the presence of God. She felt a rushing wind blow down the hallway and a heavy blanket of His glory enveloped her. Overcome, she began to worship Him right there in the hallway.

She confirmed in her testimony that the rushing wind had occurred at the same

160

time the billows began moving out over the people. God used the motions of the billows to send waves of His glory throughout the whole building, even down the hallways. I was humbled and so thankful to have been a part of this experience as God moved to touch His people.

COLOR & SOUND

Color is a fun subject to delve into. Color is such an amazing way through which God can speak to us visually, and to impact a person's mind and body without words. If you look around you, you'll see God's awesome work in full color; birds, animals, forests, crystals and gemstones, mountains, sunsets, and more.

Color and sound are very similar and they share a common fundamental characteristic; they both consist of vibration, or frequency. While most of us know that sound is made up of frequencies, we don't often think of color as frequency.

Color is light frequency, and it can have a physiological and emotional impact on us. In other words, color can have a tangible physical affect on us, prompting an emotional response. Refer back to nature and you can likely recall the emotional impact of a beautiful sunset or sunrise you've experienced.

In the first reference to light in the scriptures, we find an account involving both color and sound.

> Then God said, "Let there be light"; and there was light. And God saw the light, that *it was* good; and God divided the light from the darkness.
>
> Genesis 1:3-4 NKJV

This first account was when God spoke light into existence. This statement is quite deep because speech is vibrational frequency, or sound. When God released His words He sent out vibrational frequencies. What He spoke from the supernatural realm manifested in the natural realm.

Indeed, this is how God created. He used sound, His voice, to create, and He used color in His creation.

Science shows that light, like sound, is composed of frequency, and frequency is distinguished by its wavelength. Sound is emitted in many different wavelengths, and is sensed and distinguished by our ears.

Color is emitted in many different wavelengths, and is sensed and perceived by our eyes. Each color consists of its own unique wavelength.

Why the science lesson? Research shows us that color influences a person's mood, behavior, stress levels, etc. Like music is a composition of sound, much of what we experience in the world is a composition of color. Both can have profound physical effects on us.

As we just saw in Genesis 1:3, God can traverse the natural and the supernatural through frequency, the spoken Word and the light of His creation.

I read this quote on Wikipedia, and as I read it God revealed to me the impact His light (supernatural wavelengths of pure color) can have on us as believers amid God-worship:

> "Newton observed that, when a narrow beam of sunlight strikes the face of a glass prism at an angle, some is reflected and some of the beam passes into and through the glass, emerging as different-colored bands."

Imagine that we are like prisms. When we allow the light of God to strike our face as we worship Him, it will not only cause us to reflect His image in our creative expression of worship, but His light will pierce our heart and transform us.

His light transforms us inwardly, which is then expressed or reflected through our outward actions, even the motions of our worship. Transformed, our worship will no longer be monochromatic in nature, but it will emerge as colorful and bright, expressed through many different wavelengths of color.

The colors of our worship will transform the atmosphere as it impacts the mood and behavior of others who look upon our worship. The light of God heals. It restores. It makes us whole.

Understanding frequency and the relationship between color (light) and sound helps us understand why we are drawn to certain colors at certain times during worship. When we use a flag, banner or billow in worship, we are activating these principals in both the natural and supernatural.

Benefits of Color in Worship

Let's look at a few examples of different colors and their meanings according to the scriptures.

White

Pure light is described as the color of white. Biblically, the color white represents purity, holiness, cleanliness, innocence and honesty. (Psalm 51:7)

Gold

A gold banner speaks of God's divinity, God's glory and holiness, wealth, power and knowledge. In biblical times rulers and kings were adorned in gold, demonstrating their authority. In the construction of the tabernacle and Ark of the Covenant, God provided instruction that they should be constructed of gold. Specifically regarding the Ark's construction, gold symbolized God's deity while the acacia wood represented humanity. (Exodus 25:17-18; Exodus 28:36)

Brown

Brown symbolizes repentance, humility and the dead things in our life. When we repent with humility, our old ways die and we are spiritually reborn. (Daniel 9:3-4)

Grey

Grey symbolizes worldly wisdom gained throughout the years of our life. It is often used to symbolize weakness and foolishness also. (Proverbs 16:31; Hosea 7:9)

Blue

There are multiple symbolisms for this color. They range from heaven, holy covering and service, and chastening (to be humble or restrained). (Exodus 24:10; Exodus 28:31; Proverbs 20:30)

Red

This is my favorite color and I find myself drawn to this one almost every time I worship. It symbolizes victory and represents overcoming the attacks of the enemy. It represents the blood of Christ, the power and promise of the resurrection. (Nahum 2:3; Hebrews 9:14)

Rainbow

The rainbow, all of the primary colors, represents God's promise to never flood the earth again. It also signifies the glory, majesty and honor of the Lord Jesus Christ. (Genesis 9:13,15; Revelation 4:2-3)

Our worship is the beginning of an intimate conversation between man and God. God speaks to us in many ways. As we explored the various tools of worship in this chapter, we learned how to let Him speak to us and through us, as we allow His message to be delivered amid our God-worship.

Flags, banners, billows and color make nonverbal declarations that speak louder than words. Color is a universal language that all creeds, races and people understand. How much more powerful will our worship be when His purpose is reflected and released in truth, through us, as we display His glorious love, compassion and nature?

THE TECHNIQUE OF CREATIVE WORSHIP

I believe it is important that I conclude this chapter by exploring the technique of worship using your chosen tool. Many times, people have asked me how and where can they learn how to worship with a flag, banner, billow, or all three.

When I teach creative worship workshops I focus on how the tool, like the flag, should be one with the person who wields it. It simply becomes an extension of the person. There should be no distinction between the person and the flag. If I were to remove the flag from the person, their movements should still flow the same way.

As a creative worshiper, when our worship starts from within our spirit and explodes as an outward expression, our whole body will move. There will be emotion and feeling with every move and it will flow through the flag, banner or billow.

The motions and movements should be an emotional response that stems from our core (bosom), which is our spirit man. That is where the Spirit of God flows from and through our body. It doesn't stop there. It then pours out through our tool of worship.

There are times when I am so enraptured in His glorious presence during worship that I forget I am even holding a flag. The flags begin to move in ways that deliver God's message through a beautiful picturesque display of God's heart. This is how I become His *living canvas*, His masterpiece.

Watching someone worship in this way makes it hard to separate the person from the flag. The flag no longer becomes the focal point, but the worshiper and flag become one and the heart of the Father is displayed for all to see. The person watching is automatically drawn in and emotionally moved to also engage in true God-worship.

They are encouraged and challenged to go deeper in their worship, no longer focused on man but instead to have their eyes fixed on Jesus. The focus shifts from the person wielding the flag to the One who is being worshipped.

I want to emphasize that no one tool of worship is better than another. Whichever tool you use makes no difference, as long as you are wholly surrendered to God when using it.

From flags, banners, billows and paintbrushes, to musical instruments, each has its own unique purpose and place as part of the worship team. When a worship team understands this fundamental aspect of the creative expression of worship, and operates in humility and unity, there will be no competition or desire to seek the limelight. The only person who should stand out, the only person in the limelight, should be Jesus.

My husband Mike, flows powerfully in prophetic painting. His tools of worship are paint and paintbrushes. He is very gifted with color and is creative to his core. His talent to create amazes me. The art pieces he creates are extraordinary. Some of his creative work includes designing and building furniture for people and pets, design of home interiors, design of couture pet clothing.

These are just a few extraordinary ways he can reach people for God's glory. God uses him to reach people and share the good news of the gospel, especially with like-minded creative people, people that others might not have access to.

Both he and I love to worship together with our gifts and talents. In our marriage, we are one and we find that our creative worship brings us closer together as a couple. We made a declaration to each other that we will always put God first in our relationship. Because of this decision, our marriage grows stronger and our relationship grows deeper.

While Mike paints during worship services I flow with the flags and dance. There have been times when I glance over and look at his canvas and he is painting what I just saw in the spirit and translated through the flags and dance.

People have attested to watching a timely message delivered through Mike's paintings that spoke very clearly and directly to them. Three people would testify to three different messages that witnessed in just one painting.

There is something supernatural in the relationship between the prophetic and visual arts that emerges during worship. It's incredible how together they can deliver timely messages to multiple people all at the same time. It's amazing how these messages are delivered on a canvas that is alive, a true living canvas.

To the natural mind this sounds impossible, but God knows what He is doing and knows how the creative arts impacts lives.

I believe God is restoring the arts to the Church through people who are wholly surrendered to Him. There is a sound of the rattling bones coming together like in Ezekiel 37 where the valley of dry bones rose up as a mighty army. God is using people like you and me to breathe life back into the creative arts, bringing the bones together, ready to rise as a mighty resurrected army of God.

It is important that the purity of God and His holiness remain at the forefront, firmly in the hearts of those who are in the creative arts.

A worship team cannot function in unity when a creative worshiper has a lone wolf mentality, seeking fame and recognition. We must surrender and always present ourselves humbly before God.

We must leave our agendas and worldly ideas of grandeur at the altar of sacrifice. We must allow the fire of His Holy Spirit to burn away the chaff that would otherwise hinder or stop us from presenting ourselves as pure and holy.

As we burn for Him in our true God-worship, let the fragrance of our burning be found pleasing to God. **A humble person is a teachable person. Always remain teachable!**

CONCLUSION

In closing, I want to reinforce that the tools of our worship are simply tools. There is nothing special or spiritual about the physical or material nature of our tools. When the power and anointing comes upon us, it flows through us.

Our flags, banners and billows reflect God's heart and purpose as He pierces and transforms the heart of the worshiper who wields the tool. Our tools must never overshadow our heart of true God-worship. Instead, they should amplify our adoration and praise for God, and reflect what the Holy Spirit is communicating in worship.

As a true God-worshiper we do not need these tools to worship. They simply amplify and enhance God's heart through our worship allowing for a shifting to take place in the atmosphere. They illuminate and reflect the heart of the Father who heals, delivers and sets His people free.

All God asks is that we are willing and obedient, surrendered with extreme submission and reverent adoration as we worship in spirit and in truth. When our heart is right, our tools will bring glory to God and prepare the atmosphere for God's Spirit to fulfill His purposes and set the captives free!

11

THE BLESSING OF ORDER
Fire Will Unlock Passion & Purpose

And He put all things [*in every realm*] in subjection under Christ's feet, and appointed Him as [*supreme and authoritative*] head over all things in the church, which is His body, the fullness of Him who fills and completes all things in all [*believers*].

Ephesians 1:22-23 AMP

Order is a topic that is not often talked or preached about in charismatic church circles. Yet is it is an essential principle necessary for a healthy Church.

God is a God of order, and His blessings and promises operate through His divine order. His plans and purposes for His Church, for each of our lives, proceed from a heavenly authority and through divine order.

Even in Heaven, there is a divine order. In Ephesians 1:15-23 Paul establishes the Godhead and its authority; God the Father, Jesus the Son, and the Holy Spirit. They operate as one, yet they are three divine persons, ordered and coordinated according to their divine roles.

God the Father is at the head of the Holy Trinity. The Father appointed Jesus as the ultimate authority over everything, including the body of Christ.

We also read in John 5:19, Jesus tells us that He can do nothing of His own accord, only what He sees the Father doing. Then, a few verses down, we see the unity of power and authority.

> Just as the Father raises up the dead and gives them life [*makes them live on*], even so the Son also gives life to whomever He wills and is pleased to give it.
>
> John 5:21 AMPC

This divine order and authority extends from the spiritual to the natural.

> Let every soul be subject to the governing authorities. For there is no authority except from God, and the authorities that exist are appointed by God.
>
> Romans 13:1 NKJV

God's divine order naturally extends to our churches as well. Paul reminds the Church in Galatians of his assignment and authority.

> PAUL, AN apostle--[*special messenger appointed and commissioned and sent out*] not from [*any body of*] men nor by or through any man, but by and through Jesus Christ (the Messiah) and God the Father, Who raised Him from among the dead--
>
> Galatians 1:1 AMPC

As worshipers, we must respect the authority and order within our churches. God has appointed our pastors and leadership. And if we expect to be a productive part of the church, we must honor God's Word, and we must honor the leadership and authority in our churches.

We each have a place in the plans and purposes of God, a place for which God created and prepared us, even before we were born. God is ready to use us. So the real question becomes, are we ready to be used by God?

To be used by God we must know our place, role and part in the body of Christ. Just like with the puzzle analogy mentioned earlier, we can't all be the same shaped piece. That would deem the puzzle useless and incomplete.

We are each a uniquely shaped puzzle piece, assigned a specific spot, a spot no other puzzle piece will fit. When we aren't placed in the right spot, we also prevent other puzzle pieces from being placed in their assigned spots.

The goal is to bring together each of the uniquely shaped pieces to reveal God's vision, His plan and purpose. God works through order and authority to accomplish this, often through churches and other Christian organizations.

This divine order creates an environment for the blessings of God to flow and produces the fruit of the Spirit; love, joy, peace, patience, kindness, goodness, faithfulness, gentleness and self-control. This is an essential principle through which God works.

Where order is lacking the devil has room to operate. A door to confusion is opened and a spirit of rebellion can take root, causing people to step outside of the protection godly order provides. We become easy targets for the enemy.

A mother hen that protects her baby chicks keeps them safe under her wings. If someone were to pick up the mother hen, the baby chicks would scurry around in confusion looking for the warmth and protection of their mother. The baby chicks are vulnerable to predators looking for a meal.

When we ignore or turn our back on godly order in our lives and the Church, we step out from under the shadow of the Almighty. We become vulnerable to the devil, who is forever on the prowl, seeking whom he can devour. (1 Peter 5:8)

The order of God extends from the supernatural into the natural. This is important to understand, because God works from Heaven. He delivers His will from Heaven through the Holy Spirit to accomplish it here on earth. (Matthew 6:10)

God is the ultimate authority to which man submits. God puts leaders of authority in place to hold us accountable, to keep order and maintain unity. This point cannot be overstated. It is so important that we submit to our God-appointed leaders, to those leaders who are submitted to God and His Word, and whose lives reflects what God's Word teaches. This is so that we can receive the fullness of God's will for our lives.

If you yourself are a leader, it is important to note that others are following your lead. I believe there are many in leadership roles that are unaware of this simple dynamic. As a leader, you must be submitted to God first. You must submit to your leadership and the vision of your church. You must be humble and attend to the needs of those following you. Remember, your actions speak louder than words, because most will learn by observing.

There's a saying that comes to mind from when I was a kid. When my dad did something that set a bad example, like licking the knife at mealtime, he would always tell us "Do what I say, not what I do." It didn't matter how many times he told us this, we still did what he did rather than what he said.

As a leader, I am happy to tell you I have leaders in my life that I submit to, who hold me accountable, so that I don't walk down a path that leads to pride and arrogance.

In our home we have a picture frame hung in a special spot we can plainly see each day. In it is the order we follow in our home: God, spouse, family (kids), career (job), calling. It establishes our focus and priorities.

Pastors, evangelists, missionaries, teachers and prophets have God-appointed leaders over their lives who hold them accountable and challenge them to go deeper in their walk with God. When we respect our leaders, it makes following godly order easier.

Understanding our place and purpose within the "chain of command" will bring us freedom and liberty, not restriction and confinement.

Sadly, there are leaders who have gone astray. They have lost sight of their role, responsibilities and from where their authority comes. They have fallen out of order and opened the door to attacks of the enemy. Through this open door, they have invited pride and arrogance into their hearts.

Signs of this are when titles and reputation become more important than their relationship with God. Instead, **pride picks up a mirror and all the leader can see is the reflection of self**, not of those they are leading.

Mirrors lead people to self-reflection. They judge their own appearance and compare it to those around them. This view opens the door to comparison, which causes division to creep into churches and causes horrible hurt and destruction.

Godly order turns that mirror into a window. It allows others to see in, while you look out. You cannot hide anything. A window keeps you honest and vulnerable. This window maintains humility that produces spiritual growth, not death.

Consider a different analogy for a moment. An army is preparing to go to war. The army's general is placed in a position of authority to establish and maintain order and unity. This order and unity is the strength of the army. It is also the means through which the battle plan is delivered and executed.

If someone steps out of order and begins barking orders, it would create confusion, bring division and ultimately lead to the destruction of the army. Order and authority are essential for victory.

As creative worshipers, we must respect and submit to authority, because it not only benefits us individually, it also benefits those around us. A rogue soldier will do more harm than good. He might survive, but his rebellion could bring injury and death to those around him.

The same applies within the Kingdom of God. When we go rogue we may experience momentary success, but we will leave a trail of hurt and destruction in our wake. God never intended for us to go rogue. He has called us to join the army of God, His Church.

In the context of a local church, the pastor is the general. He has been placed there to lead a group of people, the members of his church. When the pastor invites a guest speaker to preach at his church, he is giving the guest speaker the authority to speak into the lives of the members of his church, trusting the speaker will honor his authority.

Imagine what would happen if the guest speaker went rogue. He would undermine the authority and trust the pastor has with his members. The speaker would undermine the authority God has given him. This would lead to confusion, to hurt and possibly the loss of church members.

As creative worshipers, we must beware of operating outside of the leadership of the church. To find our place, we must be careful to find it under authority, and we must take care to operate under godly order.

THE BLESSINGS OF GODLY ORDER

Godly Order Creates a Protective Environment

As people operate in their gifts and talents in a safe and protected environment it will build confidence in them, whether it's worship or other activities.

Within a church worship service, when there is godly order we will experience the power and presence of God as we enter into the posture of God-worship. The atmosphere will be perfect for people to step out of their comfort zones and allow themselves to be vulnerable to the Holy Spirit.

As they experience the manifestation of His glory they will hear His voice, feel His transforming touch, see visions, and even smell the beautiful fragrance that sacrificial worship releases. (2 Corinthians 2:15) It is important that we carefully guard this environment by embracing godly order. Otherwise, worship will be powerless, chaotic and void of these things.

Would grabbing a guitar and joining the band without an invitation be right? Would interrupting the pastor in the middle of a sermon to share a revelation you just received seem appropriate? NO!

Likewise, it is inappropriate to jump up and dance, run around the building, wave a flag or banner at the wrong time. That would disregard and disrespect the authority of the pastor, the worship leader and the worship team.

These might be extreme examples, but they make the point that it's not only disrespectful and inappropriate but also completely out of order. God has a time and place for everything, and when we feel the urge or need to share or participate we need to follow the godly order that is already in place.

Godly order promotes a spirit of teamwork. As a creative worshiper, particularly those who dance, use flags and banners, we are to minister as unto the Lord. Our purpose for dancing, flagging or waving our banners is not to draw attention to ourselves. It is to reflect the heart of God, to echo His heart, to draw others in and point them to Jesus.

> My sons, do not be negligent *and* careless now, for the Lord has chosen you to stand in His presence, to attend to His service, and to be His ministers and burn incense."
>
> 2 Chronicles 29:11 AMP

Godly Order Builds Relationships of Trust

Personally, as someone who is called to creative worship with dance and flags, I am submitted to the authority placed in my life. My pastor may not understand all the technical ins and outs of the flags, but by the Spirit of God he understands the purpose and impact of creative worship.

I work hard to ensure that I have sound relationships with my pastors, through which I am able to build trust and understanding. Trusting relationships provides us with accountability, humility, and above all, freedom in worship. It ensures that I am accountable to both God and my leadership.

Godly Order Builds Faith

If you are a creative type and feel that you are called to worship in the creative arts but find yourself in a church that does not embrace the arts, go to God in prayer first.

Through prayer we untie God's hands and give Him access to the circumstances that are standing in the way. Allow God to prepare the hearts of your leadership by building a relationship between you and them. Over time a trust will develop. Prayer also opens the door of grace and favor in your life.

> For whoever finds me (Wisdom) finds life and obtains favor and grace from the Lord.
>
> Proverbs 8:35 AMP

Godly Order Creates a Healthy Respect for Authority

Once you have sought the Lord in prayer and God has released you to meet with your pastor, share your heart with him about worship and your desire to worship through the creative arts. Then leave it in God's hands.

Don't force anything to happen. You have just given your pastor a lot to digest, especially if he or she has very little knowledge of creative worship, or if others who have used the creative arts as a platform to promote themselves to seek self-gain and recognition have put off your pastor.

Godly Order Improves Interpersonal Relationships

Once the lead pastor or your leadership grants you permission to worship in the creative arts, meet with the worship leader/pastor and share your heart again.

Unless there is a relationship between you and your pastor, a trust has not been developed yet. So, it is important that you show that you can be trusted by your actions and that you have a respect for the leadership.

The worship leader/pastor may invite you to join a worship practice session. It is one way for them to see what creative worship is about, and to start building a relationship of trust. Worship practice is a great place to become familiar with the worship team, and them with you.

It is important to remember that we are to impress God, not people. Our focus should always be on Jesus and to please Him.

As I worship, I envision Jesus looking down upon me with a great big smile of approval and how pleased He is with my worship.

Godly Order Leaves a Remnant of Jesus

Creative worshipers should not be selected to impress people or visitors. A leader that understands the importance of pointing people to Jesus and submission to

God's authority will be wise in selecting creative worshipers like dancers, painters and flaggers.

The creative worshipers that leadership selects will, through their true God-worship, draw others unto the Father and point them to the One whom they worship.

In summary, as creative worshipers, we must do the following to establish godly order in our lives and our churches:

- Pray, and submit your gifts and talents to God;
- Pray, especially when there seems to be no way to express your gifts in worship;
- Pray, and build trust through relationship with your leaders;
- Pray, humbly serve and submit to your leaders;
- Pray, remain sensitive, become aware of God's heart, and leave it in His hands.

Yes, I said to pray with each step. It's essential. Prayer is simply talking to God and listening to Him. Prayer humbles us, frees us of pride and arrogance. Through prayer we acknowledge that in our own power we are inadequate, but in Christ we are more than able.

Prayer takes our minds and hearts off our own struggles, thoughts and agendas, and shifts it onto Jesus who will exalt us in His perfect time.

> ...and when the Chief Shepherd appears, you will receive the crown of glory that does not fade away. Likewise you younger people, submit yourselves to your elders. Yes, all of you be submissive to one another, and be clothed with humility, for "God resists the proud, But gives grace to the humble." Therefore humble yourselves under the mighty hand of God, that He may exalt you in due time...
>
> 1 Peter 5:4-6 NKJV

SENSITIVITY TO THE HOLY SPIRIT

Sensitivity to the Holy Spirit benefits humankind in many ways. It creates an emotional awareness, empathy, fairness and justice. It allows us to be passionate and generous.

When we become sensitive to the Holy Spirit we become aware of the heart of God. When we become sensitive to the Holy Spirit these benefits will begin to manifest within our leadership and our church.

It is this sensitivity among our church leadership, as well as those who aren't in positions of leadership, that will bring discernment to differentiate between devoted true God-worshipers and those who perform to seek recognition and self-glory.

I read a story years ago that has stuck with me. The account tells of a dance group that was doing a worship dance number in a church service. As they were worshipping in front of the church, a lady from the congregation who was not part of the dance group stepped out and joined the dancers.

To a leader who was not submitted and sensitive to the Spirit, this would not only be inappropriate but unacceptable. Thankfully, the dance leader's heart was in the right place and was sensitive to discern the direction of the Holy Spirit.

Instead of stopping the lady, the dance leader instructed the rest of the dance group to circle around the lady and kneel. The lady continued to dance in the middle of the circle. While she was dancing, the Lord showed the dance leader that He prompted the lady to step out and join the dance group because He wanted to heal her from years of rejection.

This lady may not have been graceful or trained, but that didn't matter to God, the reason was to bring her inner healing and acceptance.

PROTOCOLS & PROCEDURES

Protocols and procedures are an important part of godly order. They provide us with direction, limits and constraints in the order of authority. Having them in place eliminates a trial and error approach. They establish a clear understanding of our responsibilities.

Protocols and procedures free leaders from micromanagement and they create an environment for healthy spiritual growth. A respect for order and authority are formed when leaders spend time to teach and communicate proper procedures and protocols to their teams.

Under the laws of the Old Testament in biblical times, following proper procedures and protocols was often the difference between life or death. In the book of Exodus 36:8 through 39:43 we read about the particular procedures and protocols that were to be followed in building and preparing the Tabernacle.

From the perspective of a creative worshiper, when the church leadership does not embrace or have an understanding of the purpose of creative arts as worship, we should not cast judgment.

Or if we ever find that our leadership is in error, we must never take it upon ourselves to confront or challenge them. There is always more to a story than what we might know or see. They might not be at the point in their walk with God to understand creative worship.

Growing up, my dad always told me that there are three sides to a story; one side, the other side and the truth. So how do we handle leadership that is in error? Pray for them! I can't stress this enough.

> The heartfelt and persistent prayer of a righteous man (believer) can accomplish much [*when put into action and made effective by God—it is dynamic and can have tremendous power*].
>
> James 5:16b AMP

This brings to mind another personal story that took place at the first church I attended shortly after I immigrated to the States. When I first started to flow in dance during worship at this church, the senior pastor refused to allow group dance as part of the worship service.

I didn't know the whole story at the time, but I am glad I didn't confront him. I could have blurted out multiple reasons and scriptures why dance should be embraced as a creative expression of worship. But instead I chose to pray.

Our dance group met faithfully and spent at least half of our practice in prayer. I strongly believe now that if it weren't for our faithful and fervent prayers, we would not have had the breakthrough in that church like we did.

The part of the story I didn't know was that a lie about the pastor and the leadership once held them captive. This lie was a stronghold that prevented the people in this church from experiencing the fullness in their worship. However, the lie was destroyed through the fervent prayers of a few, and the church experienced a breakthrough.

We must be vigilant in our walk with God and not allow the influence of the enemy to use us to bring division to the church. Always approach everything in prayer first. Our prayers must be from the Spirit of God and not of our own will. Sensitivity to the Holy Spirit will lead us so that we don't end up like Judas.

I will expand upon this story in the next chapter, but for now I've revealed it in part to highlight the importance of praying for our leaders instead of calling them out.

Protocols are not meant to limit us, but rather provide us with a framework on which we can stimulate healthy spiritual growth. It promotes order in the church. It allows our leadership more free time to grow in their personal relationship with God and to advance the Kingdom of heaven.

THE CREATIVE WORSHIPER RESUME

As a creative worshiper, we should consider whether we are ready to worship with creative expression. There are some important considerations we must weigh before we approach our pastor for permission to worship with creative expression using the arts.

Our purpose should be pure. Our intent should be to enhance or add to the dynamic of worship. Our goal is to shift the focus from the arts to the creator of the arts, God the Father.

Leaders should recognize the gifts and talents in others. They should help them recognize and tap into their unique gifting. They should celebrate their unique identities and callings.

As leaders, when we promote conformity, we become a stumbling block for believers pursuing God's plan and purpose in their lives. While the world tries to conform us to it, effective godly leaders help facilitate the transformation that brings spiritual maturity and breakthrough. Leaders can only accomplish this through the

Holy Spirit.

I have leaders in my life that I serve and submit to, not because I want to be like them. It's because I want to be like the One whom they reflect, Jesus. In each of them I see God working in their lives, and I am confident their wisdom comes from the Holy Spirit.

Qualified leadership and order are essential. To serve in leadership, or to serve as part of the worship team, there are certain requirements. The same goes if you are a creative worshipper on the worship team. As a dancer, flagger, painter, poet, etc., your spiritual resume should include the following:

- Born again;
- Baptized in the Holy Spirit;
- Skillful in the things of the Spirit;
- Able to flow in the prophetic;
- Be an intercessor;
- Be comfortable with silence.

As creative worshipers, before we even set foot into a worship service, we should first pray and seek the Holy Spirit. We should ask Him to prepare us to be willing and obedient vessels used by Jesus.

In worship, when God instructs us to stand still, we should be willing and quick to obey. We must be comfortable in our inactivity, even though everyone around us is singing, dancing, crying or laughing. We must trust and know that God's plan and purpose for us at that moment is greater than our own.

A prophetic anointing may enter a worship service and God will instruct us to deliver the prophetic message through movement. Be quick to respond. A spirit of war might arise as God propels us into the spiritual front lines of warfare worship, or *warship*. God has a specific and strategic time and place for everything. You and I are part of His plan, not our own, and we are here to fulfill His purposes on this earth as part of His army.

There is a time for everything. Here are just a few of the scriptures from Ecclesiastes 3 that reinforce the point I am making; that we must be willing to obey the Holy Spirit when He prompts us to do something, even though it may seem contrary to what is happening around us.

> A time to weep, and a time to laugh;
> A time to mourn, and a time to dance;
> A time to embrace, and a time to refrain from embracing;
> A time to keep silence, and a time to speak;
>
> Ecclesiastes 3:4,5b,6b NKJV

The key is to keep your spirit connected with the Holy Spirit during our worship. By doing this you will receive clear instruction as to what you are to express or fulfill.

A Bluetooth speaker can only play audio if it stays connected and receives the signal from the device transmitting the audio. We must stay connected with the Holy Spirit. We must humbly submit to the authority of Jesus and respect the earthly leadership and authority that He has placed over our lives.

Prepare your heart first by emptying yourself of your own plans and agendas and lay them at His feet. Humble yourself before God. Embrace your leadership, and embrace the Holy Spirit so that you don't miss the opportunity to be used by God during these times in worship by stepping out of order.

CREATIVE WORSHIP DRESS CODE

Generally, proper dress and attire apply to dancers and those who require movement using flags, banners or billows. Establishing a proper dress code or attire will command respect for the dancers and give the dancer a personal confidence.

A proper dress code will also prevent them from becoming a distraction to others, and it will free the dancer to express themselves without fear of inappropriate exposure.

Attire should be comfortable and reverent. Proper wardrobe functionality is important because there is nothing more distracting than a creative worshiper wearing ill-fitting or inappropriate clothing. It is not only distracting but also inappropriate for those watching, as well as for the dancer.

Personally, I wear long dark colored tops over jeans or leggings that are long enough to be considered a short dress. I like dark for two reasons; to cover or hide any perspiration, and so that the focus is not on me but rather to emphasize the flag or fabric as I worship and point others to Jesus.

This is where our church leadership, protocols and procedures can be very helpful in guiding us to appropriate dress so that we don't distract but direct attention upward to Jesus and the Father.

Our purpose as creative worshipers is to reflect the heart of the Father, and through our worship we point others to the one whom we are worshiping. When this is done without distractions we can be used to encourage others to follow suit in their free expression of worship.

We must use wisdom and understanding in everything. When we neglect one area, like how we dress, we will have a negative impact on others. We could pose as a stumbling block or obstacle. (Proverbs 4:7)

As believers, when we accept Christ as our Lord and Savior, we surrender our earthly body. Our bodies became the temple of the Holy Spirit. (1 Corinthians 6:19) We must treat our bodies accordingly and keep the focus on God, not us. We are merely vessels or channels through whom the Holy Spirit flows through for the benefit of others and us.

And so, dear brothers and sisters, I plead with you to give your bodies to God because of all he has done for you. Let them be a living and holy sacrifice—the kind he will find acceptable. This is truly the way to worship him.

Romans 12:1 NLT

CONCLUSION

In closing, I want to emphasize that the heart of a worshiper is the key to true God-worship. It is our heart in worship that will echo God's heart. It will draw others to Him and into the glorious experience of worship.

The motive of our heart should seek to be pure, humble and honest in our intention so that we can fulfill God's plans and purposes.

Keep these four things in mind to maintain the right heart and attitude as a creative worshiper:

- Obedience: Be obedient and willingly submit to the authority of those God has placed over us.
- Dedication: Be dedicated to study God's Word. It will grow us spiritually. It will bring us revelation and knowledge that will propel us deeper into His presence.
- Humility: Be humble. Never seek recognition, self-promotion or fame. God will move mountains on our behalf when we remain humble.
- Commitment: Be Committed. Our commitment to faithfully attend practices and services regularly will open doors for us.

The blessing of order sets a framework in place that benefits us in many ways. As worshipers, we are part of God's army. In the book of Chronicles, we see how the worshipers were sent out ahead of the army singing praises to the Lord and giving thanks.

After consulting the people, the king appointed singers to walk ahead of the army, singing to the Lord and praising him for his holy splendor. This is what they sang: "Give thanks to the Lord; his faithful love endures forever!"

2 Chronicles 20:21 NLT

As creative worshipers on the front lines of the battle, we must be so grounded in the Word of God, we must know who we are in Jesus Christ, so that when the fiery arrows of the enemy come our way we will not be pierced, wounded or defeated.

Those that go ahead of the army are those that face the attacks first. So, remain in Him. Our God is faithful and He will wipe out the enemy for us.

So fix your eyes on Jesus. The storm can rage around us and the enemy can try to distract us, but Jesus will keep us in perfect peace. Our storms, struggles, and the battles of life will not destroy us.

Instead, God will use each one of them to raise us up from glory to glory, to strengthen us and to multiply our mighty testimonies.

Just as we see in 2 Corinthians, we are transformed by these things:

> And all of us, as with unveiled face, [*because we*] continued to behold [*in the Word of God*] as in a mirror the glory of the Lord, are constantly being transfigured into His very own image in ever increasing splendor and from one degree of glory to another; [*for this comes*] from the Lord [*Who is*] the Spirit.
>
> 2 Corinthians 3:18 AMPC

When we look back and reflect on all our victories, we will be glad that we were transformed in our willingness to obey, submitting with humility and stepping out in confident boldness.

At the beginning of this chapter I emphasized the importance of order and how as creative worshipers we must respect order if we expect to find our place in our churches. It's worth revisiting again, here at the end.

God is a God of order. His plans and purposes for His Church, proceed from a heavenly authority and through divine order. As worshipers, we must respect the authority and order within our churches. God has appointed our pastors and leadership. As difficult as this is to believe sometimes, it's the truth. It's written in the Word of God.

To be a productive part of the Church, we must honor God's Word, and we must honor the leadership and authority in our churches. Otherwise, we become a hindrance to the work of God. Or worse, we become instruments of destruction. We must honor and respect order in the house of God so that "a little folly" doesn't foul the delightful aroma of worship.

> DEAD FLIES cause the ointment of the perfumer to putrefy [and] send forth a vile odor; so does a little folly [*in him who is valued for wisdom*] outweigh wisdom and honor.
>
> Ecclesiastes 10:1 AMPC

Every good thing comes into order, and through God's divine order we receive the blessings of God in our lives. Our prayer and worship are how we engage in relationship with God. Prayer and worship are how we honor God. Through prayer and worship we enter into a heavenly place and express our love for Him.

God selected David to be king of Israel, not because of his might, but because of his heart. And all the days of his life, David was a man after God's heart. (Acts 13:22) Let us learn to honor and worship God the way King David did, so that the aroma of our worship is pure and pleasing to God.

> Let my prayer be set forth as incense before You, the lifting up of my hands as the evening sacrifice.
>
> Psalm 141:2 AMPC

12

READY FOR LOVE

Tests & Trials Produce Beauty in Our Lives

Heart-shattered lives ready for love don't for a moment escape God's notice.

Psalm 51:17b MSG

I am excited because I see God restoring the arts back to the Church through you and me. He is refining the hearts of His people and restoring the purity to the hearts of true God-worshipers.

A pure heart of worship is a humble heart surrendered and submitted to God with extravagant adoration. It is a heart that pursues virtue and righteousness. The heart of a true God-worshiper is a heart that is ready to receive love and share it with others.

Have you ever considered the characteristics of the olive tree? An olive tree is described in the scriptures as being beautiful and attractive.

I, the Lord, once called them a thriving olive tree, beautiful to see and full of good fruit.

Jeremiah 11:16 NLT

His suckers and shoots shall spread, and his beauty shall be like the olive tree and his fragrance like [*the cedars and aromatic shrubs of*] Lebanon.

Hosea 14:6 AMPC

A Christian in love with Jesus is both attractive and beautiful.

THE GOOD FRUIT OF THE OLIVE TREE

I also believe that the olive tree represents the life of a Christian who has embraced God in His fullness with pure love. It's a relationship rooted in spiritual maturity. It is ever sprouting new life that produces good fruit. It is productive, resilient and long-lived.

> But if some of the branches were broken off, and you [*Gentiles*], being like a wild olive shoot, were grafted in among them to share with them the rich root of the olive tree, do not boast over the [*broken*] branches and exalt yourself at their expense. If you do boast and feel superior, remember that it is not you who supports the root, but the root that supports you.
>
> Romans 11:17-18 AMP

Whereas the olive tree represents the Jews, the grafted branches from the wild olive shoot represent the Gentiles, those who are not Jews. In other words, we are grafted into the Body of Christ because we have accepted Jesus Christ as our Lord and Savior. We are born-again, purchased by the blood of Jesus.

As a born-again believer, you are now a child of God, part of the bloodline of Jesus Christ. As you are grafted into the good olive tree, you become a good branch and will bear good fruit.

> You, by nature, were a branch cut from a wild olive tree. So if God was willing to do something contrary to nature by grafting you into his cultivated tree, he will be far more eager to graft the original branches back into the tree where they belong.
>
> Romans 11:24 NLT

We can see here in verse 24 that this grafting process is contrary to nature. That means God did something extraordinary here. By simply trusting and submitting our lives to Jesus, we allow God to use us to bear good fruit in our lives.

The Life-giving Olive Tree

It is 7 years before an olive tree produces its first fruits. It takes an additional 7 years before the olive tree reaches maturity and produces a mature harvest.

Olives are harvested by hitting the branches with sticks to drop its olives. This knocking is so injurious to the olive tree that it only produces a harvest once a year, yet olive trees will live and bear fruit for centuries.

When I visited Israel in November of 2016, I was intrigued with the olive trees, particularly all the wild shoots that spring up from the ground around the tree's mature roots. The mature olive tree not only produces fruit, but it also produces new life from its roots.

The Symbolic Olive Tree

Our Christian walk is like an olive tree. God has given us all that we will need in this life through His Word and the Holy Spirit to reflect the same characteristics of the olive tree: maturity, good fruit, resilience, longevity and new life.

Maturity develops greater self-control, encourages forgiveness, shields us from offenses and cultivates in us a generous spirit.

Good Fruit manifests as kindness, patience, joy, peace and hope, which is rooted in a healthy understanding and practice of God's Word. It also fulfills the will of God in each of our lives.

Resilience sustains us through the troubles and hardships of life, allowing us to walk through it while maintaining our peace and joy, and continuing to produce good fruit.

Longevity comes when we allow God's glory to renew our minds and transform our bodies, transforming daily our spiritual and physical health, slowing the aging process.

New Life is what happens when the beauty and fragrance of our lives attract the lost and draw the prodigals back to Jesus.

The Resilient Christian

One thing we should all recognize, accept and even embrace in our Christian walk: It is certain we will face "troubles, hardships, and calamities of every kind." (2 Corinthians 6)

As believers, living in a fallen world we cannot avoid them. They are part and parcel of our Christian walk. It is our faith and the condition of our hearts that will determine how we will respond to troubles, hardships and calamities. They will either knock us down and defeat us, or they will build us up and strengthen us.

If we look at scripture, we see again and again that God is a God who creates. He is a creative God. The very first verse testifies to this: "In the beginning, God created…" (Genesis 1:1)

Every believer is an unfinished work of God's creation. We are His work of art. When we become a child of God, He begins the work of finishing what He started.

> And I am convinced and sure of this very thing, that He Who began a good work in you will continue until the day of Jesus Christ [*right up to the time of His return*], developing [*that good work*] and perfecting and bringing it to full completion in you.
>
> Philippians 1:6 AMPC

If we look in Hebrews, we see more evidence of this work that God continues in us. Even more compelling, in the latter part of this verse, we can see a display, an example of Jesus' resilience, as He endured the cross.

Looking away [*from all that will distract*] to Jesus, Who is the Leader and the Source of our faith [*giving the first incentive for our belief*] and is also its Finisher [*bringing it to maturity and perfection*]. He, for the joy [*of obtaining the prize*] that was set before Him, endured the cross, despising and ignoring the shame, and is now seated at the right hand of the throne of God.

Hebrews 12:2 AMPC

This scripture is a ***mini playbook*** that instructs our walk through trials. Instead of focusing on our difficulties, we are instructed to focus on Jesus, who we know is working to perfect us.

In our walk, as we are blessed through this perfecting process, we must be careful to remain humble, remembering that our perfection only comes when Jesus returns. Pride has a sneaky way of infiltrating our lives when we think we are a perfected and finished work of art. Believers who fall into this trap will begin to operate in pride, believing they can achieve perfection apart from God.

It is only when we allow God to shatter our pride that we can be ready for His pure and unadulterated love to flood our heart and soul. This love is the living color that adorns the canvas of His enduring work in each of us. Indeed we are His living canvas.

SHATTERED PRIDE

What does a heart that is shattered and ready for God's love look like?

The gifts on an altar that God wants are a broken spirit. O God, You will not hate a broken heart and a heart with no pride.

Psalm 51:17 NLV

A true repentant and broken heart is a bare canvas, an unfinished person who has relinquished control over all things to God. When we give God the broken pieces of our heart, God takes those pieces and makes it whole. He not only makes it whole, but He fills our hearts and souls with His glorious and passionate love. This kind of person has a teachable spirit and has a broken and contrite heart toward the Lord.

As a creative worshiper, it seems that creative people often tend to face a lot of opposition and judgment. This kind of judgment comes from those who have not allowed their hearts to be broken and contrite before the Lord.

When our heart is not shattered and ready for love, instead of acceptance we pursue competition and compare ourselves with others, hoping to achieve recognition, promotion or fame.

Luke, the travel companion of the apostle Paul, warns us not to pretend to be something that we are not since God knows our hearts.

Then he said to them, "You like to appear righteous in public, but God knows your hearts. What this world honors is detestable in the sight of God.

Luke 16:15 NLT

Often we misunderstand the word *broken*, associating it with hurt, disappointment, failure, rejection, etc. But this is not what God means by being broken. David understood this as he went to God in prayer. He had nothing to offer but his broken spirit.

My sacrifice [*the sacrifice acceptable*] to God is a broken spirit; a broken and a contrite heart [*broken down with sorrow for sin and humbly and thoroughly penitent*], such, O God, You will not despise.

Psalm 51:17 AMPC

The biblical meaning of the word broken, as it relates to one's heart towards God is a heart that is submitted, teachable, pliable, useable, separated, qualified, obedient, consistent and in agreement. A contrite heart is one that is humble and repentant.

This quote by Leonard Ravenhill, English Christian evangelist and author, makes a profound statement about what I believe is the condition and motive of the current Church's heart.

"Most Christians pray to be blessed few pray to be broken."

When we are broken, we are in the right place for God to renew and mold us. If we want to enjoy a delicious omelet we must first break the egg's shell. God needs us broken and contrite before He can use us powerfully for His glory.

So when we find ourselves on the receiving end of unjust and unfair judgment it is not an excuse for us to crawl back into the closet and lick our wounds, or to run back to the world.

Instead, we should forgive those who cast judgment on us, pray for them and allow God to use these circumstances to fortify our spirit and build our resilience.

The condition of our heart will shine through as we walk through "troubles, hardships, and calamities of every kind." Our response to them, our actions, emotions and words, will become the evidence of our heart's condition.

As creative worshipers, we must ensure our worship reflects the heart of God and not our own.

HARDSHIPS. DO THEY MAKE US OR BREAK US?

Troubles, hardships, and calamities are not to be feared or avoided. We should welcome them with joy and allow them to prepare us for life and ministry.

Our response to hardships will make or break us. It is up to us whether we allow tests and trials to make us bitter or better. It is up to us whether we accept tests and trials as opportunities to build our character. It is our choice whether we allow misfortune to imprison us behind walls of fear and defeat.

Hardship is something that causes pain, suffering, or loss. In the Bible hardships are usually described as troubles, trials, tests, tribulations, calamities or persecution. Worshipping God during our trials and tribulations without giving up produces perseverance and builds character. In the book of Romans, Paul explains how tests and trials are there for us to learn.

> We know that troubles help us learn not to give up. When we have learned not to give up, it shows we have stood the test. When we have stood the test, it gives us hope.
>
> Romans 5:3b-4 NLV

A person who has perseverance will not resign or quit. Having a persevering heart unlocks the door of our own heart to receive God's love which gives us hope. We must block out the voices of criticism and judgment. These come from the flesh and they only bring fear and confusion.

Instead, we must keep our ears finely tuned to the only voice that counts, the voice of the Holy Spirit.

> For the desires of the flesh are opposed to the [*Holy*] Spirit, and the [*desires of the*] Spirit are opposed to the flesh (godless human nature); for these are antagonistic to each other [*continually withstanding and in conflict with each other*], so that you are not free but are prevented from doing what you desire to do.
>
> Galatians 5:17 AMPC

If we are to do what we desire to do, to serve God and to produce good fruit, then we can only be connected to one voice. The Holy Spirit must be our guide.

Why Hardships Are Necessary

Troubles, hardships and calamities are necessary because they build us up and strengthen us in the face of persecution.

Today, a culture of political correctness has crept into the Church, targeting the creative types. Because creative types tend to be sensitive and emotional in their expression of worship, it is easy for political correctness to bring confusion and keep them from walking in the fullness of their purpose.

This spirit of political correctness is a spirit of control. Among Christians, it will try to control anything that goes against the Church's norms. The creative expression of worship clearly goes against what is considered normal or comfortable in a politically correct church.

Personally, I have faced this kind of opposition, indirectly. Instead of targeting me personally, those close to me were targeted. Thankfully, they understood how to respond in love and not offense.

When our heart is broken and contrite before the Lord, ready for His Love, and keeping the Lord continually as our focus, we will not be moved by any hardship or persecution we face.

> I have set the Lord continually before me; because He is at my right hand, I shall not be moved.
>
> Psalm 16:8 AMPC

If King David allowed the persecution and ridicule of Goliath to offend him, if he allowed his brothers' lack of confidence in him to affect his self-esteem, he would never have defeated the giant with a sling and a stone.

David didn't use the armor and weapons of those around him. Instead, he was confident in his gift and ability with a sling.

Samson, although blessed by God, was not a perfect man. He made a big mistake when he allowed Delilah to rob him of his strength by cutting his hair. If he allowed Delilah's betrayal to offend him, or his eyes being gouged out to defeat him, he wouldn't have slain more Philistines at the time of his death than in his lifetime.

A holy and prayerful man, Daniel was committed to following God. He was considered a good and devoted man by all accounts. Had he allowed the jealousy and deceit of his peers, the other men who served King Darius, affect his faith in God, he would have been devoured by the lions.

It was Daniel's devotion and committed lifestyle to God that paved the way for King Darius to write into law that Daniel's God was the one true God and that His Kingdom must submit and accept Daniel's God as their own.

Judgment and persecution are rooted in a lack of knowledge and understanding. It appears as ridicule, betrayal and jealousy. Its intention is to stop what it doesn't understand. When we do not rely on God, this results in the hurt and destruction of God's people.

When judgment and persecution come against you, remain humble and committed to God. In humility and with understanding the root and intent of judgment and persecution cannot stop you or hold you back.

Instead, allow it to propel you forward into a deeper intimacy with Jesus, who is your vindicator.

> He who vindicates me is near. Who will contend with me? Let us stand up together. Who is my adversary? Let him come near to me.
>
> Isaiah 50:8 ESV

Embrace tribulations and allow them to strengthen you, through God's strength. Surrender to the one who fights the battles for you.

SURRENDER

God will open the door for the creative types only when we "let go and let God," when we surrender to God's will. A great example of this occurred in my life shortly after I immigrated to America.

God had just healed me from bulimia and it was shortly after that my mom introduced me to Joy Tate. It was that introduction that gave birth to a long-lasting friendship between us.

That friendship grew over the years and recently began to bear good fruit. A few years ago, we started ministering together; teaching and training in creative worship workshops.

When I first met Joy, she asked me if I would like to do a little part in a mini production she was preparing for a ladies' conference at our church. She needed someone to carry a crown to the throne.

With my background and training in ballet, I was prepared and able to do a whole lot more, but was just so happy to be involved, no matter how small a part.

At the time, the pastor of our church was strongly opposed to dance in the context of a church service. However, his wife was not. With the pastor's consent, he granted his wife permission to use Joy to organize a group of ladies and present a dance at the upcoming ladies' conference. This was a big deal because of the strong opposition the pastor had toward dance.

Shortly after the conference Joy approached me again. The pastor's wife had given her permission to hold worship meetings with a handful of young girls and ladies from our church. The meetings were held at the church, but in a private setting where we could pray and worship in dance together.

Looking back, this was a pivotal breakthrough, instrumental in what happened next at this church.

As our little group met weekly in one of the youth halls, Joy felt a strong urgency in her spirit that we should begin to prepare ourselves by learning a choreographed dance. She believed God was in the process of softening the heart of our pastor toward dance, and that an opportunity was going to present itself soon.

So, we knuckled down and began learning a dance choreographed to the song "Hail to the King" by Vineyard Worship.

Each of us in our little group was walking through some personal hardships. As we gathered privately to pray and worship with our gifts and talents, victory over these hardships began to manifest in each of our hearts.

We began to have victory over fear, insecurity, depression, and even hurt from being misunderstood. A hope began to rise in our hearts as we persevered through it all, no matter how hard it was at times. A godly character began to grow in each of us, which became evident in our worship.

Our dance group meetings served as our training ground, a place where we began to grow spiritually.

I did not know it at the time, but God was preparing me, maturing me to be a leader. I was a student first, and because my heart was teachable, God grew me and promoted me into a leadership role.

I like what Jack Welch, former CEO of General Electric says in his book, *Winning*:

> "Before you are a leader, success is all about growing yourself.
> When you become a leader, success is all about growing others."

Even though I became a leader I never lost sight of remaining teachable. A leader cannot lead successfully if she hasn't been to the place where she is leading others. If I wanted our group to go deeper in our relationships with God, I needed to go there first. I needed get there first to know what to expect so that I would know how to lead and teach others to get there too.

Our pastor's opposition to dance didn't stop or intimidate our little group from praying for him. In prayer, God showed us that we needed to remain constant and faithful with our weekly worship get-togethers.

It was not our place to judge, but rather to pray for the pastor and his leadership. We knew the source of opposition was several bad experiences with dance in the church previously. We knew the opposition stemmed from a lack of knowledge of the real purpose of the creative expression of worship.

Both the pastor and those dancers from the past lacked the knowledge of true God-worship. Despite all of it, we were slowly overcoming this opposition through prayer and our faithfulness to God.

If our team had chosen to operate according to worldly standards, we could have taken matters into our own hands. We could have approached the pastor, telling him we received a word from the Lord about dancing in church. We could have explained all the reasons we believed we should dance at the next Sunday service.

Or worse, at the next service, we could have just stepped out and began dancing during the worship service without the pastor's approval, knowing that we were operating outside of the blessing of order.

Operating in this manner would not only break trust but it would increase opposition and jeopardize what God was doing in the heart of our pastor.

If we allowed our own motives and desires to override what the Holy Spirit was showing us, we might have destroyed the potential for the creative arts to be restored back to this church.

> But you are not doing what your sinful old selves want you to do.
> You are doing what the Holy Spirit tells you to do, if you have
> God's Spirit living in you.
>
> Romans 8:9 NLV

This scripture in Romans is wisdom we can apply to every area of our life, and especially in this case. By remaining in Him through the Holy Spirit, God gives us direction and He can effectively use us in the restoration of the arts back to the Church.

Worshiping God creatively through the arts may be burning in your inner most being. In your mind's eye, you can envision yourself expressing your worship through the most heavenly and spectacular movements, drawing people to God.

But, be sure to allow the Holy Spirit to make a way for you, especially when there seems to be no way. The Holy Spirit breathes life into situations that seem to be dead.

HAIL TO THE KING

Our little dance group remained faithful and prayerful as we met weekly. Looking back, I believe God was patiently watching to see what were the true motives of our hearts.

Soon our pastor's wife approached us about possibly doing a dance for another ladies' conference she was hosting. We were super excited, and without hesitation we accepted because we knew that we were ready!

We began meeting a couple times a week to tweak the choreography for our dance to "Hail to the King."

It was a challenge at first because I was the only person in our group with formal dance training. Joy had some Jewish dance training, but the others had no formal training or experience. Prior to the decision to start working on a choreographed dance, our previous meetings were mostly freestyle.

Every time we met to practice we started in prayer. We prayed and prayed, and only after we felt a release in the Spirit did we begin to practice the dance.

Because these ladies had never formally danced, never learned choreography and had to overcome some personal hardships, their confidence needed to be found in prayer first. It was a big step for them to even think about worshiping in front of a large group of ladies.

So each time we met we prayed until the release came, and we began the learning process of the choreography. Through this process, we had some profound moments in our personal spiritual growth and character.

Angelic Encounter

The ladies' conference was drawing near. We moved our practices into the church sanctuary so we could become familiar with the space. During these practices, we experienced some amazing moments in worship.

One of these moments was during a practice session in which I experienced an angelic presence. This particular presence felt tangible and holy.

At this practice, just as in practices before, we only used the lights at the front of the sanctuary, over the platform. The rest of the sanctuary was dark. We practiced the choreography again and again, until we decided to go through it one last time. At this point we were very familiar with the choreography, so we would allow ourselves to let go and worship with our whole self in true God-worship.

As we got into position, I hit play on the boom box and we began the worship. While we were dancing, I sensed a presence in the sanctuary. I looked out into the darkness and there appeared to be a figure standing in the back.

All this seemed to happen in slow motion, but in reality it was just a few split seconds. Instead of stopping I continued, thinking I would later ask the others if they had seen anyone.

As we continued dancing, I sensed the same presence again, a second time. This time I squinted my eyes, hoping to see through the dark sanctuary. But I could not see anyone.

Afterward, puzzled by this experience, I asked the others if they had seen it. Joy's daughter confirmed that she had seen it too.

As dark as it was in the back of the sanctuary, we wondered if someone may have heard the music playing and come in through the side door to watch.

Curious, I figured I'd go and look outside to see if there was anyone out there. There was no one. The only cars in the parking lot were ours. We were the only people on the church property.

While I was "investigating" I felt God prompt my spirit, saying that it was a heavenly being, an angel attracted to our worship that came in to watch as we danced.

To this day, I cannot provide any worldly evidence, except for the confirmation of Joy's daughter. But by the Spirit of God I know that as we entered into a realm of worship, our dance attracted an angel.

Because of our unity in worship, it created an atmosphere that was inviting and welcoming for this angel to join and watch over us. We never prayed or fasted for angels to be present in our dance practices, but we did ask God to release His heavenly hosts to fill the church grounds and to prepare the atmosphere so that when we would present our dance at the ladies' conference, that His power and glory would be released through our worship.

Our hearts were purely focused on Jesus and honoring Him with our dance. It never dawned on us that our worship would attract heavenly beings. This encounter was such a boost to our self-confidence that a holy boldness arose in our spirits. At that point, we could confidently say that God was truly making a way where there seemed to be no way.

Our posture of true God-worship will always create a shift in the atmosphere that gives glory and honor to God alone. **There is no room for self in true God-worship.**

After the second ladies' conference, we received a lot of positive feedback. Many were touched and impacted to go deeper in their personal worship. This was the beginning of an interest in worship dance among the members of our church. It sparked a fire, a desire to know more about the creative arts as an expression of worship.

Our dance group grew by a few more ladies after the conference. Joy and myself were very careful with whom we invited into the group. The arts will attract all kinds of people, and if their hearts aren't yet in the right place, it could hinder the power and anointing that comes from being humble and unified in spirit.

When something is so well received, it tends to be normal for others to want to be part of it. Most didn't see what took place in the background; the preparation within our hearts and lives, the hardships we walked through, the time spent in prayer allowing our spirits to connect with the Holy Spirit, and the trust that was built in our relationships.

It was the culmination of all these things that brought us to this point, dancing at the ladies' conference. So, when others approached us to join, we sought God in prayer, asking for His guidance as to whom we should add to our little group. This little dance group was not ours to begin with. It was the Lord's.

The moment the Holy Spirit gave us peace about someone, we knew that we had God's stamp of approval. With the Holy Spirit, it is easy to discern and know whether a person is seeking fame, recognition or promotion, or whether they are submitted to the Holy Spirit.

Those submitted to Him are humble and will be immune to offense. They will welcome submission to leadership and accountability. Above all, they will understand the difference between a performance and true God-worship.

The Small Things

Our dance group remained faithful. We continued to meet with prayer and worship. Even though we didn't have any prospects of dancing anytime soon, we loved our times of prayer and worship together and decided to stick with it. We enjoyed the freedom to express ourselves in creative worship free from judgment.

Many months later, our pastor approached Joy. He invited our group to dance in church on a Sunday. It was not a Sunday night service, but the main Sunday morning service.

This came as a shock. It was a miracle! God made a way where we didn't see a way and He softened the heart of our pastor. By remaining faithful in the small things, God saw our hearts and so did our pastor. He saw our character and passionate love for God. That softened his heart and he decided to set aside his own understanding, his own feelings, even if it was for just a moment. He gave worship dance another chance in the church.

Needless to say, we were elated. If we had chosen to confront our pastor right in the beginning, this opportunity would never have been available to us. God had a bigger plan in mind for this church and we were so excited to be part it.

If you find yourself in a church that might be in the same place this church was before the breakthrough, be encouraged and know that God will make a way where there seems to be no way.

First, determine in your heart whether the church you are attending is a church you are invested in. If the answer is yes, then take the matter to God in prayer. Remain in prayer as long as it takes. Stay faithful, humble and consistent. Begin worshiping God in preparation for the moment the opportunity arrives. Be ready, but don't be stagnant. Continue to pursue a deeper intimacy with God.

Our dance group was so focused on pleasing Jesus that if we never had the opportunity to dance at a service we would still have met to pray and worship together. But we knew through prayer, we had a promise from God that the arts would be restored back to our church. So we rested in Him and enjoyed the journey. (Luke 12:34)

No man can stop what God wants to accomplish through us when we are faithful. Keep your heart focused on Jesus. Seek His face and allow your heartbeat to come in sync with His heartbeat.

Mountains Will Tremble

In preparation for this awesome opportunity to dance in the main Sunday morning service, Joy shared with us the song God had given her; "Did You Feel the Mountains Tremble" by Delirious.

Joy met with our worship leader and asked him if he and the worship team would be willing to learn the song. He agreed and was super excited because he was open to worship dance too.

As we met for practice there was such an excitement in the hearts of our dance group. A revival fire was burning in us and it was hard to contain. We knew that this opportunity was going to release something big, but we had no idea how big. Nor did we know how well it was going to be received.

Instead of worrying about any of this, we remained focused and we stayed prayerful and worshipful.

What happened that morning was so extraordinary, I want to share the account through two different perspectives; my own and Joy's.

My Account

Sunday arrived! The worship team and our dance group were ready. We could feel the electricity in the air. Our dance group met for prayer in a little room beforehand. Intercessors joined us and anointed each dancer's feet.

Initially we were supposed to dance at the start of worship, but when we arrived we were informed that we would be dancing a few songs later.

Worship began. We waited patiently. But the signal for us to take our places at the back of the sanctuary didn't come. About three songs into worship, one of the youth delivered a message to our group noting that we needed to be ready for when the offering was to be taken.

Now, as the offering ensued, we were more nervous than excited. We took our places and waited for the song to start.

Then the first note sounded. Immediately the presence of God filled the sanctuary. As we stepped out and began worshiping with all our heart and spirit, it felt like the roof split open for God's glory to fall in the sanctuary.

The people jumped to their feet and began worshiping with us. Their hearts came alive as the powerful presence and anointing of God washed over them. There was dancing, leaping, people falling on their knees, some lying flat on their faces weeping before the Lord.

Our group struggled to dance under this powerful anointing. One of the newer ladies collapsed right at the beginning, right in front of the altar. We had to dance around her.

It was a tremendously powerful experience. My physical body struggled to dance under that anointing. By the time we got to the end of the song we had more "casualties" to the power of God. Overcome with emotion, I found a spot in the foyer, laid on my face and wept.

I don't remember what happened after that. All I remember is that revival hit our church and people were radically changed and transformed. The Holy Spirit had complete freedom that day. God used a faithful few to usher in a spirit of revival. God impacted our community and many people fell back in love with Him!

Joy's Account

Dance as ministry began to flourish both in the women's ministry and the youth ministry in our church; but choreographed worship dance was not allowed in the adult services.

With adult women and some teenagers, we were presenting anointed movement and worship for Women's Ministry meetings. With only 2 adult women and many teens, we were presenting dance as worship in many of our young group meetings at a local high school and various churches in another state.

The day came when the senior pastor asked for this worship dance team to bring its presentation to the adult church service. When we arrived at church, we were so surprised to learn that we were the presentation for the "offering" part of the service.

The worship band began playing our song by Delirious, "Did You Feel the Mountains Tremble." We began our presentation of banners. Then the worship dancers came bursting down the aisles and ran up into the front altar area with joy, celebration and worship fabrics.

The once seated congregation responded by standing, clapping and worshiping to the joy that just entered the room! One adult dancer went out in the power of the Lord and was lying on the floor.

At the close of the song, all flaggers and dancers exited the sanctuary through the back doors. The young flaggers and dancers were all going down on the floor, out in the power of the Lord's presence.

I watched the service on the TV in the foyer; church as usual was interrupted! Instead of preaching his Sunday sermon, the pastor began inviting people to come forward and receive Jesus as their Lord and Savior.

This went on for the entire service with many young people from the young group coming forward to be "born again."

Then I heard the pastor say, "let's bring that song back again!" I looked at the flag and worship dancers and they were all on the floor enjoying the presence of the Lord. "Get up! Get up!" was all I could say.

We began the presentation again, exactly as before. But this time was different. This time, instead of the congregation being a spectator to a worship dance presentation, they were all on their feet participating in the joy and exuberance of the presence of God.

They not only used our worship fabrics to worship, they were using every handkerchief or fabric they could find to join in a glorious time of praise and worship; flag, dance, music, joy and celebration to the Lord. In that moment in time we were all in one accord. The atmosphere was heavenly!

PEOPLE ARE ALWAYS WATCHING

A bestselling author and life coach, Rob Liano was quoted saying:

> Each day you are leading by example. Whether you realize it or not or whether it's positive or negative, you are influencing those around you.

Whether we know it or not, people are always watching us. In fact, people watch more than they listen. Whether we are within the four walls of the church or outside in the world. Our lifestyle will either reflect the heart of God or our own agendas and ideas of life.

In the first book of Timothy, Paul tells us how important our lifestyle and walk with God is, not only for our own good, but for others too.

> Watch yourself how you act and what you teach. Stay true to what is right. If you do, you and those who hear you will be saved from the punishment of sin.
>
> 1 Timothy 4:16 NLV

CONCLUSION

The key to all the God-experiences in my journey as a creative worshiper is being wholly surrendered to God. I embraced the Holy Spirit and got to know Him more intimately. My selfish ideas and agendas began to fade away, and as a result I developed an attitude of humility and submission to my leadership.

Anytime I heard pride knocking on the door of my mind, or when insecurity tried to climb through the window into my heart, I turned my back on them and lifted my eyes to the Father, locking my gaze with Jesus!

Every story or experience I shared with you here was not a result of my own doing. It was simply the thread of God's plan woven into the fabric of my life.

As Jesus continues to lead me, I will continue to follow His lead. With my heart in His hands He can do whatever He wants with my life. I have walked through some tough times, tests and trials; from bulimia to a broken vertebra in my neck. But through it all, I never blamed God or doubted Him.

God shattered my pride, which prepared me for His love, His unconditional love. God has touched my heart and moved me to share my story with you through this book so you too can experience all that He has for you.

When you come to Jesus in worship, face to face in the throne room of God, His glory will transform you!

We are His living canvases. We are His unfinished masterpieces. As the unfinished work of Jesus, we can go from glory to glory.

> And all of us, as with unveiled face, [*because we*] continued to behold [*in the Word of God*] as in a mirror the glory of the Lord, are constantly being transfigured into His very own image in ever increasing splendor and from one degree of glory to another; [*for this comes*] from the Lord [*Who is*] the Spirit.
>
> 2 Corinthians 3:18 AMPC

Call to Arms
WE ARE A GREAT ARMY!

So I prophesied as He commanded me, and the breath came into them, and they came to life and stood up on their feet, an exceedingly great army.

Ezekiel 37:10 AMP

When we look at our culture, our politics, our faith and the division in our country, its clear we live in an age of rebellion. One could argue today's Church is losing the battle for souls.

But there is a new wind blowing. There's a shift in the supernatural that is manifesting in the natural. This shift is the breath of God. His Spirit is breathing life into the dead, dry and parched bones of the Church.

Now is the time! There is a "shaking and trembling and a rattling" coming from the dead, dry and parched bones as they are raised back to life. Can you hear it? It is the wind of the Holy Spirit reviving a great end time army.

What will this look like and what will be the evidence?

The Word of God will once again return as the foundation of every believer's life. God's blessed order will take root at the heart of every family and families will be restored. Relationships will be made whole. The once estranged will be reunited.

We will see the hearts of those once dead and dying in the clutches of religion set free and revived. They will desperately seek a true encounter with God, an intimate relationship with Jesus.

The prodigals will return home and the lost will turn their hearts back to the Father. A heart of purity and holiness will brightly burn in the lives of God's body of believers.

The world will depart from its ways; it's own models for success. Instead, they will turn to the Church. They will glean from it, embracing biblical principles as the foundation of their success.

Secular strongholds, such as marketplaces, businesses, the creative and the arts communities, and other worldly domains, will be torn down and set free. They will be restored back to God to advance His Kingdom.

We will bring down demonic strongholds over territories and regions by restoring and rescuing gifted and talented individuals from these very places.

Instead of rebellion, we will see the breath of God blow a reviving wind into these territories and regions, transforming the lives of dead, dry and parched believers.

True God-worship will "set us down in the midst of the valley." Our praise and worship will be like the "thundering noise" that precipitates the gathering of the dry bones.

> So I prophesied as I was commanded; and as I prophesied, there was a [*thundering*] noise and behold, a shaking and trembling and a rattling, and the bones came together, bone to its bone.
>
> Ezekiel 37:7 AMPC

The opening of Ezekiel 37 is about revival. I believe God is calling upon His true-God worshipers to take their positions in His army and to prophesy through their worship. I believe through our true-God worship God is calling us to prophesy revival.

> Then said He to me, Prophesy to the breath and spirit, son of man, and say to the breath and spirit, Thus says the Lord God: Come from the four winds, O breath and spirit, and breathe upon these slain that they may live.
>
> Ezekiel 37:9 AMPC

As I have shared throughout this book, I believe God is calling us to rise up above our perceived limits and to break out of the mold of normal religious worship services.

> So don't turn a deaf ear to these gracious words. If those who ignored earthly warnings didn't get away with it, what will happen to us if we turn our backs on heavenly warnings? His voice that time shook the earth to its foundations; this time—he's told us this quite plainly—he'll also rock the heavens: "One last shaking, from top to bottom, stem to stern." The phrase "one last shaking" means a thorough housecleaning, getting rid of all the historical and religious junk so that the unshakable essentials stand clear and uncluttered.
>
> Do you see what we've got? An unshakable kingdom! And do you see how thankful we must be? Not only thankful, but brimming with worship, deeply reverent before God. For God is not an indifferent bystander. He's actively cleaning house, torching all that needs to burn, and he won't quit until it's all cleansed. God himself is Fire!
>
> Hebrews 12:25-29 MSG

When we answer His call in this glorious way, freedom and liberty will fill the hearts of God's people, people of all ages who are wholly and totally surrendered to the Holy Spirit. We will go from glory to glory as we are transformed in His glorious presence, in a face-to-face encounter in the throne room of God.

This revival will restore God's people by returning them to their true identity in Christ, setting them free to use their gifts and talents to achieve the plans and purposes of God for which He predestined for each of us. (Ephesians 2:10)

God is ready to use you for the advancement of His Kingdom. Are you ready to take your place as a worshiper in His army? Are you ready to take a stand as part of this great army of God?

In Isaiah 6, God comes to Isaiah in a vision, seeking someone to deliver His message.

> Also I heard the voice of the Lord, saying, Whom shall I send? And who will go for Us? Then said I, Here am I; send me.
>
> Isaiah 6:8 AMPC

Can you hear God's calling? Can you prophesy the breath of God breathing life back into a once lifeless Church?

Accept God's calling and surrender to Him as He breathes new life into your bones, bringing them together, connecting them with sinews, muscles and skin.

God is restoring us. He is gathering a great army and preparing us for battle. As worshipers, we must march ahead of the army and prepare the way, just as God instructed Joshua in the battle of Jericho (Joshua 6:4), just as Jehoshaphat appointed worshipers to sing and praise God ahead of the army in the Wilderness of Tekoa. (2 Chronicles 20:21-22) In both cases, neither army fought. God fought both battles.

Embrace God's calling and allow your spirit to become sensitive to the voice of God's Holy Spirit. It is important to be sensitive and humble as He puts us into position among fellow warriors in His great army.

There is a "shaking and trembling and a rattling" arising from the valley of dry bones. Listen! Can you hear the thunder?

Lift your eyes to the Father. Surrender every aspect of your life to Him. Put down your worldly weapons. Take up the weapons of the Holy Spirit. Embrace your identity in Christ and your God-given gifts and talents, and begin to roar in true God-worship!

It's time to take your stand! We are His great and mighty army!

ABOUT THE AUTHOR

ILSE R. SPEARS

Born in South Africa, Ilse R. Spears has traveled the world in missions and ministry, teaching creative worship. In 1997, she moved to the U.S. with her mother, father and younger brother.

Since her arrival in the States, she has traveled to the Philippines, Haiti and India sharing her creative worship and teaching others how they too can use their God-given gifts and talents in creative worship.

Ilse is a wife and mother to two daughters, London and Dakota and works fulltime in the health and wellness industry. She is an ordained minister of the Gospel and works part-time in ministry, teaching worship through creative worship workshops.

Ilse holds an Iridology certification through the International Iridology Practitioners Association. She also has 12 years of ballet training, completing her Elementary level from the Royal Academy of Dancing, based in England.

Finally, Ilse loves to bake and she holds a 1st kyu Brown belt in Goju Kai Karate.

69345022R00126

Made in the USA
San Bernardino, CA
14 February 2018